Harpo Marx
as Trickster

Harpo Marx as Trickster

CHARLENE FIX

*For Jack,
with mutual
admiration for those
Marxs, especially
Harpo!*

Charlene Fix

McFarland & Company, Inc., Publishers

Jefferson, North Carolina, and London

LIBRARY OF CONGRESS CATALOGUING-IN-PUBLICATION DATA

Fix, Charlene.
    Harpo Marx as trickster / Charlene Fix.
      p.   cm.
    Includes bibliographical references and index.

    ISBN 978-0-7864-7147-8
    softcover : acid free paper ∞

    1. Marx, Harpo, 1888–1964—Criticism and interpretation.
I. Title.
PN2287.M54F59 2013
791.4302'8092—dc23
[B]   2013001547

BRITISH LIBRARY CATALOGUING DATA ARE AVAILABLE

On the cover: Harpo protects a seal, his friend, checkers coach,
and disciplinarian, from the rain, never mind that a seal's habitat
is water. Harpo Marx as Punchy, *At the Circus*, MGM, 1939

Manufactured in the United States of America

McFarland & Company, Inc., Publishers
  Box 611, Jefferson, North Carolina 28640
  www.mcfarlandpub.com

For my mother,
Anne Kobrinsky Cohen
September 23, 1912–March 4, 2012

Table of Contents

Preface

My subject is Harpo Marx: the Harpo, that is, in the films. Though the man behind the persona was much loved, and I'm sure I would have been tremendously fond of him, this study is focused on Harpo in the films. Beyond inviting you, reader, to spend time in the pleasure of his cinematic company, I am also offering a lens to view Harpo through: the trickster archetype, including the implications of that archetype's resurrection in the Marx Brothers films for the culture. Tricksters remind us, writ large, what it means to be human. They also show us how to make necessary adjustments to our values, institutions, and cultures. So Harpo Marx as trickster has timeless, historical, and contemporary relevance.

I think I have always been interested in Harpo in the Marx Brothers films. Long before I conceived of this book, before I was even conscious or sensible, I watched them because they made me laugh: truly, madly, and deeply. My interest in Harpo began in childhood when he was already so iconic that one child or another would be accused of resembling him (a compliment, to my mind). He's the sweetest, wildest, most magical, and most poetic Marx brother, and compelling to observe because his antics are deeply resonant. For much of the time I was working in earnest, no one had yet devoted a book to Harpo in the films. So in part I set out to fix (pun intended) this critical neglect. Writing about Harpo in the thirteen Marx Brothers films felt like my homework from the universe.

As I was completing this book, I learned of Wayne Koestenbaum's forthcoming *The Anatomy of Harpo Marx,* now out from University of California Press, a brilliant close reading of Harpo's physical wonders in the films. We were studying Harpo at the same time, and I wasn't looking over my shoulder, so engrossed was I in the subject. But never mind: Harpo deserves many books and will no doubt have them. There's Harpo's own *Harpo Speaks!* and his son Bill Marx's *Son of Harpo Speaks,* and critical studies of the Marx Brothers that pay some attention to Harpo (*Groucho, Harpo, Chico, and Sometimes Zeppo* by Joe Adamson; *A Century of the Marx Brothers*, edited by Joseph Mills; *Hail, Hail Euphoria!* by Roy Blount Jr.; and *The Marx Brothers: Their World of Comedy* by Allen Eyles). But only Koestenbaum's book and my own focus on investigating Harpo in the films. Our eyes are glued to him the way he glues the newspaper to Ambassador Trentino's bum in *Duck Soup*.

I set out to compare Harpo to tricksters in folktales, myths, and legends from all over the world, and the idea yielded big time. I stood upon the shoulders of Lewis Hyde, whose *Trickster Makes This World* helped me build scaffolding for this study. I also stood upon the shoulders of Paul Radin, whose *The Trickster: A Study in American Indian Mythology,* along with Richard Erdoes and Alfonso Ortiz's *American Indian Myths and Legends,* took me deep into cycles of trickster tales from the native peoples of the North American continent whose spirits surely animated Harpo whether he knew it or not. I studied trickster Hermes in Greek mythology and tricksters in Caribbean, Arabic, and Jewish folklore. In all of them, I found parallels to Harpo's luck, foolishness, cleverness, mania, hunger, lust, thievery, shape-shifting, gender-bending, alliance with the underdog, attacks on the powerful, musicality, connection to animals, magic, and all-around mischief. In addition, from time to time I discovered parallels in Harpo's craft to the work of a number of poets and writers. You will find most of the specifics of all of these comparisons in the chapter notes.

I offer a two-part introduction: an "Establishing Shot" of Harpo as trickster in his historical context, and a "Preview of Coming Attractions" summarizing Harpo's trickster characteristics in the films, followed by thirteen chapters examining Harpo's trickster persona closely in each particular film. The final chapter, *A Concluding Montage*, weaves aspects of Harpo's trickster essence manifested in the films into a composite impression that, with a little luck, will resonate beyond the covers of this book and leak out into the world, making it a more just, flexible, resilient, amusing, and magical place.

I thank my husband Pat for living patiently with this work, for keeping our lives running in myriad ways during the years it took to complete, and for help with research. I thank my daughters Madeleine and Sonya, and my son Daniel for sharing my time and attention with Harpo. Maddie, thanks for your contagious creative energies, for the meditative image of floating in an inner-tube in Harpo's pool, and for coining the phrase "prone to nudity": I have applied it to Harpo within. Sonya, thanks for your deep and illuminating intelligence: you pushed me beyond my abilities and comfort zone, asking relevant questions that obliged me to undertake research to make this a better book. And Dan, thanks for bringing the spirit of wildness and fun into our lives from the moment of your birth, and for your many funny stories of mischief that I'm glad I didn't know about at the time: surely you primed me for this project. I thank my pets for being, as always, peaceful and non-judgmental. Thanks to Columbus College of Art and Design for a Faculty Enrichment Award to help defray the costs of stills. Also at CCAD, thank you Palmer Pattison for endless patience, technical support, and access to your cell phone number, and thanks Maria Spiess at CCAD's IT Help Desk too. Thanks to Eric Homan, Ron Saks, Dante Kinney, and Steward McKissick for technical expertise with screenshots. Thanks to my colleagues at CCAD, Nanette Hayakawa and Sophia Kartsonis, for inviting me to present my Harpo work in the Visiting Artists Series, and to Susan Josephson, George Felton, Ed Lathy, Lesley Jenike, Joshua Butts, Robert Loss, Joan DeMartin, Kim Landsbergen, Char Norman and other wonderful CCAD colleagues and friends for assistance, emotional support, and confidence, especially when I mislaid my own. Thanks to my poetry group, the House of Toast Poets: (Jerry Roscoe, Fred Andrle, MJ Abell, Jacqueline Smith and Linda Fuller-Smith) for years of listening, for books, for hook-ups, and for solid advice. Thank you Dollie at Jerry Ohlinger's, Ron Mandelbaum at Photofest, Kristine Krueger at the Margaret Herrick Library, and Tom Lisanti at the New York Public Library for assistance and advice with images. Thank you Wayne Koestenbaum for kindness and advice. Finally, thanks to my sister Laura (Cohen) Truxall and my buddy Barb (Davis) Weiss, the two people, next to the Marx Brothers, who make me laugh most in this world.

Introduction

Establishing Shot

"Where is the dirt work of democratic mass society? Where has trickster's spirit settled?"
— Lewis Hyde, *Trickster Makes This World*[1]

Consider this. In 1936, Harpo Marx was waiting in a reception line to shake hands with the Prince of Wales, uncrowned King Edward VIII of England. When he stretched out his hand, Edward handed him his leg.[2] It was a gesture Harpo had enacted many times in the Marx Brothers films and personal appearances, even eventually on television, this slipping of his leg to strangers and familiars, friends and foes alike, and momentarily disarming them, no pun intended, into holding it as it swung casually at the hinge of his knee.

It is one of Harpo's most eloquent tropes, for it demonstrates the power of the hinge, Harpo's mischief calling attention to the efficacy of flexibility and maneuverability. Perhaps it caught the attention of the Prince of Wales because in the first Marx Brothers film to introduce the trope of the proffered knee, *The Cocoanuts,* various characters repeat the come-on: "Did anyone ever tell you look like the Prince of Wales?" But more significantly, at the historical moment when the prince handed Harpo his leg, England was heading toward war with Germany, though Edward would abdicate and his brother, King George VI, would lead England into the conflict. Nevertheless, if we juxtapose Edward's imitation of Harpo's trick to images of the hinge-denying Nazi goosestep, the metaphor seems even more striking.

Another story, unrelated to the Prince of Wales, one I remember from undergraduate days involving classical conditioning, also seems relevant to Harpo's trickster persona. Students in an auditorium lecture class were told

5

Notice the locked knee of the death-delivering Nazi goosestep. United States Holo-caust Memorial Museum, 1933–1939, courtesy Bechoefer.

to look bored except when their professor unconsciously put his hands in his pockets, at which time they were told to perk up and take notes. By the end of the semester, they had the professor lecturing with his hands constantly in his pockets.

I recalled this story when I learned that Arthur (Harpo) Marx stopped speaking during the Marx Brothers' stage performances as a result of a bad review. But he consistently received good responses when he mimed and gestured with props, so he kept these in his repertoire and continued to develop them. One could say, then, that Harpo's stage persona was in part shaped by his audience and critics. In fact, while making their first films at MGM, the Marx Brothers would take skits on the road and play them before live audiences, adjusting timing and content. In this way, the public had a part in eliciting and honing their genius.

That is because audiences angle to get their needs met, and one old collective need is for a figure to refresh their world with cleansing chaos. That figure is trickster. Indeed, Groucho and Chico are, to some degree, tricksters too (Zeppo's just a guy), but Harpo, as we shall see, exhibits the widest range of trickster traits. Arthur Marx's genius and good nature shaped his persona, Harpo, along with his audience, who summoned and encouraged the wild, hilarious, disruptive trickster archetype he expressed in that persona.

The trickster figure tends to emerge during cultural and historical moments that call for healing, cleansing, and corrective chaos. This especially resonates when we consider that all but the last Marx Brothers films were made between 1929 and 1946, a decade and a half of international economic depression, rising, then entrenched fascism, and World War II. If ever folks needed death-dealing order to be tempered by life-affirming disorder, this was it.

Trickster figures, by being unpredictable and disruptive, tend to fight against humanity's potential to turn against itself.[3] They take on power, complacency, rigidity, injustice, and snobbery. Theirs is an assault on power, but less to overthrow it than to recalibrate it, to clarify and reinvigorate the lively creative forces that helped develop culture in the first place. For the chaos is

Groucho (left) and Chico (right) gaze at Harpo as if they know he is the trickster kahuna, central to the mischief and mayhem in the films, while Harpo gazes at us. MGM, 1935.

temporary. Harpo, for example, steals if the impulse strikes him — in many of the films, he is the consummate thief, not his brothers — and by stealing he makes us rethink who owns what and by what right. But he distributes or returns what he steals if the impulse strikes him; covetousness is clearly not his motive. Similarly, he violates boundaries of personal space and social protocol, not to offend or cause harm but because of his excessive affection, vitality, and mischievousness. Again, consider his generosity with his leg. Like trickster, he blurs the distinction between animal and human, maintaining affectionate terms with horses, seals, ostriches, and frogs, to name a few — and in doing so, he expands what it means to be alive. Harpo wanders from place to place with his hyperbolic appetites; no Marx brother devours more food, not to mention non-food items, than Harpo does.

With Groucho and Chico, his trickster cohorts, he serves the procreant urge by helping young lovers prevail, he disturbs boundaries based on social class, and he is, significantly, the only Marx brother in the films to step lightly over social barriers based arbitrarily on race or class, to be accepted into the lives and hopes of marginalized people. His is an egalitarian spirit, manifesting affinity with and sympathy for the poor, for immigrants, for minorities, for those with underappreciated talent and character, and for sweethearts kept apart by unjust social or economic barriers. He helps turn institutions inside out, making mayhem of power's penchants, most memorably its penchant for war.

Although Groucho and Chico are allied with Harpo in his efforts, Harpo is, again, more the consummate trickster than are his brothers for he manifests the full range and multiplicity of trickster traits. Groucho and Chico are more like the trickster cohorts who sometimes pal around with Coyote and Hare in American Indian legend.[4] And though Groucho may seem dominant because of his vigorous verbal wit, and Chico may steal fire because of his role in such exchanges in addition to his goofy sexiness, Harpo, examined in light of the trickster gestalt, is clearly the Marxes' trickster kahuna.

In addition to his bond with animals and with the oppressed, Harpo turns silence into speech, cross-dresses, farts, steals, eats, sneezes, and lusts hyperbolically, all the while violating personal space and social protocol. And when he arcs from lowly to angelic playing his harp, when he demonstrates the power of the hinge, and when he transcends the laws of physics, entering the realm of the surreal, we sense the ancient and quasi-divine attributes of trickster.[5]

It is easy, in retrospect, to see to what extent the most vulnerable (often immigrants, minorities, and the poor) needed the cleansing disruption of social and political order during the years the Marx Brothers films were conceived, and it is easy, in retrospect, to see how much American institutions (along with the world's) needed to be jolted, cleansed, and renewed. Yet Harpo's trickster has traveled beyond his own time, enacting his cleansing chaos in our own time as well, and that is part of the wonder. For while Arthur Marx was channeling the persona of trickster and transforming himself into Harpo, first on the vaudeville stage,[6] then in the relatively new medium of film, that medium, undergoing its own process of refinement, was plucking Harpo from the flow of time, preserving his antics, and carrying him into the future. Now we have only to play or stream a film or attend a Marx Brothers retrospective to resurrect trickster for whatever in contemporary culture or our own personal lives calls for trickster's corrective chaos.

In order to elucidate Harpo's trickster nature, we must first investigate the nature of the trickster archetype. Known to the ancient Greeks as Hermes,[7] whose own stringed instrument, the lyre, was a prototype of Harpo's harp, trickster appears in various guises throughout the folklore of the world. In both Sephardic Jewish and Arabic folklore he is Joha, a simultaneously childish and astute fellow who exposes hypocrisy, and in Ashkenazic (Eastern European) Jewish folklore he is Hershele Ostropolier,[8] a hungry goofball in his own right, intent on survival and, like Harpo, coiffed with curly hair. Trickster appears all over the world: in Mexico, Peru, Chile, Argentina, Venezuela, Alaska, India, France (whose trickster, the Lutin, has, like Harpo in the films, a special bond with horses), to name a few places. Trickster is best documented in this country in American Indian cycles of tales like those about Hare or Coyote, and Eshu, the Afro-Caribbean trickster with his double-sided hat.[9] And while Harpo mirrors qualities of tricksters from everywhere, he may have the most in common with Hare, Coyote, and Eshu.

In most tales, trickster is a wanderer who is hard to arrest and examine for he is playful and busy and chaotic. He can also be lazy: His is a fun-and-games rather than a work ethic, offering an interesting corrective to America's Puritan ethic, though he gets involved in many a tangle to satisfy his need to eat. In fact, he is ravenous for food. He is also highly entertaining and hilarious, lustful and lecherous, and sometimes ambiguously or outlandishly gendered. He can seem simultaneously foolish and wise, a clumsy buffoon who stumbles upon solutions but also knows how to exploit what chance affords. At times he is barely differentiated from an animal; at other times he seems to partake of the divine. He gives humans fire. He debases in order to cleanse, clowns around, releases tension, challenges power, fights for the underdog, and is a facilitator of renewal. His stories arc between disorder and balance; they pass through chaos.

And that happens to be the plot arc of the Marx Brothers films, with Harpo at the heart of the disruption. In Harpo, we see trickster at work. It's

Harpo gives his leg to Joe, who is amused to accept it, the litmus test of a good guy. Harpo's flexible leg bends, in contrast to the Nazi goosestep. Chico Marx (left) as Chico, Rockliffe Fellowes as Joe, and Harpo Marx as Harpo. *Monkey Business*, 1931, Paramount Studios. From the collections of the Margaret Herrick Library.

problematic to lay a template so old and varied on a modern cinematic character who is by nature so unwilling to hold still, so essentially mysterious, and so utterly distracting and disarming as Harpo; but the trickster template fits him remarkably well. This becomes apparent when, in each film, the sediment of culture cracks open and trickster rises from the exposed vein in the incarnation of Harpo Marx, the persona that he, with a little help from his audience and critics, created and handed down to future generations.

A Preview of Coming Attractions

> "No generation understands him fully but no generation can do without him."
>
> — Paul Radin, *The Trickster*[10]

Harpo Marx blended so thoroughly with Arthur Marx that he himself said his public never heard him speak,[11] though his fellow members of the

Algonquin Round Table and his family and friends were another matter. And he claims to be no one but himself when he plays the harp in the films. Nevertheless, this study concerns itself with his film persona. And we have only to examine the Marx Brothers films to witness the variety of trickster traits concentrated in Harpo, from the moment he arrives in picaresque style — usually appearing once the need for cleansing chaos has been established in the world of the film — all the way to the end.

Harpo often carries or wears a prop (a belt, a lollipop, or his great shoplifter's trenchcoat) from one film into the next, making him recognizably that trickster fellow, like coyote on the road wandering from adventure to adventure. And he spins his mischief all the way to the last word, which, paradoxically and silently, he often delivers. With his trickster cohorts Groucho and Chico he dismantles institutions: the microcosms of duchies, ships, colleges, opera companies, hotels, and department stores. He humbles powerful individuals and he discombobulates value systems and enterprises like land speculation, classism, colonialism, art high and low, collegiate sports, prohibition, war, medicine, horse racing, and even, especially in the last two films *A Night in Casablanca* and *Love Happy,* cinema itself.

Harpo's persona, like trickster of myth, seems to be not quite of the world of men. This is due to his tantalizing complexity: simultaneously undifferentiated from animals yet manifesting the divine. He is often a buffoon, like the clumsy Mudheads of American Indian lore,[12] foiling himself along with his antagonists yet somehow managing to remain cunning. Then his magic renders him surreal: He runs up curtains; he steals a birthmark; he brings statues to life; he plays in a trio with his own mirrored reflections; he hosts a tattoo of a doghouse with a real dog barking from it. In addition, Harpo's virtuosity on the harp suggests an angelic nature even while connecting him to the ancient Greek trickster Hermes, inventor and master of the lyre, the original stringed instrument that won him both approval from Apollo and acknowledged paternity from Zeus.

Harpo's silence, the highest volume aspect of his persona, is the most complex in terms of his trickster essence. Like an animal he is mute; and animals from horses to seals to frogs bond with him. He is inarticulate as a child; and children love him. He doesn't speak, yet his muteness is sophisticated. He puns with props; and he overhears dire plots against good people and communicates the danger by means of mime, his cohort Chico seemingly the only one capable of translating. The process is amusingly complicated by Chico's newly acquired immigrant English, itself a work in progress.

In fact, we come full circle here: Harpo's language of gestures and props is inclusive: It doesn't privilege English but instead offers the immigrant and even the babbled world direct access to his utterances. In this way Harpo takes an important stand in support of the outsider, the newcomer, the stranger, and takes a stand against exclusionist nationalism at a time when it was on its lethal rise and legislation was being drafted — as it is being drafted here today — to stem the flow of immigrants to America. That the Marx Brothers are twice cast as stowaways on ships — which is to say, illegal immigrants — is worthy of mention here.

Moreover, Harpo, being mute, straddles both the silent and sound film eras. In the Marx Brothers' first film, the early talkie *The Cocoanuts,* only Harpo was relatively free of the problems of early sound technology. Groucho and Chico had to wet the Why-a-Duck map, for example, so it wouldn't crackle.[13] But ultimately, Harpo's silence offers a critique of the limits of language and a protest against powerful people who sometimes distort language for their own use. At times Harpo's silence feels like a refusal to be like Job, arguing with God against injustice.[14] Harpo's silence even suggests an Adorno-esque despair of language, and in the early films a prescient pre–Holocaust refusal to speak.[15] Having taken what is essentially a vow of silence,[16] Harpo also seems linked to religious and spiritual traditions of silence found within Buddhism, Hinduism, Sufism, and Catholicism in monastic orders like Benedictines and Trappists and Carmelite Nuns. Yet the irony of Harpo's silence is also part of the fun, for culturally, Jews tend to celebrate loquaciousness. Therefore, it is fitting that Harpo's silence is also, true to his ethnicity, rambunctious and effusive and loquacious in its own way.

Finally, Harpo's silence helps us see. In the midst of the quiet, we focus. In spite of his refusal to speak, Harpo communicates information and expresses humor, protest, irony, and even awe in a few rare close-ups of his face when he responds to human generosity, like in the feast-in-steerage scene in *A Night at the Opera,* or when he is disarmed by Polly's heartache when he finds her weeping alone in the garden in *The Cocoanuts.* Harpo's silence has much trickster resonance: It is, essentially and paradoxically, speech. And while Harpo's mischief connects him to the baser essence of trickster, the silence itself, being, as Hyde suggests,[17] sacred, connects him to trickster's divinity.

Harpo's hungers, also loaded with hyperbole, especially resonate with the trickster archetype. Trickster personifies the body's vitality; likewise, food and sex are huge aspects of Harpo's persona. He is pretty much insatiable. In *Room Service,* he eats like a ravenous machine, consuming more and continuing long after his hungry cohorts are sated. And in that joyous steerage spaghetti dinner scene in *A Night at the Opera,* an astounded Harpo has finally found a dinner consummate with his capacity to hunger. Sometimes he is so indiscriminately hungry that he eats things that aren't food, like a telephone in *The Cocoanuts* and a necktie, with condiments of course, in *A Night at the Opera*. Like trickster, who in Native-American legend is a notorious poacher, Harpo steals a live turkey for his starving friends in the hotel room in *Room Service*. And Harpo's woman-chasing lusts are a constant motif in the films. He often drops other nonsense to take off after a blonde, or several, once even on a bicycle, a moment celebrated in a poem by Jack Kerouac.[18]

Harpo also expands the perimeters of gender. In *A Night at the Opera*, he waves around a salami reminiscent of the external phallus Coyote had to lug around in his early inchoate days.[19] Conversely, Harpo is the only Marx brother to appear in drag in several films. His occasional cross-dressing — wearing women's clothes or shoes — reflects trickster's androgyny, part of his shape-shifting capacity. And it should come as no surprise that he enthusiastically hugs and kisses both men and women in the films.

He expands the perimeters of identity in other ways as well. For example, Harpo seems, at times, to be one with animals, on more intimate terms with them than with humans, wedded to or besotted with or collaborating with them, and is therefore reminiscent of animal incarnations of trickster like Spider, Great Hare, and Brer Rabbit. In *Duck Soup* Harpo is in bed with a horse; in *The Cocoanuts* he kisses a photograph of his sweetheart, also a horse; in *At the Circus* he tames lions with his piccolo, is coached at checkers by a seal, and fights evil from the back of an ostrich; in *Monkey Business* a frog abides under his hat, close to his mind.

Harpo also impersonates others, in *Monkey Business* becoming Maurice Chevalier when he lip-syncs "You Brought a New Kind of Love to Me" more convincingly than his brothers with a phonograph strapped to his back. He disguises himself and his cohorts with beards stolen from aviators in *A Night at the Opera,* and he makes himself indistinguishable from Groucho in the mirror scene in *Duck Soup* by means of a nightshirt, night cap, and mustache. So Harpo's persona is malleable, a quality summed up metaphorically in *A Night at the Opera* when he strips off layers of Lassparri's costumes, from *Pagliacci* clown to sailor all the way to female, as if the *anima* resides on his innermost layer.

Significantly, Harpo and only Harpo of his trickster cohorts is the consummate thief that trickster of myth and legend is, starting with Hermes' clever theft of Apollo's cattle and Krishna's theft of his mother's butter.[20] With his big shop-lifter's trench coat as repository, Harpo steals his way through the films, often just for the fun of it, sometimes returning what he has stolen, sometimes stealing to help others. With trickster's tendency to destabilize fixed notions, Harpo causes the viewer to rethink the concept of ownership, and to enjoy the fun-loving spirit and dexterity of his thefts along with the good they sometimes accomplish, like feeding the hungry. We are warmed by Harpo's generosity with what he has stolen, and we appreciate the pragmatic utility of the contents of his deep pockets, also presumably stolen, like the hot cup of coffee, ice cream, a swordfish, a blowtorch, scissors, or a five-card flush, to name a few.

Harpo's trickster nature is also suggested metonymically in gestures that offer testimonial to the sophistication and eloquence of his silent tongue. One prop he carries often is a horn on a stick. Because he honks at women using a rigid stick with something round and squishy at one end, the implication is clear. Yet Harpo's horn is also involved in a trope suggesting trickster's legendary flatulence. His horn is his mouthpiece both in and beyond the films, but it is also his *tuchus*-piece, a joke hinted at in the very first film, *The Cocoanuts,* when Harpo honks his horn and his cohorts run out of the room. In the stateroom scene in *A Night at the Opera*, the flatulent nuance of his horn reaches full swell when Groucho keeps adding hard-boiled eggs to the dinner order each time Harpo honks his horn, an olfactory (sulfurous) metonymy that is especially humorous given the small size of the stateroom. This culminates in Harpo's multi-toot crescendo, provoking Groucho to order twelve more hard-boiled eggs, and is punctuated by a half-toot, causing Groucho to cap the order with a duck egg, thus expanding the metonymy to include the auditory resemblance of a fart to the distressed quack of a duck. So by means of his horn, Harpo reminds us of the often hyperbolic flatulence of trickster in American Indian legend.[21]

Another metonymic gesture that is even more frequent and perhaps more deeply significant involves Harpo's leg: the way he tricks the unsuspecting into holding it in many of the films and even beyond the films. Because he swings the lower part of his leg while the upper part is held aloft by surprised and affronted individuals who at first unconsciously accept it, then drop it impatiently, our attention is drawn to his knee, the hinge of the leg. While the hinge suggests the hidden and vulnerable space within a god's or culture's or institution's power, and thus the place to attack, the hinge, according to Hyde, also represents flexibility.[22] In this way, it represents an ideal to aspire to. In fact, Harpo reminds us that the hinge or joint, with its internal space, its capacity for movement, becomes a kind of symbol, not only for how to manipulate power but also for how to hold an efficacious posture in a troubled world. Moreover, we instantly recognize as sympathetic the few characters who accept Harpo's leg with good-natured amusement rather than outrage. The outraged tend to be antagonists.

These implications coalesce when we consider that joints must be lubricated and exercised to move well and painlessly, which is trickster's work in cultures. Exploiting vulnerability, going for the joint, is only part of the lesson. Hanging loose, remaining flexible and relaxed, being able to swing to alternative rhythms and breach destructive protocols — these are important too. Harpo is well nigh floppy at times, he seems so relaxed, and he is lovably and indiscriminately generous and promiscuous with his leg. His proffered leg is his most frequent trope in the films. He insists upon it, enacts the gesture as if it were normal and his leg ultimately desirable and welcome. He drives the lesson home to us, reluctant learners that we are, by repeating it like variations on a melody. The lesson goes down easily with laughter.

Finally, all of the films are driven by trickster's perennial conflict with the gods on high, whether those gods are anointed by wealth, political or institutional power, or even crime.[23] While Groucho often plays some sort of dubious professional and Chico an Italian immigrant working odd jobs and wearing poorly fitting clothes, Harpo is a tramp, ranked socially beneath even Chico. Yet Harpo has an interesting and complex relationship with the gods on high. He satirizes them in attire and swagger, sometimes wearing vestiary markers of wealth like a top hat, albeit at times a smashed one. Nor does he kowtow to the wealthy or powerful, who anyway tend to ignore or dismiss him until he does something obtuse like trick someone into holding his leg or otherwise violate social protocol or breach the boundaries of personal space. When he enters in a top hat and cape in *Animal Crackers*, for example, then strips down to his underwear at a formal party, he is essentially removing the "shame covers,"[24] also known as "clothes" that people wear to hide various truths about themselves. And Harpo doesn't mess around; when his shame covers are removed, they come away in one fell swoop. This happens in *Horse Feathers* too: When he is deprived of his clothes by Mullins and MacHardie, Darwin players, his clothes, attached to each other, also come off at once. Even so, members of the upper class tend to react to the superficial aspect of his gestures, missing the deeper critique.

Nevertheless, Harpo succeeds, with help from his cohorts, in disrupting the equilibrium of the highly placed — perpetrating physical outrages in vestibule, on trapeze or examination table upon the wealthy dowager played by Margaret Dumont, for example, or taking on institutions, even the relatively benign or sacrosanct like the U.S. mail, when he turns letters into confetti. The chaos Harpo creates with his cohorts is, in the end, good for all: Relationships are refreshed and realigned, some sort of justice is accomplished, lovers are united, and the powerful are humbled and chastened even if they're not overthrown.

Harpo exhibits other trickster traits in the films: his picaresque and feral nature, his tendency to inhabit liminal spaces (if the film itself isn't set where

Harpo wears the vestiary markers of wealth, the elegance only a tad belied by his loquacious horn and bedroom slippers. Harpo Marx as The Professor. *Animal Crackers,* Paramount Pictures, 1930.

land and water meet, Harpo hangs around doorways, elevators, and stairways), his talent for discovering opportunities, his accidental good luck, his spontaneous ethical impulses even while ignoring ordinary notions of *good* and *bad*, his penchant for falling asleep at inopportune times, his response to difficulties with silliness like making the Gookie face (an expression Arthur Marx perfected in youth, imitating a man rolling cigars in a store window),[25] his casting his luck with oppressed or marginalized people, his zany impulsiveness, his alliance with the procreant urge implied in his helping young lovers, and his bending and stretching of physical reality unto the surreal.

These traits will reveal themselves as we examine the five films the Marx Brothers' films: made for Paramount: *The Cocoanuts, Animal Crackers, Monkey Business, Horse Feathers,* and *Duck Soup*; the one they made for RKO: *Room Service*; the five they made for MGM: *A Night at the Opera, A Day at the Races, At the Circus, Go West,* and *The Big Store;* and the two released by United Artists: *A Night in Casablanca* and *Love Happy.*

1

The Cocoanuts (1929)
TRICKSTER APPEARS

"Eshu and Legba are both wanderers, living in spaces between things; their special areas are crossroads, thresholds, and boundaries."
— Voth, *Myth in Human History*[1]

In *The Cocoanuts* (1929), Harpo's character name is Harpo, but no matter what his name is or how little he's differentiated from the man who plays him, this first Marx Brothers film introduces suspicions about the character's identity and nature that will be reinforced in subsequent films until the accumulated evidence makes it impossible to deny that the being we have before us is none other than a resurrected archetype, trickster: ancient, ubiquitous, and necessary, surfacing in this then-new medium of film, and due to the magic of technology, a trickster for our time as well. And goodness knows we need him.

Like the American Indian trickster Hare with his friends Iktome and Coyote and Crow, who sometimes help, sometimes impede one another but always recognize their kindred natures and seek each other's company, Harpo has trickster cohorts, Chico and Groucho. Their sympathy is established in this film when they trip over themselves and others, circling and shaking hands in the hotel lobby; or when Groucho (playing Hammer, the manager of the hotel) hands Harpo more mail to tear up instead of stopping him, or watches undismayed while Harpo ingests a blotter with paste and washes it down with ink. All three are tricksters, Zeppo is a straight man, and these identities are reinforced in various scenes, like when Chico carries Hammer's bidding-up scheme to an extreme that undermines the land auction. But of the three, only Harpo exhibits the full spectrum of trickster traits.

19

The trickster cohorts recognize their kindred natures in the lobby of a hotel where land and water meet. Left to right: Zeppo Marx as Jamison, Groucho Marx as Hammer, Chico Marx as Chico, and Harpo Marx as Harpo, *The Cocoanuts*, Paramount Pictures, 1929.

Who is Harpo in this film? Detective Hennessey and even Hammer wonder. But much in the film shapes a response. He's a fellow who likes to hang around liminal spaces — in this film, doorways and elevators in a hotel that is situated where land and ocean meet, undeveloped beachfront property being the basis of the film's satire on land speculation. Harpo is a fellow with hyperbolic appetites for women and food, and he offers some gender-bending innuendo. He exhibits an animal-like repertoire of responses along with outlandish charm and an unequivocal allegiance to life. In addition, like antiquity's trickster Hermes, Harpo is a versatile musician, and like Hermes, an audacious thief.

Ultimately in *The Cocoanuts*, Harpo, in trickster style, helps correct inequities in the social universe he finds himself in, destabilizing superficial assumptions about wealth, status, ownership, and law enforcement. For this thief likes to return what he steals, and he advocates for the impoverished though talented Bob, aligning himself with the sweethearts and therefore the procreant urge. Finally, within his own character he fuses the elevated and lowly, for he is sometimes a tramp yet is often sublime both in sympathy and musicality. He's even poetic: Two of Harpo's most brilliant tropes are introduced in this film, his honking horn and his swinging knee. Both have profound trickster resonance, but more about those later.

Harpo appears about twenty minutes into the film, a delay that establishes his typical entrance in Marx Brothers films. Before we meet him, we are introduced to the milieu — the moral, social, and ethical fabric in need of trickster's remediation — in this film, a world too keen on money and status and impervious to genuine worth. When Hammer tries to convince his unpaid bellhops to "forget all about money," arguing that they can't be "wage slaves" without "wages," he may seem like a chiseling prevaricator. Yet lucre and what it defines (happiness, social class, and human worth) is very much a target in this film, especially when we meet the *bad* money-hungry schemers, Harvey and Penelope, and the *good* impoverished lovebirds, Bob and Polly. The latter pair introduces the film's theme song, "When My Dreams Come True," a song with meta-textual implications given that film-viewing in a theater is like collective dreaming in a huge dark room.

Bob may be short on cash but he's long on worth. Nevertheless, Polly's dowager mother, Mrs. Potter, played by Margaret Dumont, is on the side of status and therefore opposed to this match. We know that she must change. And though Hammer woos her, Harpo precipitates the elevation of her consciousness and even assures that Bob's bid on a lot for his dream home for Polly prevails by knocking the rival bidder out of the auction with a cocoanut to his head from high in a tree.

Only after the need for adjustment in the values of this milieu is established does Harpo appear, chasing a woman into the hotel, then ringing for more and more female bellhops so he can chase them too. Trickster's flatulence follows his lust, for when Hammer shakes his hand, a kind of "pull my finger," Harpo honks his horn — a loud blast that seems to be metonymy for a fart because everyone scatters.

Human beings need to eat, and when they're hungry they may eat a lot, but Harpo exhibits trickster's hyperbolic hunger, eating, in the course of registering at the hotel, the bellhop's buttons, the blotter (after first spreading paste on it), and a buckwheat flower. He drinks the ink and eventually munches on the telephone (a specially made chocolate prop). This last snack introduces a satire on verbal communication that Harpo will repeat in other films. Here, this particular gag is even more amusing when we consider that in this early talkie, problems of sound synchronization had to be resolved,

which is the reason why the map in Groucho and Chico's "Why a Duck" dialogue, the wanted poster for "Silent Red," and the scheming note by Harvey
Yates had to be wetted down to inhibit crackling.

When Hammer refers to Harpo as "a groundhog," and Detective Hennessey calls Chico and Harpo "birds," when Harpo swims out of Penelope's
room spitting water, and when he uses his mouth instead of his hands to steal
handkerchiefs from both Penelope, Hammer, and Bob, we see that like American Indian and other tricksters, Harpo is not differentiated from animals. At
the auction, Detective Hennessey conflates Harpo's identity with a dog's, saying, "I don't know where he's from; he has no license on." Harpo even rows
away on dry land, like trickster's transcending the laws of physics.

Similarly, Harpo shares trickster's mysteriously inchoate nature, suggested
when his cohort Chico says they'll "take a vacancy but not a room," and when
he hands a bellhop his leg, they exit together, and Harpo reappears exiting

Harpo eats a blotter with paste, washes it down with ink, and munches on a flower
and the telephone in this scene too. Chico Marx as Chico, Groucho Marx as Hammer,
and Harpo Marx as Harpo. *The Cocoanuts*, Paramount Studios, 1929. From the collections of the Margaret Herrick Library.

the elevator while playing the theme song, "When My Dreams Come True" on a clarinet. The bellhop, now running the elevator, not only looks on with satisfaction, but he closes the elevator door before Harpo can get back in to pursue Penelope. Is he jealous? Then, after depositing Penelope on her floor, he opens the door Harpo is leaning on, causing him to fall into the elevator. Did they have a tryst?

But it is trickster's lesson of flexibility that is most poetically conveyed by Harpo's signature proffered leg with its capacity to bend and swing at the knee. The offer or imposition of his leg, a trope repeated over and over again in Marx Brothers films and beyond, suggests trickster's ability to hang loose in tight situations, to go for the joints of his enemies, and to find and inhabit the flexible joint. Yes, Harpo crosses boundaries when he gives his leg, most often to strangers. It is socially inappropriate yet a harmless intimacy. And the laughter his repeated gesture evokes softens us up for the lesson. For in offering his leg to others — actually tricking them into holding it for him — he demonstrates the flexible joint no less than nine times in this film, first to the bellhop, then to the crook Harvey Yates, next to Detective Hennessey, again to the bellhop, then to a woman he meets in the lobby, then to Margaret Dumont's Mrs. Potter's, to his familiar Chico, and finally in nifty overlapping leg pile-ups, to Chico and the crook Penelope while seated at a formal dinner. His leg may be interpreted as an affront, an invasion of personal space, but Harpo is as relaxed when handing it over as if he were offering a hand for a handshake. And to an animal, a leg is no different than an arm. Most important is the visual emphasis on the knee's hinge, for much depends upon the power of the hinge. Not only is "humor in the hinge," but also refreshing insights come from "the hinged mind."[2]

One of Harpo's most salient trickster traits in this film, however, is his penchant for stealing. Like Hermes, antiquity's trickster, Harpo steals, and he steals a lot. Hermes committed his theft of Apollo's cattle out of desire to be acknowledged as Zeus' son, and he accomplished the theft with adroitness, making the cattle walk backwards so their hoof prints would confuse. In *The Cocoanuts*, Harpo steals, often just for the fun of it, never to cause harm, and with a similar adroitness. When he attacks the bellhop for picking up his bag, we note not only his sublime ignorance — *sublime* because Harpo doesn't understand the caste system of the workplace, and *ignorant* because, well, bellhops are paid to carry bags. But the main joke involves his assumption that the bellhop is stealing his bag, for it evokes the adage "It takes one to know one." The joke is confirmed when the suitcase falls open, Hammer remarks on its emptiness, and Chico says, "That's all right; we'll fill it up before we leave."

In spite of Harpo's unabashed thievery, we are aware of the contrast between his candor — we know he has stolen because he returns what he steals — and the sneaky and damaging thefts of Harvey and Penelope. Registering at the hotel desk, Harpo "types" on the cash register and pockets a wad. Later in the film, he steals a man's suit coat from under his overcoat even as they discuss train schedules, and he helps ease the fit for Chico by removing the wallet. He eats the bellhop's buttons. And in one antic scene (significantly the scene where Harpo also plays savior by giving Bob the [also stolen] evidence he needs to clear his name and implicate the real crooks), Harpo steals again and again Hammer's tie and Bob's watch and somehow Hammer's false teeth and underwear. Apparently Arthur Marx, like his persona Harpo, asked director Robert Florey if he could borrow his belt one day on the set, wore it all through the movie, and never returned it.[3] He may still be wearing it in their next film, *Animal Crackers*.

Eventually so much stuff falls out of Harpo's big shoplifter's coat that Groucho calls for someone to go upstairs and count the rooms. Harpo seems unable to repress his urge to steal, and we seem unable to repress laughter at the excess and inconsequence of his thefts. Clearly, we are abiding in a place where stealing may be joyous just as it may be damaging (try to explain that distinction to a magistrate). Because of this, we are challenged to consider who owns what, according to whose laws, what those laws are based on, and what a thief hopes to accomplish.

Reinforcing our dawning awareness of the limitations in the letter of the law, Detective Hennessey turns out to be the film's biggest buffoon. Harpo steals his badge and later his shirt while he is wearing it. When Hennessey asks Harpo his name, Harpo leans against him with his belly and honks a reply, another metaphor of flatulence. When Hennessey asks to see his face, Harpo makes the Gookie face. Not only does Harpo interrogate the investiture of power when he steals Hennessey's badge, but he also, in a later scene, steals the key to Bob's prison cell, frees him — though not before making a racket by dropping shovels, picks, and hoes, then accidentally locks himself in. It's a quintessential trickster savior-buffoon moment, but he frees himself by transcending physical laws, easily bending one of the iron bars.

In the beginning of the final sequence, when Harpo steals Hennessey's shirt while he's wearing it, Harpo has a quick game of tic-tac-toe with Chico on Hennessey's undershirt. The loss of his shirt inspires Hennessey to sing a *Carmen*-esque aria, "I want my shirt," an allusion the Marx Brothers' bull fighting costumes prepare us for. And the restoration of the shirt results in a grateful and humbled enforcer of the law, one who is now able to recognize the real villains.

One of the nine times Harpo gives his leg to others to hold, not that they asked for it. Sylvan Lee as bellhop and Harpo Marx as Harpo. *The Cocoanuts*, Paramount Pictures, 1929. From the collections of the Margaret Herrick Library.

At one point in *The Cocoanuts,* Hammer says about Harpo, "Don't talk — he'll take the voice right out of your mouth," but it seems rather that someone has taken Harpo's voice, though we have to rewind back before this film to the Marx Brothers' earlier stage career to discover the origin of Harpo's muteness. Of relevance here are the ramifications of Harpo's silence, a staple of his persona that liberated him from problems of early sound in this film but that doesn't inhibit him from answering the telephone twice, once tasting it and once honking his horn into it. In fact, Harpo's muteness has important trickster resonance, connecting him to the underdog by expanding access to his comedy in a country of immigrants with their babbled tongues, a theme addressed more explicitly in *The Big Store*. The language Harpo speaks, a language of props, gestures, facial expressions, rudimentary sounds like whistles and lip pops, and later tattoos, is commonly accessible. So Harpo's silence offers a more universal speech.

Significantly, Harpo also speaks the language of music. For Harpo, like Hermes, is adept at playing a stringed instrument, the harp a cousin of the lyre that made Hermes a little god.[4] It may be true that sometimes Harpo plays the harp backwards,[5] but his technique fascinated harpists and won him amused admiration. Harpo's face is beatific in the harp-playing interludes in this and subsequent Marx Brothers films. By his own admission, the distinction between Harpo and Arthur Marx dissolves when, enraptured and enrapturing, he plays. Moreover, epithets like "bum" flung at him by the likes of Harvey — after Harpo dances Penelope and him around the hotel lobby and inspiring a musical exit full of Revolutionary War iconography to make sure we get the revolutionary thrust of the Marx Brothers comedy — are contradicted when he plays the harp.

Even heartbreak is on hold as Harpo plays the theme song, strumming a superior dreamed world into existence for the duration of his solo. Also like Hermes, who made music on a pipe after giving Apollo the gift of his lyre, Harpo plays a clarinet in *The Cocoanuts*, though it is Harpo's transcendent repose on the harp that renders him angelic and thus connects him to trickster's divinity. Harpo's musicality helps realize his complex trickster nature, part buffoon, part animal, but also part angel.

Finally and most importantly, Harpo's mischief, like trickster's in many a tale, is crucial to helping the underdog by loosening destructive social attitudes and thus rectifying the culture's values. Mrs. Potter, for example, needs to have her goddess-on-high social vision cleansed in the little universe of this film, a theme first suggested by the negative print of women dancing during the film's title sequence. This visual trope reminds us that sometimes we see through cellulose darkly, that truth may be the opposite of appearance, and that even the high life may not be what it seems. This is why trickster's attack on rigidity and smug certainty — and who can seem more wonderfully smug and certain than Margaret Dumont? — matter deeply and perennially.

Necessary to this work is Harpo's irreverence for the gods on high that, like trickster's, ultimately shows the way to healthier and less rigid values. Who would tamper with the U.S. mail? Trickster would, his spirit of mischief and mayhem in the face of authority established early in the film when Harpo breaches the barricade of the hotel counter to tear up hotel guests' letters in the little boxes. This is a federal crime, and letters are potent symbols of the social contract, links in the chain of humanity, so there is something breathtakingly shocking about Harpo's behavior. But envelopes can also contain bills, draft notices, summonses, and all sorts of bad news or obligations, including news of illness and death. Perhaps for this reason we feel, in addition to shock, a curious ebullience watching Harpo destroy mail: He shows us how easy it is not only to break rules but also to free ourselves from entanglements. For this interlude, Harpo makes us feel like kites, strings snapped, sailing up and away. He even advances to a telegram while Hammer, sympathetic to the madness because he is trickster's cohort at heart, hands him more letters. (Harpo also tears up a telegram in *Duck Soup,* possibly forestalling war.) Treating the sacrosanct irreverently can be cleansing: In this scene, federal authority and social obligations are jolted and reconsidered by Harpo's mayhem with the mail.

Furthermore, despite his tampering with the mail, we never really doubt Harpo's benevolence. When he comes upon Polly weeping alone in the garden because her beloved Bob has been arrested and her mother has announced her betrothal to the schemer Harvey, Harpo tries to console her by offering her a lollipop. He licks it first to demonstrate what to do with it, a charmingly childlike gesture. But when Polly weeps on his shoulder, a close-up of Harpo reveals his wide-eyed dismay in the face of human sorrow.

Harpo also exhibits those wide eyes the entire time the schemer Penelope is trying to seduce him to visit her room, but this time they're wide with skepticism and he is anything but childish. While she is trying to trick him, Harpo is busy stealing her handkerchief with his teeth, and listening to her without believing a word she says. In the scene in her hotel room, he is especially crafty in the way he steals the written evidence of the Potter-necklace-theft plan by deftly catching it in his top hat, an incongruous, ironic, and resonant article of his wardrobe that satirizes the upper class while positing a different and unexpected kind of nobility, one attached to lowliness. Then he swims on a carpet, hops up on Mrs. Potter's bed in the adjoining room and gestures for her to join him there, gives Penelope an unwanted embrace or two, and goes in and out and in and out of doors, often unseen.

In fact, Harpo shares trickster's attraction to liminal spaces, the kinds of intermediate locations where change and accident can occur. In this film, he hangs around doorways, lobbies, and elevators, all in a hotel where land and water meet. And the sequence in Penelope's room exploits the liminal for humor because Penelope and Mrs. Potter's rooms, though they have their own hall entries, have a connecting door. So they are places of potentially violated space where mischief can be accomplished or thwarted.

In this scene, all three Marxes, Mrs. Potter, Penelope, Harvey, and Detective Hennessey enter and exit through the front and adjoining doors of these two rooms while we watch them suspect the presence of, yet fail to catch each other in a scene of escalating confusion. Finally we are led to understand that identities as well as fate — future successes or failures — are in flux. And when Penelope steals Mrs. Potter's necklace in order to entrap Bob, we know that no matter their frequency, Harpo's thefts are essentially harmless while Harvey and Penelope's one theft is bad to the bone. When at last the two rooms empty out and the scene winds down, Harpo emerges from under a bed with the incriminating evidence bagged, thank goodness, in his hat.

The bad thieves are busted in the final scene, compliments of Harpo's clowning. Excessively thirsty, drunk, and utterly annoyed by the phoniness of speechifying, he stalks away from the dinner table each time someone rises to speak, his grimace a hyperbole of disapproval and disgust. When Hammer, Groucho, Mrs. Potter, or Harvey get up to speechify, Harpo slinks to the punch bowl for escape and fortification, each time returning to the table a little more sloshed. After a while, a trip to the punch bowl becomes Harpo's conventional response to anything: He stalks off for wine when Hammer announces "music" and Chico rises to play the piano, thus implying his preference for his own harp serenade and giving us a peek beyond the fourth wall at their sibling rivalry, the latter also alluded to in Harpo and Chico's fake fistfights in several of the films.

The picaresque is a big part of trickster legend: trickster wanders from place to place, having adventures. In *The Cocoanuts,* Harpo and Chico arrive at the hotel from wherever they were elsewhere — that undisclosed location often implied in the films — likewise in picaresque style. In subsequent films, Harpo will turn up at a Long Island mansion, a college, a circus, a duchy, an ocean liner, the opera, a racetrack, a department store, the wild West, even in Casablanca — to make messes and to clean them up, to correct imbalances social or political, to unite lovers, to have a little fun, chase some women, love some members of the four-legged nations, shape-shift, eat some food and some non-food, and leave when the work is done. Here Harpo turns up at a Florida resort, and the stolen items that fall out of his coat imply prior sojourns at hotels in other states.

The main work to be accomplished in this film is the revelation of Bob's talent as an architect and the cleansing of the widow Potter of snobbery so that the lovers, Bob and Mrs. Potter's daughter Polly, can unite. This is accomplished via Harpo's exposing both Harvey's duplicity and Bob's worth. Along the way, *The Cocoanuts* introduces many motifs that establish Harpo's identity as trickster, and more fully a trickster than Groucho or Chico. Some clues to his archetypical nature are embedded in gags he will repeat in subsequent films, whether filmed in Queens or Hollywood: his appearing from nowhere or anywhere, an unabashed thief with excessive appetites and a complex animal-human-angelic nature, a player of stringed and wind instruments who treats institutions and powerful people with irreverence, cleanses them, and thus corrects injustice and recalibrates culture, especially when he comes down on the side of young love and against social class snobbery. He chases women, offers his leg with his trope of the hinged knee to all and sundry, and communicates with his flatulent horn. And this film is just the beginning.

2
Animal Crackers (1930)
THE PROFESSOR PROFESSES

"My clothes made all the difference. Since they were invited in,
I'm feeding the dinner to my hungry clothes."
— Schram, *The Hungry Clothes*[1]

Like trickster in folklore, Harpo deflates the inflated. He does this in
The Cocoanuts by undermining Mrs. Potter's premises about status, thereby
removing barriers to the love between Polly and Bob. And his accomplishment
is similar in the Marx Brothers second film, *Animal Crackers*. But in this film,
Harpo's trickster essence expands to include magic and the surreal. He animates the inanimate and even steals what a mere human cannot steal: Roscoe
Chandler's birthmark. So in addition to standing up for the underdog, Harpo's
character, the Professor, challenges our assumptions about the nature of reality,
an attack on philosophical idealism that offers its own kind of renewal. For
once destabilized, what is real expands to admit the mysterious and surreal,
and our vision is broadened. In *Animal Crackers*, Harpo shows us that
expanded reality is not a bad place to be, and expanded vision is not a bad
way to see.

Groucho, playing Captain Spaulding, and Chico, playing Ravelli, are
trickster cohorts who share his adventures and facilitate his accomplishments.
But here, as in other Marx Brothers films and despite Groucho's compelling
verbal audacity, the trickster essence is concentrated, distilled, and made multi-
faceted in Harpo, who, in this second film, returns with renewed energy to
the task of democratizing, expanding perimeters, and cleansing a society of
myopic snobbery so that it is able to recognize and celebrate genuine worth.
He carries his lollipop from *The Cocoanuts* into *Animal Crackers,* and he may
even still be wearing Robert Florey's belt.

In the world of *Animal Crackers,* the need for trickster's remediation is established in the fifteen minutes, before Harpo's entrance. It is a world of division, social and financial. Margaret Dumont's Mrs. Rittenhouse introduces the presumptions of the upper class with her trilled *r*s, her mansion, and her social-event-of-the-year party. On the other hand, Groucho and Chico simultaneously initiate the deconstruction of such pomposity, preparing both her millieu and the audience for the Professor's instruction.

Before Harpo's entrance, delayed like in *The Cocoanuts,* Mrs. Rittenhouse's world is shown to be snobbish, prudish, and full of beneath-the-veneer contradictions. Captain Spaulding, for example, is celebrated as "a moral man who hates dirty jokes unless they are told by someone who knows how to tell them," and the musician Ravelli charges a fee for playing but a higher fee for not playing, a fee for practicing but an even higher fee for not practicing, implying that silence is more valuable than sound and thus tipping his hat to Harpo's mute eloquence. In listening to Harpo's cohorts, the liberation of the viewer's mind begins: Absurdities undermine premises, creating a receptive — a hinged — state of mind.

At this point, the Professor swaggers in wearing a top hat and cape, vestiary markers of the wealthy. He ostentatiously blows dense bubbles of smoke with his cigar: smoke solidified, his first trope on the nature of reality. His second is chocolate smoke produced at Groucho's request, a meta-cinematic joke in a black and white film, as are references to his red hair in several of the films. He is compared not to an animal, as in *The Cocoanuts,* but to a Fig Newton, a cookie with exotic fruit between its layers. And we are about to see that fruit, for when the butler takes Harpo's hat and coat, his clothes come away with his coat, and lo, Harpo stands in the center of the shot in his underwear, challenging propriety with his shame covers removed even while reminding us that no matter how superior our apparel may be, once stripped of it, we are only ourselves. Moreover, his unabashed response to the removal of his clothes suggests that his exposure may seem shocking to others but not to himself. He couldn't care less what he is wearing or not wearing. It's summertime, and the strippin' is easy.

Yet Harpo in his underwear in a formal social setting does suggest vulnerability of the kind that flesh and spirit work hard to cover. So we are also taught a lesson by his nonchalant response to his state of undress. Because he is utterly at ease and it seems all the same to him: top hat and cape or underwear, and because, moreover, Harpo in his underwear may be more interesting than Harpo in top hat and cape, he teaches us that the essential self is more engaging than the layers we construct to cover it. Furthermore, the stripping of Harpo introduces the thematic motif of unmasking in this film: The loyal and proper butler is an ex-con in cahoots with a scheming guest; the dealer of fine art, Roscoe Chandler, is really Abie the Fishman.

With Harpo's entrance, the mood established by Groucho's verbal wit rapidly deteriorates into slapstick and mayhem. The guests, shocked by the Professor's undressing, flee. So the sudden assault on proper decorum creates space, physical space that parallels the psychic space Groucho and Chico liberated in the first scene with their nonsense logic. Here the audience can float as if gravity were suspended, pun definitely intended. In rapid succession, Harpo offers his leg to Groucho, he brandishes a pistol which causes the guests to scatter, he shoots the cuckoo bird from the clock, and he fires at a statue that, in self-defense, comes alive to draw a pistol and fire back.

The bird and the statue erase the distinction between animate and inanimate, and this gets added to the rapidly growing list of eroded distinctions: those between hero and *schnorrer,* hello and goodbye, clothed and naked, music and silence, order and chaos. The Professor shoots hats off of women and shoots the butler's tray from his hands. Closing the scene, Harpo reprises a moment from *The Cocoanuts,* marching Revolutionary War–style to piccolo notes and reminding us again that trickster's is a revolutionary sensibility. He closes the scene chasing a blonde, exhibiting trickster's hyperbolic lust, a motif that helps *Animal Crackers* cohere as did Harpo's many thefts in *The Cocoanuts.*

Of course, the Professor is a thief in this film too. His thefts comprise its other major motif, especially the confusing succession of thefts of the Beaugard painting, including thefts of the bogus Beaugards. All the paintings pass through Harpo's hands and end up in his possession. This complex core of the plot, the multiple identities of the painting, the original *After the Hunt* and its imitations, is hard to follow. Furthermore, the similar sounds of *bogus* and *Beaugard,* the film's fictional artist, suggest that art is an object of satire here: not genuine art, perhaps, but the failure of upper crust art collectors who attempt to gain status by owning fine art to recognize artistic genius.

Harpo is the pivot of this art-centered plot, and it is worth noting that the better artist, John Parker, is also the better person: that he, though unknown, is as skilled as the recognized master, Beaugard. Harpo ultimately helps reveal this truth. It is also worth noting that *After the Hunt*'s subject matter not only rhymes with Captain Spaulding's spurious African safari adventures but also presupposes a distinction between humans and animals that runs contrary to much trickster lore and one that Harpo repeatedly deconstructs in Marx Brothers films, starting with *The Cocoanuts,* his being a dogcatcher in *Horse Feathers* notwithstanding. His animal simpatico is ramped up a notch here. For though Harpo comes to possess every version of the Beaugard, bogus and otherwise, he treats them all, fake or genuine, with the same benign irreverence, caring more for a photograph of his sweetheart, a horse.

Because of his connection to all of the paintings (the Beaugard, John Parker's masterful imitation, and Grace Carpenter's inept one), Harpo moves to the center of the plot. Mrs. Whitehead apparently wants to create a diversion to embarrass Mrs. Rittenhouse — snobs battling snobs — by replacing the Beaugard with her friend's unskilled imitation, so she convinces the butler Hives, her loyal former employee — "my soul is yours though my body belongs to Mrs. Rittenhouse," says he to her — to switch them. But she is not the only character motivated to substitute a bogus Beaugard. In the sequence that introduces the theft-of-the-Beaugard plot, we also meet Arabella Rittenhouse and her sweetheart John Parker, an impoverished painter. Our sympathies align with young love as easily as with unrecognized talent. Chico's Ravelli agrees to help them, involving the Professor in the effort and thus placing him on the side that trickster tends to favor anyway: young love and its inevitable consequence, the procreant urge.

Arabella's scheme to substitute John's copy for the Beaugard, unlike Mrs. Whitehead's, has the more honorable motive of revealing John's talent to the world. The fate of these young lovers rests in Harpo and Chico's hands, even while Harpo is engaging in other trickster antics: stealing silverware, cross-dressing, creating chaos, playing the piano, flute, and harp, and chasing blondes in bathing suits or summer dresses up and down the elaborate stairway of Mrs. Rittenhouse's Long Island summer mansion with its vacation ambiance reminiscent of the hotel in *The Cocoanuts*.

But mischief isn't all Harpo engages in while helping these marginalized sweethearts. He accomplishes by far the most impressive theft in the film and perhaps in all Marx Brothers films when he steals art dealer Roscoe Chandler's birthmark. Ravelli is the first to notice that Chandler looks familiar. But it takes the Professor to reduce Chandler to his essential identity as Abie the Fishman. The Professor professes volumes when he tackles Chandler, rolls up his sleeve, and points to the identifying birthmark.

What does it mean that Roscoe W. Chandler is Abie the Fishman from their village in Czechoslovakia? For one thing, it means that the immigrant experience in America includes the magic of reinvention: one can don a new identity with little likelihood of exposure. This, of course, is the opposite of Harpo's wearing the cape and top hat, then ending up "exposed." Harpo not only jumps on Chandler, picks his pocket, and steals his handkerchief, but he also steals, with surreal finesse, Chandler's birthmark and affixes it to his own arm, an act that solidifies Harpo's status as magician and shape-shifter, though here he shifts someone else's shape as well.

Suspecting that art dealer Roscoe Chandler is really Abie the Fishman from Czechoslovakia, Harpo and Chico tackle him to see his birthmark. Harpo Marx as The Professor, Louis Sorin as Roscoe Chandler, and Chico Marx as Emanuelle Ravelli. *Animal Crackers,* Paramount Pictures, 1930. From the collections of the Margaret Herrick Library.

And Chandler's is not the only unstable identity in the film: Hives, the proper butler, has a criminal past, and Groucho replaces "Captain Spaulding, African Explorer" with *schnorrer*. Even the painting at the center of the film has multiple incarnations. For although we know that the lovers, John and Arabella, have enlisted help in substituting John's copy for the original Beaugard painting, and we may assume that Chico and Harpo accomplish the swap before Hives and Whitehead substitute Grace Carpenter's copy, we aren't entirely certain. Do Chico and Harpo remove the genuine Beaugard? Does Hives have John's masterful imitation?

The scene in which Chico and Harpo replace the Beaugard with John's copy as a favor to John and Arabella has multiple trickster moments. When the lights go out in a thunderstorm, the mute Professor satirizes language, specifically the potential for misunderstanding in immigrant pronunciation. For when Ravelli asks for a flashlight but pronounces flash *flesh*, Harpo offers him a flask, a fish, and a flute, all from the deep pockets of his coat, and, incidentally, reprising one of their stage skits. The chaos intensifies when Captain Spaulding and Mrs. Rittenhouse, groping in the dark room, find Harpo's fish. Yet although Harpo and Chico are making a racket, Spaulding and Mrs. Rittenhouse seem unaware that others are in the room, let alone are there swapping paintings.

Harpo makes more magic at the end of the scene when he opens the door on one side of the room to night and a storm but opens the door on the other side of the room to a sunny day. This may be a meta-cinematic joke on the weather in California where this film was being shot. Or it may be meta-cinematic commentary and not a joke at all, given that night and day, rain and sun, are occurring somewhere on the vast continent where the film is playing. The conditions of the setting beyond the set and studio, in other words, are other identities that are not fixed or stable.

In *Animal Crackers,* between every scene that advances the plot, an inter-

At the end of a dysfunctional bridge game, Harpo has somehow stolen and is wearing Mrs. Whitehead's shoes, and oh how they fit him! Left to right: Margaret Irving as Mrs. Whitehead, Chico Marx as Ravelli, Margaret Dumont as Mrs. Rittenhouse, and Harpo Marx as The Professor. *Animal Crackers,* Paramount Pictures, 1930.

lude advances the spirit of chaos and mischief, reminding us that we are in trickster's world. While the core of the plot thickens around the painting, Harpo continues chasing blondes, gives Chico and others his leg, honks his horn, and whips a card game into chaotic froth. When he and Chico sit down with Mrs. Rittenhouse and Mrs. Whitehead for a game of bridge, a refined and orderly pastime with upper class associations, Harpo's first deconstruction involves folding as Hives unfolds the card table, at last smashing in on Hives' head and literally framing him. Then Harpo and Chico monkey with the rules of bridge. Harpo, with an endless supply of aces of spades, peeks at the women's hands, switches cards on them, disposes of cards, insults Mrs. Rittenhouse, satirizes card shark gestures, and makes nonsense bids. In fact, Harpo is so out of control in this scene that both women ask, "What is the matter with him?" By the end of the scene, Harpo has stolen and is wearing, though we cannot imagine how, Mrs. Whitehead's shoes, the first but not the only example of his cross-dressing in the film.

Mrs. Rittenhouse's soiree for Captain Spaulding also gets cleansed with chaos. When Spaulding tells a story about bagging six tigers, saying *begging* instead of *bagging*, we have more satire on immigrant pronunciation of English along with an example of how a profound change of meaning and even ironic truth can emerge by means of a single altered letter. When Mrs. Rittenhouse calls for "three cheers for Captain Spaulding," Harpo carries in three *chairs,* his understanding influenced either by poor spelling, Groucho's explanation, or by his habitually hearing English spoken by immigrants. Then follows typical Marx mayhem, Ravelli exasperating the guests with a monotonous tune on the piano, Harpo spinning the piano stool and scorching his bum, all three roughhousing and playing football with a pillow, and Harpo reprising his *Cocoanuts* grimace when Chico plays. At the end of this scene, Harpo bangs together horse shoes, punctuating with a clang the well-deserved deconstruction of upper class colonial values: Rittenhouse and company's celebration of a *schnorrer* explorer. Harpo implies that a horse is better company.

Then, as often happens in the films, Harpo goes from the ridiculous to the sublime by playing a serene harp solo, shifting our awareness to the divine in his trickster nature. And the impression not only endures but also works proactively. The painting is unveiled and Chandler recognizes a forgery, apparently Grace Carpenter's unskilled imitation; the lights go out, then the forgery too is stolen; Mrs. Whitehead, Grace Carpenter and Hives suspect the Professor but we still trust him, our sympathy reinforced when the young lovers sing a duet, "Why Am I So Romantic?" and the Professor plays the melody on his harp, whistles it, and puts himself to sleep with his music as if he were his own innocent baby.

Even scenes in this film that do not involve Harpo have the Professor's lessons embedded in them. Arabella asks Ravelli to return the original painting but they discover it is missing; Ravelli suspects Chandler, and we remember who Chandler really is, thanks to Harpo, who revealed and is wearing the evidence of Abie the Fishman's birthmark. When Zeppo, Spaudling's secretary, takes a letter for him, with satire coming as early as the salutation "Gentlemen" followed by a question mark, we are reminded of the question raised by the vision of Harpo in his underwear at the formal party: Who is a gentleman? The Professor? Roscoe Chandler, who is really Abie the Fishman? John Parker, unrecognized genius? Captain Spaulding, African *schnorrer*? Ironically, all of these Rittenhouse mansion conundrums transpire while Harpo sleeps peacefully on a bench outdoors where his feathered and hoofed friends abide. The painting is his blanket — he treats whichever version of it this may be with casual irreverence even while others are searching for it. The singing birds are his clocks.

In this way Harpo's animal nature, akin to trickster's, is hinted in *Animal Crackers,* to be developed more fully in subsequent films. For example, Mrs. Whitehead, tipped off by Hives that the Professor did not sleep in his room all night, seeks him outdoors to angle for the painting. When she asks whom he loves, the Professor shows her a picture of a horse and kisses it while simultaneously hiding the folded canvas in a newspaper to keep it from her. When she tries to take the bundle, he gives her his leg, twitting her with the power of the flexible joint. He also mimes that he is five years old, smacks her when she touches his leg, then kisses her hand, typical trickster multitasking.

Harpo often operates on multiple levels. For example, when Hives chloroforms him and he loses the painting to Whitehead, he is not unconscious for long because when a blonde passes by, he revives to chase her, lust overpowering chloroform, even while he is clutching a lollipop that seems to have been transplanted from *The Cocoanuts*. When John says that there is a painting on the terrace, Harpo runs upstairs to retrieve it and comes down nonchalantly, the painting under his hat. He steals Groucho's watch and, aware that he is a suspect because of a suspicious red hair, disguises himself as an inspector and drops a "left-handed painting," diverting focus to a "left-handed painter." Granted, none of this makes much sense. The Professor seems to be the thief of all the paintings, but a hinged mind might also understand that he's gathering them.

And he is preparing to reveal more than which one is the original. The final sequence reinforces aspects of the Professor's trickster nature though it feels more like a comic interlude than a conclusion. Instead of helping the lovebirds, the Professor is playing around with chloroform and a bug-sprayer.

He even pauses to join Groucho, Zeppo, and Chico in a rendition of "Old Kentucky Home," standing behind them and moving his lips though presumably not making a sound, then emerging from behind them dressed in what may be an upside-down union suit but looks more like a woman's dress, the second instance of gender-bending reminiscent of the sometimes ambiguously gendered trickster of legend, an aspect of Harpo's persona more fully developed in subsequent films.

The fake Beaugard is found in John's room and it looks bad for him: Like in *The Cocoanuts,* the innocent guy has been framed, and he needs someone with special powers to save him. Then an inspiring thing happens: Characters reveal a selfless disregard for consequences that is also sometimes part of trickster lore. To protect John, the Professor, Ravelli, Spaulding, and even Mrs. Rittenhouse and her daughter Arabella confess to the theft of the Beaugard. But the Professor saves the day — after, that is, a bit of buffoonery. When Inspector Hennessey asks to see "the picture," meaning the Beaugard painting, Harpo shows him the picture of his beloved horse. Then he pulls John's masterful imitation and the Beaugard original rolled up in tubes from under his big coat and unfurls them. They are indistinguishable. So thanks to the Professor, John Parker's artistic genius is recognized, he gets a commission on the spot from Roscoe Chandler, a.k.a. Abie the Fishman, and John and Arabella exit the scene in one other's arms.

The most amusing part of the conclusion, though, involves Harpo's return to his nature as hyperbolic thief. When Inspector Hennessy asks him, "Do you want to be a crook?" Harpo's face lights up and he eagerly nods assent, for trickster *is* a thief: Stealing is part of his nature as is lust, sympathy for the underdog, animal simpatico, magic, shape-shifting, gender-bending, working the hinge, and charming others with music played on a stringed instrument. Many of these traits are expressed in the penultimate scene. When the inspector shakes the Professor's hand and tells him a sentimental story about his mother, hoping to dissuade him from a life of crime, stolen silverware falls from Harpo's sleeves. After a query from Spaulding, even the prodigal silver coffee pot descends. Harpo's stealing, like trickster's, is unabashed and unrestrained.

In the final scene, the film's denouement, the Professor, knowing he is about to be arrested, sprays Hennessey and everyone else with Whitehead and Hive's leftover chloroform. He has to spray Groucho's leg a few time to put *it* down. But when Ravelli suggests that they escape, perhaps to wherever they came from in picaresque style in the first place, Harpo sprays Chico, then positions himself next to the blonde he has been chasing throughout the film, and sprays himself. At last he has caught up with her.

3

Monkey Business (1931)
NOT QUITE CHEVALIER

Trickster's is a "spirit of disorder, enemy of boundaries, a mighty life spirit."
— Radin, *The Trickster*[1]

In *Monkey Business,* some of Harpo's trickster characteristics are reinforced and even more fully realized, among them his playfulness in the face of peril, his lust for blondes, his deep connection to animals, his irreverent treatment of the upper class, and his generosity with his leg, symbol of playful flexibility, an ideal to aspire to. The film also contains numerous riffs on facial hair amounting to a submerged allusion to our animal natures, for the autonomy of hair and its capacity to transform others by means of its removal (or its addition, as in *A Night at the Opera*) is emphasized. Harpo even reverses the animation-of-the-inanimate motif developed in *Animal Crackers,* for here we have the in-animation of the animate. And as usual, Harpo's trickster impact lingers, following us out of the film and calibrating our lives.

Groucho worried that this first film he and his brothers made in Hollywood for Paramount would flop at the box office. But it didn't, for though its plot is loose, its charms get under the skin like Marx Brothers films tend to do, offering their double dose of liberation, both social and psychological. Here the four brothers (Zeppo is still in the act), bearing their own stage names, play stowaways on an ocean liner. As the credits roll over rolling barrels, each brother's face appears in a knothole, making us think of barrels of monkeys. The milieu being satirized this time is the luxury liner: its command structure, shipboard protocol, and especially its bureaucratic processes at ports of entry involving customs, passports, and the stamping of paperwork.

39

Of course the ship is a microcosm, so the satire applies to institutions on terra firma that have arbitrary social constructs predicated on status and rank divisions that separate those with authority from ordinary people, in this case passengers, and that separate ordinary passengers from the underclass, in this case stowaways, a trope repeated when the Marxes are again stowaways and join the Italian immigrants traveling in steerage for a feast and music in *A Night at the Opera*. Furthermore, like any other, this ocean-liner world has its breakers and benders of rules, here represented by both the stowaways and the gangsters who happen to be traveling legitimately as paying passengers. And because those gangsters, in fact, are not all the same, this film, like others, develops a distinction between *good* bad and *bad* bad. One must be capable of negative capability,[2] or have a hinged mind, to grasp the distinction.

Harpo's entrance is not delayed in this film. He simply appears with his trickster cohorts Groucho, Chico, and Zeppo, who in this film is more than just a guy: He's the romantic lead. They all seem to be wanderers. Where do they come from? We know only that they are in the ship's storeroom, and they are somehow related to one another, broke and inhabiting barrels, yet not particularly concerned about their insecure tenure on board. In the opening scene, in fact, they are singing in harmony, their voices rising from separate barrels labeled "kippered herring." These herrings sing "Sweet Adeline" in the four-part harmony of a barbershop quartet, and this, of course, injects the absurd implication that Harpo is singing too. Is his part silence, like the ideal sound of pipes on Keats' Grecian urn?[3] In addition to presenting us with this conundrum, their foolish-under-the-circumstances singing alerts the ship's authorities not only that there are stowaways hiding on board but even, one could argue, how many there are.

This is the first joke that celebrates Harpo's muteness in the film, a muteness that hasn't disqualified him yet from participating in voice-dominated activities: in *The Cocoanuts* liberating him from problems of early sound film but not preventing him from interacting with telephones; in *Animal Crackers*, letting him profess without speaking and sing without singing. And here, moments into *Monkey Business*, he's singing without singing again too.

This opening scene also introduces several of the film's motifs, starting with trickster's animal nature. Harpo and his cohorts are passing as "kippered herring" after having sent a note calling the captain an "old goat." In addition, the motif of facial hair, embedded in the gestalt of a barbershop quartet, is bandied humorously when Chico says his grandfather's beard is coming by "hair mail" to meet Groucho's mustache. The autonomous life of facial hair will be fully realized in a later scene in the ship's barbershop. And because the four are singing purely for enjoyment even while jeopardizing their concealment, we understand that for them pleasure trumps safety, and musical expression trumps practicality. We're being instructed on values here.

Harpo mimes the brushing of his hair using the barrel's lid for a mirror, and he mimes shaving with his horn whose honking gives them away. Indeed, when the stowaways are stripped of their barrels—one moment the barrels presumably have bottoms, the next, they are hoisted over their heads bottomless—the brothers respond with a nonchalance akin to Harpo's in his underwear in *Animal Crackers*: They squat in a circle on the floor, preparing food and making cocktails, maybe even shooting craps, impervious to being busted.

So far, Harpo's nature hasn't been distinguished much from his cohorts,' but that is about to change. In the chase scene that follows, his trickster antics are manifest. To keep the chase alive, a good example of tricksterly self-sabotage, Harpo honks his horn. On deck he rolls a life preserver like a child rolling a hoop, then tosses it over a man's head as if it were a peg to hang it on, reversing the inanimate-brought-to-life gag in *Animal Crackers*. In fact, in *Monkey Business* the motif consistently involves the rendering of the animate inanimate, a trope fully realized in the marionette scene. In this early sequence it is further developed when Harpo hides from the captain's goons by lying on a deck chair under a woman who seems unaware that she is reclining on Harpo and not merely the chair. And Harpo himself is gleefully sprawled on top of a man who may be her husband or even a stranger. The unfortunate man, squished deeply into the fold of the chair, is the bottom slice of bread in a trickster sandwich.

Harpo and his cohorts disguise themselves by shape-shifting too. During the chase, they hide in full view, posing as the ship's orchestra, picking up instruments and playing them raucously. That they are applauded tells us that there is a need for manic music on this ship, just as there is a need later for the lilting, lulling music of the harp. In this earlier scene, Harpo plays what looks like a soprano saxophone, again echoing trickster Hermes' musical versatility. And this prepares us for his and his cohorts' Maurice Chevalier impersonations that are yet to come.

After the chase scene, Harpo disappears for a while from the film. He isn't with Groucho and Chico when they steal into the captain's quarters, ignoring shipboard protocol in order to cop a meal. This important scene, though Harpo-less, is Harpo-esque because it involves cleaning with dirt: the lowly stowaways sullying the inner sanctum of the ship and sitting at the captain's table where they are also re-enlivening the space. It's the kind of scene Harpo is well suited for and we miss him in it, but meanwhile he is up to more dramatic trickster antics. After chasing a blonde, he hides from the authorities in a Punch and Judy[4] show by becoming part of it, using his Gookie face as his mask.

Here we have the animate Harpo becoming an inanimate puppet, but on another level we also wonder what human force is animating the actual wooden puppets because we see no puppeteer, not even when we are shown Harpo's backside behind the stage. Moreover, Harpo makes an excellent dummy; his antics sync well with those of the marionettes Punch and Judy. Both as a puppet and as a man, his silliness is much appreciated by the audience of children. In fact, in every film, children are drawn to Harpo, perhaps because children are closer to the inchoate, mischievous energy of trickster.

When the captain's goon spots him as one of the stowaways, the ensuing confusion and chase are predicated on one question: Harpo or dummy? Keeping in mind that a willing suspension of disbelief in the distinction between animate and inanimate is necessary to enjoy a puppet show, the ambiguity cast upon Harpo's nature also makes us wonder if the distinction is overrated.

As a puppet between Punch and Judy, Harpo blurs the distinction between animate and inanimate while entertaining the children and twitting the ship's authorities. Harpo Marx as Harpo. *Monkey Business,* Paramount Pictures, 1931.

It may be that we depend upon it to navigate ordinary life, yet relaxing the barrier between animate and inanimate feels liberating in this scene. Harpo opens a door to a reality whose nature and essence may be very different from, and infinitely more interesting and magical than the one we take for granted and assume. The children enjoy his antics without getting hung up on the distinction, for the imaginations of children have not yet erected barriers between animate and inanimate, real and imaginary. They are in a hinged state that is as essential to play as play is to learning.

But we aren't left to contemplate Harpo-or-dummy for long. Harpo exploits the confusion to kick the captain's goon when he turns his back. Then in a meta-cinematic spin on his own gag involving his proffered leg, he offers a leg that is not his own leg but a rigid and false limb, a mannequin leg that he and the captain and his goon have a tug of war over. Harpo even crosses over to their side to help them pull it. His joining them intensifies the visual pun on *pulling someone's leg* while it further confuses animate and inanimate, a conflation repeated in a later scene when Harpo unscrews his hand, apparently an extra one that gets in the way of his playing the harp. And we mustn't forget that Harpo's leg isn't the one being pulled here. Harpo's leg bends: It has an active and resilient hinge.

Expressing a kindred spirit, the alligator puppet honks Harpo's horn. And when the captain tries to assist in Harpo's apprehension, the children are clearly on Harpo's side, and therefore so are we, laughing and cheering with them when he escapes on a proto-skateboard, a toy, incidentally, that children and adults alike play on to this very day, not yet invented in 1931 but by trickster foreseen.

So the stowaways remain on the lam on board the ship, and the motif of facial hair is the next one to be more fully developed, this time in a scene of quiet chaos. Harpo and Chico are hiding in the barbershop pretending to be the ship's barbers when a ship's officer comes in. With equanimity, they shave him and trim his mustache while he naps in the chair. Chico keeps recommending additional "snoops" to even out the sides, and Harpo cheerfully complies, never a shy one with scissors, until the mustache is no more. In this early cinematic example of Harpo's scissor-wielding mischief, the officer remains asleep throughout the makeover, unaware that he is getting a new face.

This becomes part of the film's pattern of gags on facial hair that began in the opening scene with Chico's complaint that there wasn't room for his grandfather's beard in the claustrophobic barrel, the beard apparently on its way to visit him *sans* grandfather, as if, like Gogol's nose,[5] it can live a life of its own. Moreover, Chico hopes to introduce the beard to Groucho's mustache, the very feature, we later learn, that identifies him to the authorities and thus betrays the face it inhabits. So facial hair in this film has autonomy. It is like a little animal. And like he does with animals, Harpo doesn't fear it but establishes a rapport with it. He gets close to it, takes a scissors to it, yanks on it.

The autonomous life of facial hair is related to the theme of identity, one that Harpo and Harpo alone carries in Marx Brothers films. Sometimes it is manifested in the motif of gender ambiguity, which is one of the ways Harpo's trickster essence is made manifest, for trickster of myth and legend is not always exclusively male. Like other aspects of his identity, trickster's gender can be malleable.[6] We have an allusion to this in *Monkey Business* when Harpo stands in front of the ladies' room, his body hiding the "wo" part of "women" on the sign. When an unassuming man goes in, he gets thrown out. Only when Harpo walks away do we see the entire sign. Later in the film, Harpo disguises himself as the bustle on the back of a woman's dress, simultaneously going from animate to inanimate while, moreover, not *in* drag but drag itself.

Furthermore, Harpo and Harpo alone in this and other Marx Brothers films displays trickster's deep affinity for animals. Throughout the films, a familial bond exists between Harpo and the four-legged nations, an essential ontological connection reminding us of life's undifferentiated origin, life's universal template, and our connection to everything alive. In *Monkey Business*, when Harpo joins some children gathered around a little pond on the ship, he honks his horn to make them run away so he can coax the frog they are admiring to jump into his hat. Successful, he carries the frog on his head under his hat, a metaphor, perhaps, for shared sensibility. The frog's croak even substitutes for speech at times, the way Harpo's horn does.

Harpo chases women in this film, but those distractions seem more superficial than his devotion to this frog. Having shooed children away from the little shipboard pond to invite the frog into his hat, then having carried it secretly on his head, the relationship is threatened when he loses the frog and whistles for him but fails to find him. Harpo goes so far as to throttle a hoarse man who complains of having "a frog in his throat," then is ecstatic to find his frog in the hallway. Why a frog? And why is Harpo so devoted to it? What does he hear in the frog's croak?[7]

Harpo also offers trickster's political and social reverb in the film. For example, he develops a little satire on the sophisticated board game of chess when he comes upon two silent men playing an extremely slow match, so slow and intense that he smokes one of the men's cigarettes without being noticed, and then, with his cohort Chico, leans into the game, disrupts it, and walks off with the chessboard, chessmen intact. He and Chico resume the match as if, having stolen it, they are obligated to replicate its sluggish pace. Their satirical theft also facilitates the transition to the gangster part of this loose plot, for they start playing in what turns out to the sympathetic gangster Joe's stateroom.

Gangsters in *Monkey Business* help develop an important distinction, one that counteracts our tendency to think of the law as inflexibly black and white. Here Harpo and his cohorts are outlaws in that they are stowaways, thieves of passage on the ship. Yet they are sympathetic. So the question becomes, in part, how do they differ from the gangsters, the other lawbreakers on board? And how do the gangsters differ from each other? To resolve these questions, Harpo helps illuminate the distinction between the two kinds of gangsters on board: *good* bad Joe and *bad* bad Alky. This may actually be the distinction between *mischief* and *evil*.

For example, the racketeer Joe is a *good* bad guy because he is on the side of love, having an affectionate relationship with his daughter Mary, who is linked romantically to Zeppo. Joe's link, via Mary, to the cause of young love *de facto* classifies him as *good*. So does the amused way he receives Harpo's proffered leg, and this is no small thing: Uptight and unsympathetic characters tend to scorn Harpo's leg. Thus Harpo's offer of it becomes a barometer of the human heart. In contrast, the *bad* racketeer Alky (played by Harry Woods, whose name offers a gratuitous pun on hair), Joe's former partner, wants to have it out with Joe and maybe even kill him. Alky hires Groucho and Zeppo to help him because he is impressed by Groucho's *chutzpa* when he catches him romancing his wife. This has the potential though not the power to set trickster and his cohorts against each other.

For when Harpo and Chico wander into Joe's room with the chessboard, they are oblivious to the immanent confrontation between Joe and Alky. Unconcerned about danger or simply unaware, Harpo plays pat-a-cake with Alky, then scares him off with the stick end of his horn which Alky mistakes for a gun, a prime example of trickster's felicitous bumbling. When Harpo and Chico further impress Joe with their fighting fierceness, Harpo making his mean grimace and sending Chico flying with punches, he hires them for protection, potentially pitting them against Groucho and Zeppo. Echoing the music practice-play-pay gag from *Animal Crackers,* Chico negotiates their pay: For a little money, they can be a little tough; for too much money, they'll be too tough. That's precisely when Harpo gives Joe his leg and Joe smiles, assuring our sympathy for him because an unsympathetic character would fling the leg down. Not Joe.

Although Alky has armed Zeppo and Groucho, setting up the two contingencies for a violent confrontation, we needn't worry: Tricksters don't involve themselves in battles but are more likely to satirize the rituals of war.[8]

In this spirit, Groucho and Zeppo drown their guns in the first mop bucket they pass, and Harpo and Chico almost immediately lose Joe, whom they are supposed to be guarding, then proceed to mistake one after another passing man for him. They follow each Joe substitute sequentially — note that none of these men look even remotely like Joe — deciding that the last and this time bearded non–Joe must be Joe in disguise. Harpo even tries to pull off his beard, giving us yet another gag on facial hair. In the inevitable confrontation between the hired protectors, Harpo knocks Groucho over with a feather, offering us a double pun: the obvious one plus another that demonstrates the weight of Harpo's silence, for inside the feather is an iron rod.

The customs scene is the film's apogee, developing Harpo's talent for creating a level of chaos that is akin to trickster's in myth and legend. When the ship arrives in New York, after reporters interview an opera singer (who makes us miss the wonderfully inflated straight-woman Margaret Dumont), and after Zeppo and Mary's love scene (a farewell that must be undone according to the love-bird logic of the film's subplot), we are in for utterly raucous fun. For in an attempt to get off the ship without passports, each stowaway tries to pass as Maurice Chevalier, Zeppo having stolen or forged Chevalier's passport.

On a meta-cinematic level, it is amusing to see icons trying to pass for a different icon, but even within the fiction of the film, their attempt to do the impossible is amusing. Each Marx tries to get through the line as Maurice Chevalier by showing his passport and singing one of his most popular songs, "You Brought a New Kind of Love to Me." But Harpo is by far the most disruptive. First, he deconstructs language itself, substituting a washboard, then a pegboard for a passport. And though mute, he manages to sound exactly like Chevalier, which amounts to an auditory kind of shape-shifting.

The hilarity kicks in when Harpo gives up the failing ruse of lip syncing to a phonograph strapped to his back after it winds down once too often. At that point he throws himself wholeheartedly into disrupting the orderly bureaucratic process by means of which passengers leave the ship at the port of entry: first by getting hold of the inkpad and stamping everything in sight, including a bald officer's head, then by flinging stacks of official documents around.

Why does this scene amuse us, especially in our own era of scrutinized travel? Why should the disruption of a process that identifies passengers and makes sure dangerous criminals aren't allowed to pass through points of entry instead delight us? Because, fortunately, memory is long. We know that ink

Harpo, disguised as a bustle, cleaves to a woman's bottom and seems to enjoy it. Harpo Marx as Harpo, Maxine Castle and Rockliffe Fellows as party guests. *Monkey Business,* Paramount Pictures, 1931. From the collections of the Margaret Herrick Library.

stamps, papers, and line-ups can have their nightmare ends. And the whole notion of who is legally sanctioned and who is not must be continuously challenged, prone as such definitions are to prejudice and politics. The gathering of many into orderly lines, the relegating of some to cordoned areas and ominous transports, all so tidy and official, begs for disruption for the sake of our collective humanity. Who dares to model how to disrupt such procedures but trickster?

The stowaways find a way to get off the ship without papers when a woman calls for a doctor. Disregarding her need for help for her collapsed husband, Chico tells Harpo to take her pulse. Naturally, he takes her purse, a predictable response considering his inclinations both to hear immigrant English and to steal. When Chico says to cover her up, Harpo does so with his body, even though she isn't the one who needs attention. Somehow all four Marxes get carried off the ship under a blanket on the stretcher that is supposed to be bearing only the sick husband. In this way they actually enlist the authorities in the successful completion of their stolen passage.

The two remaining scenes, the party at Joe's mansion and the rescue of Mary in the barn, are peppered with Harpo's trickster antics. First, he injects a little gender confusion into the scene at Joe's mansion in several ways. When Joe introduces his daughter as "the sweetest little thing in the world," Harpo emerges from the wreath, stealing attention meant for Mary and posing coyly, then he resumes his lust for women, chasing a blonde on a bicycle, a moment immortalized in a poem by Jack Kerouac.[9] Just as suddenly, he partakes of the feminine again, disguising himself as a bustle and attaching himself to the back of a woman's dress, not only reprising the animate-to-inanimate trope, but also intensifying the humor by implication. For he is cleaving close to one woman's bottom, then another's, the effect of such proximity stirring our imaginations. We get some slapstick as well, for Harpo has to scurry to remain close as the oblivious women walk around. Eventually the manic Harpo tries to leap onto a woman's hoop skirt, but it collapses, unable to sustain the weight of his intensity.

Harpo calms down when, with trickster's intimations of divinity, he plays his harp, which he does in all the films but *Duck Soup* and *Room Service*. In *Monkey Business*, however, he clowns around at the onset of the performance. First, he steals his place at the harp by frightening off the harpist accompanying a female vocalist. Then he unscrews his hand before he plays, either because he has an extra one that is in the way or because he has a fake hand that must make way for the real and musically gifted hand, a gag reminiscent of his false leg in the Punch and Judy show that again confuses inanimate and animate.

Having usurped the place of the harpist, Harpo accompanies the singer in her rendition of "O Sole Mio," even while he mimes a critique of her performance by adjusting his nose while he plays, a visual pun suggesting multiple things: that she puts his nose out of joint, that she has a nasal twang, or even that the movement of his nose is making the music. Whichever it is, he finishes his accompaniment with his coat over his head as if embarrassed to be collaborating with her. Then, settling into his solo, Harpo honors Chico's request for the repetitive melody from the last film, "I'm Daffy Over You," but he embellishes it with glissandos while the frog, his kindred animal in this film, croaks approval from under Harpo's hat.

In the segue to the concluding scene involving the rescue of Mary, Harpo leaps onto a woman's back and rides her like a horse. All four Marx Brothers join the rescue, though Groucho does little more that broadcast the event while Zeppo does most of the fighting. Harpo actually gets in the way except when he wins a little hammer playing Chico's improvised wagon wheel roulette and uses it to thwack the heads of the bad gangsters. He also sits on a horse backwards, poised to ride into the future while watching the past, gazing over its rear. He is wearing a Paul Revere hat, yet another reminder that the comic antics of these films are revolutionary, an allusion repeated in each film so far and developed most fully in *Duck Soup.*

In our parting vision of Harpo, he emerges from the hay kissing the head of the calf that we earlier saw quaffing milk from its mother, a blasé mooing cow. He is holding the calf in his arms and kissing it as if he is the papa. Harpo often kisses animals in the films. And why not kiss one's kin?

4

Horse Feathers (1932)
DOGGING FOOTBALL

"All cultures have garbage heaps outside the city walls ... the trickster lives on those walls, always confusing boundaries and categories
and bringing material from one side of the wall to the other in a
way that modifies both sides."
— Voth, *Myth in Human History*[1]

Even the title of the Marx Brothers' fourth film, *Horse Feathers*, hints
at trickster's presence because the phrase is a euphemism for *horseshit,* as in
rubbish, nonsense, or *bunk,* thus signaling the film's attitude toward its
academic setting and presaging the deflation and cleansing to come. Harpo
plays Pinky, an illiterate dogcatcher and speakeasy delivery man who finds
himself enrolled to play football along with Chico's Baravelli, a rather simple-
minded Italian immigrant, at Huxley College where Groucho as Quincy
Wagstaff is the inappropriate new president. Huxley's football rivalry with
Darwin College — note the allusions to Thomas Huxley and Charles Darwin,
essentially members of the same evolution-minded team — widens the scope
of the satire to include not only student behavior and academic pretensions
but also prohibition speakeasies and the influence of organized crime on collegiate sports.

Trickster's cleansing doesn't devastate the institution: The scene of the
college burning down was cut. Instead, Harpo and his cohorts simply invade
the academic world and shake it up. They work closely together to accomplish
that, but as in earlier films, Harpo offers an intensified trickster essence. His
animal simpatico and his capacity for magic and the surreal are developed
further here. And seduction is added to the repertoire of effects his angelic
harp-playing has on others. There is, as usual, madness in Harpo's madness,

but there is also method, especially in the big game against Darwin, wherein his efforts single handedly help Huxley win.

The Marx Brothers behave inappropriately in the academic world, Harpo burning books and all three fighting with pea shooters in the classroom, an anatomy classroom expressing homage, perhaps, to Huxley. They use gags recycled from *Skool Daze*, their vaudeville skit that led to early incidents of unscripted chaos and even to the muting of Harpo's persona after a bad review.

Harpo joins the action in *Horse Feathers* about ten minutes after it begins. Prior to his arrival, Groucho sings, "Whatever It Is, I'm Against It," introducing the theme of resistance for its own sake and whetting our appetites for more oxymoronic sublime to be delivered by Harpo like feathers on a horse. So it seems natural that when we first meet Harpo, an illiterate dog-catcher named Pinky who is uninterested in book learning (perhaps because he already has ample tricks up the sleeves and in the pockets of his large coat), he is canoodling with his horse in what looks, in close-up, like a quiet off-campus picnic interlude.

It may seem to be a private if not pastoral setting in close-up, Harpo offering his horse a bouquet of flowers, eating some himself, kissing her, even sweetening and eating the oats when the horse refuses them, then nods approval for him to eat them. But we also get a surprise, a cinematic lesson on how point of view defines the reality we perceive, for when the camera pans backwards, giving us a longer and wider shot and thus revealing more of the setting, we see that the picnic is taking place on a busy city street and is moreover causing a traffic jam. Harpo has parked his dogcatcher's wagon in a traffic lane and he couldn't care less.

The many horns honking for Harpo to move his horse and wagon do not include, ironically, Harpo's own horn. In fact, Harpo doesn't use his horn to communicate in this film. But he does wear the trenchcoat we have seen before, and it is still loaded with props by means of which he both offers solutions and "speaks." In this scene, he defeats a policeman who tries to ticket him for parking illegally by writing a ticket back at him, then displaying many badges, the inside of his coat lined with multiples of the solitary badge the cop wears. In this way Harpo deconstructs the premise of power and rank, *if* their signifiers are badges and the writing of tickets. Like mirror images though otherwise not alike, they tear up each other's tickets.

And while Pinky's job of dogcatcher on the one hand casts him as an animal foe, on the other hand it allows him to obscure boundaries between species. For he leaves the scene of the arrest to chase a stray dog, just as he himself is chased. When Pinky escapes over and through other cars, then into his own vehicle, the officer pursues him right into his wagon where the other

In one of his many confrontations with police in the films, Harpo trumps the law and dogs its authority. Harpo Marx as Pinky and Ben Taggart as police officer. *Horse Feathers,* Pictures, 1931. From the collections of the Margaret Herrick Library.

captured strays are caged. Pinky locks him in, rolling down a sign that says, "Police dog for sale." The tramp has trumped the law and dogged its authority.

While Harpo's props and gestures always comprise his lexicon, in *Horse Feathers* he seems to take that language to a new level. He makes compound words like *swordfish* by pulling a fish and sword from his coat to gain access to the speakeasy, outsmarting Groucho and Chico, who find themselves on the wrong side of the door. He speaks via metonymy, ordering Scotch by doing the Highland Fling. And he puns, cutting cards with an axe. Nor do his substitutions end here. He plays the telephone when the slot machine is in use, both machines requiring the insertion of coins, and the telephone pays off big. This is an interesting variation on gags based on Harpo's interactions with telephones throughout the films. It suggests the irony that by playing differently with technology designed to facilitate communication, Harpo can reap rewards without speaking. It is a meta-gag reminding us that beyond the world of the film, Arthur Marx is acquiring wealth and fame by means of Harpo, his mute persona.

Harpo also uses down-to-earth, straightforward pragmatics, like the saw that assists his and Chico's escape from the Darwin players' room. But more often Harpo's props include the highly incongruous, even the surreal. For example, during his picnic with the horse, he eats a banana, then saves some for later, closing it with two zippers, one on each side. He pulls a steaming cup of coffee from inside his coat for a man who asks for a dime for a hot cup of coffee. And in the classroom he retrieves from his pocket a candle burning at both ends, simultaneously challenging the laws of physics and disproving Professor Wagstaff, who has just insisted that "you can't burn a candle at both ends." And Harpo's association with fire, introduced earlier when he shoveled books into Wagstaff's fireplace, continues in subsequent films. The contents of Harpo's pockets go beyond what is physically possible, thus moving him into trickster's realm, which is supra-normal or the realm of the surreal.

Harpo produces animals from his pockets too, or from some mysterious off-camera trove: a living seal in Wagstaff's office when he calls for "the official seal" on the papers enrolling Pinky and Baravelli at Huxley to play football, and a *pig* instead of a *pick* in the kidnapping scene. With the shiny seal, Harpo takes the Marx Brothers films' language gags that are often based on immigrant's misapprehension of similar-sounding words and pushes the implications much further. His language gags also include the many confusing and amusing homonyms English affords. And Harpo trumps Baravelli, who may be able to speak but confuses words like *sturgeon* and *surgeon, haddock* and *headache.*

Pinky collects and uses objects of comfort and fantasy too, like the poster of an Edwardian circus ballerina. In fact, the objects of his affections in this film evolve from his horse in the traffic picnic scene to the virtual woman on the poster, to an actual woman. We don't see as much blonde-chasing in this film as we did in earlier films and will in later ones. Instead, in *Horse Feathers,* Harpo first becomes infatuated with the image of the circus ballerina on a poster at the speakeasy. He promptly steals it to have her close. And she is always up his sleeve. He tacks her onto walls where he happens to be, like the classroom and the rooms of Darwin players Mullens and MacHardie.

Eventually his infatuation with this pop culture icon gives way to lust for a real woman: the college widow Connie Baily. He courts her along with Zeppo, Groucho, and Chico, serenading her with his rendition of the film's theme song, "Everyone Says I Love You" on his harp and embellishing it with such melodious riffs that it surpasses the lyrics Zeppo sings as well as the Lewis Carroll–like revisionary lyrics of Chico and Groucho. An enchanted Connie smiles at Harpo from the window, waving at him while he plays below. Harpo again elevates a banal tune, like he did in *Animal Crackers*, and Connie rewards him by blowing a kiss and later making a place at the altar for him in the closing scene's polyandrous wedding.

Pinky also exhibits trickster's enormous and sometimes indiscriminate appetite for food. He eats his horse's flowers and oats in his first scene, he drinks mass quantities of booze in the speakeasy, and he is frequently snacking on bananas, zipping one up to eat later in his first scene (and getting much use, both gastronomic and strategic, from bananas during the football game when he strews peels on the field and they bring down Darwin players). The only truly non-food item Pinky tries to eat in this film, having lost his hot dog but retained the bun during a tackle, is rival player MacHardie's finger, with mustard of course.

Pinky's stealing is neither as continuous nor manic in *Horse Feathers*, but he does indulge that trickster predilection adroitly, stealing whiskey in the speakeasy by ordering a shot, then using a bottomless shot glass as a funnel so as to pour himself a quart full. He also steals the poster of the circus ballerina. And we could call it *stealing* when he wins money by playing a change maker's coin belt, then playing the pay telephone like a slot machine, both quasi-surreal accomplishments that also reflect trickster's luck in myth and legend. And of course, Pinky and Baravelli steal status and legitimacy by falsely assuming the identities of football players when they agree to play for Huxley College.

Also a noteworthy theft because it so dramatizes his arrival at the big game between Darwin and Huxley is Harpo's theft of a woman's chiffon scarf along with the garbage collector's horse and wheeled can, rendering his arrival at the game classical in style: absurd, anachronistic, and memorable. But the most magical theft of all, one reminiscent of Harpo's theft of Abie the Fishman's birthmark in *Animal Crackers,* occurs during the anatomy classroom scene when Pinky helps "bear out" the biology professor, a phrase he takes literally, and returns to class wearing the professor's beard. The theft of facial hair, a motif that resurfaces now and again in the films, always hints at shape-shifting and reminds us that identity is more malleable than we may assume.

Right after Professor Wagstaff meets with two stuffy, pandering collegiate advisors, then puts in a call to Connie Baily, thickening the romantic subplot with innuendoes, Baravelli and Pinky walk across his desk, delivering ice to his safe in the wall. Delivering ice is a synecdoche for delivering booze in this era of prohibition, and Pinky and Baravelli seem to be partners in this work, though the vocational sync with Pinky's dog-catching job isn't clear. Still, we have seen Baravelli, Chico's stock Italian immigrant film persona, taking delivery orders for ice and whiskey in a back room at the speakeasy where he fills empty quarts labeled *Scotch* and *rye* from the same source. So we know what he is up to, and Pinky too.

In the scene in Wagstaff's office, the inner sanctum of Huxley College, we become more aware of our own trickster sympathies. First, we feel relief when Baravelli and Pinky replace the stuffed shirt yes-man professors flanking Wagstaff. And although this film lacks the usual subplot of sweet young lovers divided by prejudice and in need of trickster's help, a plot element that Irving Thalberg would resurrect in the MGM Marx Brothers films, we are enjoying the unsentimental world of *Horse Feathers*, a more crass and less innocent one where college widows seduce undergraduate men and may even take on their fathers and his friends. Furthermore, when the illiterate Pinky signs the contract with an X, and Wagstaff cynically congratulates him on his ability to write, we recognize a situation that endures today: athletes who lack academic credentials enrolled in colleges and universities to play sports.

It follows that Pinky pulls a volume off of Wagstaff's bookshelf, opens it, laughs silently yet uproariously, and then tosses it into the fireplace flames, though not necessarily out of disdain for learning, though his breathlessly offhand gesture satirizes a certain hot-air kind of erudition. The sympathy among these trickster cohorts is evidenced by Wagstaff's utter lack of concern, even when Harpo's actions escalate to a hyperbolic degree and he is shoveling whole shelves full of volumes into the flames. In the end, though, we see that Harpo has no vendetta against books: He merely wants to warm his hands.

After Harpo enrolls at Huxley and shovels books into the fire as his first academic gesture, his promise as a student, and Baravelli's, are fulfilled in the classroom when Professor Wagstaff interrupts the biology professor's lecture to introduce them. They fake-fight, offer illiterate responses to questions, and then, punning on the command to "bear the professor out," they each take an arm and rush the old fellow out of the classroom. Harpo returns wearing his academic regalia, a happenstance we can imagine, and wearing the professor's beard, a happenstance we cannot.

While Wagstaff lectures on human anatomy, Pinky pulls down a picture of a horse to cover the picture of the man, followed by the poster of the circus ballerina. When Pinky joins Baravelli in attacking Wagstaff with peashooters while he's lecturing — somehow the classroom's devolution into a pre-adolescent war zone does not seem farfetched, given the cast — Wagstaff pulls out his own peashooter and shoots back. Now we know without a doubt that these guys really are cohorts — why indeed else would Wagstaff have a peashooter in his pocket? The students flee the escalating battle, trickster's spirit reigning in a rain of peas.

We may have immaturity in this film, but we don't have innocence. The subplot of thwarted young lovers of past and future Marx Brothers films is here replaced with male interest in a sexually mature seductress in cahoots with racketeers manipulating collegiate sports. In fact, all of the men attracted to Connie Baily are gathered in one chaotic scene in her apartment: her gangster boyfriend and Pinky, who doesn't try to cozy up with her as do Frank Wagstaff (Zeppo); Professor Wagstaff and Baravelli. Gags repeat in this scene to the point of absurdity, like Professor Wagstaff's opening an umbrella and removing his shoes each time he enters, then exits in haste, a gesture only slightly less pointless than Pinky's repeated deliveries of unrequested ice. In fact, after Connie makes it emphatically clear that she doesn't want ice, Pinky continues to deliver it, traversing the sofa where others are wooing her and heading straight for the window with it, the block of ice crashing onto who-knows-what (or whom) below. Pinky seems dogged, pun not intended though gleefully applied, in his delivering of ice to the window. Though Frank Wagstaff was there first, his father dismisses him, and then both Baravelli and Professor Wagstaff woo Connie along with her gangster boyfriend. But again, Pinky gains her favor by playing his harp below. So this film's romantic subplot, sophisticated and morally ambiguous, isn't about tender lovers' overcoming social barriers. Instead, the resolution at the film's ending revives an idea hinted at in *Animal Crackers* when Spaulding proposes to both Mrs. Rittenhouse and Mrs. Whitehead. Only this time the solution isn't polygamy but polyandry, reminiscent of pre-code Hollywood.

In the next major sequence, the kidnapping of Pinky and Baravelli, Harpo plays the trickster buffoon. While Connie Baily is trying to get the football signals from Professor Wagstaff during their romantic row on the river, Connie doing the rowing and Groucho lounging, singing, and playing a guitar, Pinky and Baravelli attempt to kidnap Mullins and MacHardie, the hired Darwin players. Instead they get kidnapped themselves. Pinky doesn't seem to notice that he cannot overpower Mullins and MacHardie, Baravelli calling suggestions and orders from the sofa. And this is not the only time in the films that Harpo is the patsy. Harpo tries to oppose them by making mean, then meaner faces until a punch lands him on the sofa where he watches through binoculars as Baravelli gets stripped to his underwear. The stripping of Harpo is easier for the football thugs to accomplish. Again, as in *Animal Crackers,* his clothes are attached to each other, so everything but his underwear comes off at once. Apparently without his assistance, Harpo's props can manufacture humor of their own.

Throughout this sequence, Pinky squanders opportunities for escape though eventually he also accomplishes it. In order to play for Huxley, Pinky and Baravelli need to get out of the locked room, but when Baravelli says to "tie the rope to the bed and throw it out the window," Pinky throws his tie on the bed and the rope out the window. Luckily, he has a saw up his sleeve, though again he and Chico behave foolishly, not considering the consequences of squatting on the floor and sawing a circle around themselves. They land in the room below theirs, precisely where Mullins and MacHardie are getting

Oblivious of consequences like tricksters in buffoon mode, Harpo and Chico saw a circle around themselves to escape the room they are locked in. Chico Marx as Baravelli and Harpo Marx as Pinky. *Horse Feathers,* Paramount Pictures, 1931.

dressed for the game, and are again locked in. Pinky even hangs up his circus ballerina poster as though he expects to be there for a while. Nor do they learn from experience. Once alone, they sit on the floor and saw a circle around themselves again, this time landing in the room below where a bevy of startled women are playing bridge.

Always one to capitalize on opportunities, Pinky takes a chiffon scarf from one of the women and wraps it around his head, leaving a length of it streaming, then steals the garbage collector's horse-drawn collection can parked in front of the building. He rides to the field in it looking like an ancient Roman arriving at the Coliseum in his chariot improvised from the lowest of conveyances. Yet he is anything but ashamed, this anachronism of a trickster, but is timeless, amusing, and relevant.

The football game sequence is a *tour de force* of Marxian mayhem. It deconstructs a cultural icon, collegiate football, so thoroughly that it may never recover. It is a sequence legendary among football movies and utterly mad in comparison. Like the Winnebago trickster's irreverent behavior during preparation-for-war rituals, Harpo satirizes with seeming impunity and even sanction the high seriousness of football as surrogate war. Because Huxley's team is the underdog, Pinky the dogcatcher's playing on it amounts to a gratuitous pun. And all three Marxes disrespect the protocols of football, deflating its rituals and satirizing its seriousness. Pinky plays cards in the end zone, forgets about the game to chase a dog across the field, tackles the referee, eats bananas and hot dogs on the field, retrieves the ball by means of an attached elastic cord, rides to the goal in his chariot, and uses multiple footballs to score goal after goal.

Pinky and Baravelli dress for the game right on the field, Pinky pulling on a sweater that stretches over his head and across the field. They are still playing cards on the sideline when the huddle parts. Wagstaff, the college president, is absurdly though not unexpectedly playing in this game as well, all the while smoking a cigar and once pep-talking the opposing team. Baravelli hitches a ride to the fifty-yard line on a stretcher. Clearly Wagstaff and Baravelli are trickster cohorts who contribute mightily to the mayhem, but nothing tops Harpo's ancient Roman arrival, nor the elastic that allows him simultaneously to pass and retain the ball, nor his dropping banana peels that down Darwin's players, nor his putting mustard and a bun on MacHardie's finger and giving it a good bite, nor his making a touchdown and fainting after, then scoring touchdown after touchdown in the end zone with multiple footballs. By this point, the rules of the game between Huxley and Darwin have been so savaged, the quality of this football game so altered, that no one seems to challenge Huxley's winning score.

The amazing football win does not, however, wrap up the film. The academic world of the film, its main object of satire, has been roasted, satirized, and shaken up, but the romantic subplot, love almost always having relevance to the fate of institutions in Marx Brothers films, must be resolved. Harpo's trickster lust may actually achieve satisfaction after a final brief scene big in implications. In one wedding, there are three Marxes: Harpo, Chico, and Groucho (but not Zeppo, who is, after all, only an undergraduate and therefore too young for the sophisticated and irregular version of matrimony they have in mind). All three brothers marry the college widow Connie Baily; immediately after saying, "we do," they knock her down and swarm all over her. Harpo seems to be the last to dive onto the pile-up that bears a canny resemblance to a football gang tackle, implying that football may well be a metaphor not only for war but for love as well.

In the penultimate scene, a dog runs onto the field during the game, so Pinky reverts from Huxley football player to dogcatcher. In other words, he toggles between both identities. Thus he hints at the constellation of being, the plural nature of the human personality, as he chases the dog mid-game down the field with his net. In an even earlier scene, Pinky wears an engraved sign on the front of his hat that says "Kidnapper" and one on the back that says "Dogcatcher." Perhaps to a dog, these are one and the same, making this man's identity cohesive. But from our point of view, Harpo has multiple identities and is, in fact, the sum of them all. He wears various hats and plays with them — sometimes they are the basis of literal gags like in *Duck Soup* — in all of the films.

5

Duck Soup (1933)
TAKING A SCISSORS TO WAR

"He never went on the warpath — he never waged war."
— Paul Radin, *The Trickster*[1]

In *Duck Soup*, along with his inevitably coalescing cohorts Groucho as Firefly and Chico as Chicolini, Harpo as Pinky exposes the absurdities of war. And there aren't many decades in which this 1933 satire doesn't sting a nation's consciousness and conscience. Mussolini banned the film in Italy. *Duck Soup* seems particularly relevant now, after an arrogant invasion of Iraq during which reporters sometimes behaved like cheerleaders, the enthusiastic tone on the local evening news not unlike the film's musical scene's "To War," its chaos replacing the geometric order of a Busby Berkeley musical number. In fact, the film's close-to-the-bone impact may explain why *Duck Soup*, upon its release in 1933, became simultaneously a box-office failure and an enduring classic.

Harpo's role in the satire on the surrogate war of football in *Horse Feathers* prepares us for his role, trickster's in essence, in the satire on actual war in *Duck Soup*. While fascism is rising in Europe, Harpo gathers his energy and wits to lend his hand, his leg, his horn, his hat, and the contents of his coat pockets to join his cohorts in this send-up of nationalism and war. In *Duck Soup*, Harpo again wears many hats. He is the Freedonia president's driver; he is a spy for Sylvania; he is a peanuts and popcorn vendor. Having anticipated the incendiary power of scissors when he tore up mail in *The Cocoanuts* and snipped away the ship officer's mustache in *Monkey Business*, Harpo wields scissors far more often in this film than he has before. He seems to love the quick pragmatic they offer, including intimations of castration that can reduce both irritants and tyrants to manageable size, cutting things from coat tails to feather pens to helmet tassels.

When Harpo enters the film with characteristic nonchalance after his typical ten- minute delay, the world of the film has already been established. The setting is a small fictional country, Freedonia (offended officials of Freedonia, New York, tried to get the name of the film changed[2]) that flatters itself with the illusion of its own freedom even though the wealthy widow Mrs. Teasdale, played by Margaret Dumont (returning after a two-film absence) is blackmailing government officials to fire Freedonia's current president and install in office her choice, Rufus T. Firefly, in spite of his promise: "If you think that things were bad before, wait 'till I get through with it!" The pre–Harpo scenes also introduce the film's conflict: Trentino, ambassador of neighboring Sylvania, is scheming to marry Mrs. Teasdale in order to gain control of Fredonia. And Vera Marcal, a dancer, intends to seduce Firefly to keep him out of the way so Trentino can woo Teasdale.

Thus the *mishegoss* of this place and its politics is well established before Harpo's entrance. Firefly is already out of the way, asleep in bed with a cigar when he should be attending his own inauguration. Awakened by the fanfares announcing him, he slides unceremoniously down a pole and waits at the back of the crowd for his own entrance. Whose side should we be on? We don't yet have Harpo to help us decide. Trentino's duplicitous wooing of a widow to gain political power seems repellent, so the better choice must be Firefly, a man with little regard for power even though he happens to have it, who is frank and not scheming about his interest in Mrs. Teasdale's money, and who, moreover, is unpredictable and amusing.

With Freedonia and its discontents made familiar, Harpo enters the film. After Firefly has simultaneously romanced and insulted Mrs. Teasdale, met Vera, insulted her too, asked Zeppo to take a letter to his dentist, and shared a song with Mrs. Teasdale, Harpo's Pinky pulls up at the curb wearing a black top hat and driving "his excellency's car," a motorcycle with an officially decorated side car. The oddly formal hat of the president's driver is but one of the hats Harpo wears.

With a beatific expression to accompany his silence, Harpo plays a trick he will repeat with variations several times in the film, a slapstick motif of sorts: He leaves Firefly at the curb. In this case, Firefly hops into the sidecar, but it is apparently unattached to the motorcycle, because Harpo, told to make haste, revs up the engine and zooms away, leaving Groucho behind. If we appreciate Firefly's disregard for power, how can we not appreciate Pinky's disregard for the man *in* power? As for whose side we should be on, we have our answer.

Again, the hat of president's driver isn't the only hat Pinky wears. In the next scene, we learn that he and Chicolini are working for Trentino as spies.

But they are so inept they may as well be double agents. They help take apart not only the logic of war but the logic of espionage, and even the reliability of information taken in through the senses. The latter critique creeps in under the radar and short-circuits any seeming logic to come. This happens when Pinky arrives at Trentino's office in a wig, a beard, and strange kaleidoscopic eyes, meta-cinematic homage, perhaps, to the depiction of eyes in surrealist films, sliced or painted on eyelids. And in another meta-cinematic hat tip, pun intended, Harpo is also wearing a Sherlock Holmes plaid wool hat. Yet Pinky aspires to be not only Sherlock Holmes but also Holmes' dog, for Chicolini, delighted with the success of the disguise, says Pinky has "a nose like a bloodhound." Then he spins Pinky around, demonstrating how unreliable perception can be. For what we thought was Harpo's face is really the back of his head; his actual face is wearing no disguise.

This seems clever until we consider that spies should not draw attention

In the inner sanctum of power in Sylvania, Harpo tries to light a cigar with the telephone before he discovers that a blow torch works better. Left to right: Chico Marx as Chicolini, Harpo Marx as Pinky, and Louis Calhern as Trentino. *Duck Soup,* Paramount Studios, 1933.

to themselves with outlandish disguises. With Harpo we have, in essence, a spy announcing that he is a spy, thus undermining his utility as a spy and therefore placing Chicolini and himself on Firefly's side. Yet which team they are on — and in spite of the sports metaphor, the plot is heading not to surrogate war but war itself— seems not to matter: Pinky and Chicolini have no real fidelity to either Trentino of Sylvania nor to Firefly of Freedonia. They are as uninterested in and inept at war as they were at football.

In the scene in Trentino's office, Harpo establishes his credentials as trickster by exhibiting numerous trickster behaviors. He redefines hierarchies and gender by sitting in Trentino's chair, putting his feet on his desk, pulling Trentino onto his lap, and trying to answer his telephone. Here we have again the mute guy's encounter with a telephone, and in *Duck Soup* Harpo has his best success yet answering one, for in the next parallel scene in Firefly's office, Pinky actually manages to participate in a telephone conversation. But here in Trentino's office, Pinky uses the telephone to challenge sensory perceptions again, for the telephone's incessant ringing turns out to be an alarm clock ringing in his coat pocket. Pinky then tries to light a cigar with the telephone, making a buffoon of himself. Next, in two hyperbolic moves, he lights his own and Trentino's cigars with a blow torch, then extinguishes the torch with his own breath. This, incidentally, reinforces Harpo's trickster connection to the elements of wind and fire running through the films. And when he wads up a telegram delivered to Trentino, a *Cocoanuts* mail gesture whose stakes seem greater here, we recognize trickster's irreverence for protocol, power and the games of power.

Harpo reprises other familiar trickster antics in *Duck Soup*. Mesmerized by Trentino's blonde female secretary, he has to be restrained from chasing her, though he rings for her after she exits. He plays stickball with Chicolini and puns with props, pulling out a phonograph record when Trentino asks them to share their record on Firefly, again celebrating the wealth of homonyms in English that make it rich for puns. Finally, while Chicolini is giving Trentino an absurd rendition of their spying activities so far, Pinky brandishes a pair of scissors. He cuts Trentino's hair, which is amusing because Trentino seems unaware that he is losing control over his appearance. This may even foreshadow his losing the war if we associate hair, as in the Biblical Samson narrative, with power.

When Trentino expresses disappointment in their work and shames them about failing, Pinky and Chicolini hang their heads like children. But this too is a ruse, for in the next breath Pinky snips Trentino's coat tails: a metaphor, formal attire being associated with wealth and wealth with power, for cutting Trentino's status and aspirations down to size. Pinky offers a mouse-

Harpo applied paste to Trentino's bum, creating a visual pun on heads of state and where news events are conceived and set in motion. Louis Calhern as Trentino. *Duck Soup*, Paramount Studios, 1933.

trap when told to trap Firefly. But in the most eloquently resonant of all his gestures, he paints glue on the seat of Trentino's trousers so that when he and Chicolini leave and Trentino sits down, then rises and turns, the newspaper sticks to his bottom, headlines showing. This amounts to a visual trope connecting the *tuchus* of a head of state and current events. The syntax suggests whence sometimes shattering political events are conceived and issue.

Harpo's popcorn vendor scene — we might wonder at this point why the president's driver is moonlighting in this way — contains a meta-cinematic encapsulation of the film's own theme of war. Intercut with Firefly's cabinet meeting wherein he plays jacks like a child and moves the tariff from old to new to old business, provoking one member to resign in disgust, we have a sidewalk battle between Pinky, the popcorn and peanut vendor, and the lemonade vendor. The scene explores alternatives to anger and how conflict can escalate and cause destruction. After cutting Chicolini's hot dog, Pinky gives him his leg, thus simultaneously ruining his lunch and offering him the antidote to anger: the lesson of the flexible joint that models hanging loose and not getting uptight. Chicolini calls our attention to Pinky's muteness, as if we hadn't noticed, then he and Pinky have a fake fight, a motif in each film so far, taking us beyond the fourth wall to see the fun in dysfunctional sibling rivalry. In spite of Harpo's efforts, the lesson of the proffered leg doesn't successfully transfer to his nemesis, the lemonade vendor. Nothing is going to avert their battle.

Although the lemonade vendor next to Pinky's wagon is about to enter into a war with him on a minute scale compared to the one escalating between Freedonia and Sylvania, this little war is nevertheless significant for the vendors themselves. And it is especially absurd and unfortunate because thirst-inducing peanuts and popcorn go well with lemonade. In other words, the two vendors should be allies capitalizing on their potential for mutual benefit instead of fighting. So why are they fighting? Because, with trickster's impulse to steal, Pinky reaches his hand deep into the lemonade vendor's pocket, takes his knife, then gropes around in his customer's pocket as well. Furthermore, he honks his horn when they bump bellies, metonymy of farting, then he and Chicolini double-team the vendor, though it is almost entirely Pinky who juggles their hats. He takes the vendor's hat, kicks both him and his hat, gives him his leg while yo-yoing the hat with elastic cord left over, perhaps, from the football game in *Horse Feathers*, and moves all three hats from head to head to head until both vendor and viewers are flummoxed about whose hat is whose.

Hats are signifiers of identity, yet once a hat is removed from a person's head, it can perch on someone else's head just as easily, changing that person's aspect and translating him or her into someone else. So hats affect a kind of shape-shifting. And the vendor may never be the same, may never return to his original shape, for Pinky tosses his derby, an aspect of the lemonade vendor's identity, into the flame of his popcorn popper, warming his hands as gleefully as he did while burning books in *Horse Feathers*. But Pinky, as does trickster in numerous tales, also gets his comeuppance. When he fills his horn with lemonade to squirt the vendor in the face, the vendor sticks it down Harpo's pants and honks it. Given the color and consistency of lemonade, the vendor metonymically makes Harpo piss his pants.

In the scene in Firefly's office that follows, Harpo and Chico reprise tricks from the earlier scene in Trentino's office. When Chicolini announces that the popcorn wagon on the street below Firefly's window is a front for spying, Firefly, *sans* logic, makes their job easier by inviting Chicolini up and offering to make him secretary of war, an offer breathtaking in its absurdity even while implying that only a maniac and a fool could be placed in charge of the madness and folly of war. Then Chico reinforces the theme of unstable identity when he answers Firefly's telephone and says Firefly isn't there. He does this twice, prompting Firefly to "wonder what became of me."

When Harpo joins them, he answers the ringing telephone, distracting us from the identity conundrum by introducing the meta-theme of communication, both the shortcomings of spoken language and the superiority of muteness, mime, and music as facilitators of understanding. For spoken words are trumped by Harpo's horn here, its direct leap from sound to emotion, which is also the premise of music, in his animated telephone conversation with an unknown party. He communicates joy, laughter, dismay, sorrow, and finally curtness with his horn. He uses his face too, but his facial expressions are for us, not the person on the other end of the line.

Harpo also wields his scissors in this scene, snipping Firefly's quill pen, literally cutting it down to size, a joke at the expense of writers everywhere, not to mention the iconic scribes of American history who drafted and signed historic documents with such pens. But the most amazing example of Pinky's trickster commentary on language occurs when he responds to Firefly's question, "Who are you?" by showing Firefly a tattoo of himself, then a sexy-woman tattoo complete with her tattooed telephone number, and continues to converse with Firefly by substituting tattoos for words, an addition to Harpo's lexicon that is unique in the Marx Brothers canon, notwithstanding Lydia's eloquent tattoos celebrated in song in *At the Circus*. Only Harpo actually speaks *tattoo*. And at least once his utterance is censored, for when Firefly wonders if his grandfather is stained on Harpo's backside and Harpo attempts to show him, Firefly stops him.

Harpo's language of tattoos culminates in one of those rare but memorable manifestations of magic and the surreal that elevates Harpo's trickster status beyond that of his cohorts. When Firefly asks Pinky where he lives, Harpo shows him a tattoo of a doghouse, connecting Harpo to trickster's animal incarnations. But when Groucho leans toward the doghouse meowing, a real, not a cartoon dog lunges from it barking. Here we are about as close to Marianne Moore's famous esthetic standard for poetry as a medium that must provide "imaginary gardens with real toads in them"[3] as it is possible to be. Translated, Harpo's tattoo responses to Groucho say that he is who he is, that he is a lover of women, and that he is a dog. They may say more; we never get to see his bum.

Harpo's hands, or more precisely, his scissors, are felt even when he is not the focus of a scene, such being trickster's influence. For example, when Firefly summons Zeppo to take a letter so he can invite himself to the party Trentino is attending at Mrs. Teasdale's, a party to which Firefly has not been invited, he passes, on his way in, the scissors-bearing Harpo who is on his

Harpo's tattoos are added to his lexicon in this scene. This surreal tattoo of an imaginary doghouse with a real dog in it tells Groucho/Firefly where he lives. Harpo Marx as Pinky. *Duck Soup,* Paramount Studios, 1933.

way out. Then Zeppo enters wearing half of a hat. It is cut to appear whole in profile, or no hat at all in profile from the other side, reality here depending on point of view, and it functions as both a metonymy for Pinky's mischief with scissors and an uncanny though perhaps coincidental — if there are coincidences when dealing with archetypes — allusion to the Afro-Caribbean trickster Eshu, who causes confusion and sometimes fights between witnesses by wearing a hat that is white on one side and black on the other, the seen and recollected color of Eshu's hat depending upon their point of view.

Pinky, summoned again to drive Firefly to Mrs. Teasdale's party, reprises his trick with the motorcycle, leaving Firefly behind at the curb in the side car and zooming off. But somehow Firefly arrives at the party, discovers Trentino romancing Mrs. Teasdale, insults him, prompts a declaration of war, then attempts to outfox Pinky by getting on the motorcycle instead of into the side car. Yet off Pinky zooms in the side car, against logic or rather consistent with trickster's surreal logic, leaving Groucho seated on the motorcycle but stuck nevertheless at the curb.

When Harpo appears again as a vendor, we are wise to the fact that his wagon is a front for spying on Firefly. Still, in his capacity as popcorn and peanut vendor, he provokes an escalation of the mini-war with the lemonade vendor, who may well be an agitator for Trentino or for Firefly: it's not clear which. The lemonade vendor is wearing a new straw hat, but the head under it isn't renewed: the grudge remains. On the offensive, he takes peanuts and refuses to pay for them, instead greasing Pinky's open hand with butter, a pun, perhaps, on "grease my palm" and the film's accidental though sensuous echo of the Indian trickster god Krishna smeared with stolen butter.

Pinky wipes his hand on the lemonade vendor's towel, snips it, and then burns the vendor's new hat as he burned the old. After the lemonade vendor turns over Pinky's cart, finishing off his business, Pinky washes his feet in the vendor's lemonade, causing the immigrant laborers queued up for a drink to leave in disgust, thirsty though they are. With trickster's spirit, Harpo finds an obnoxious way to fire the last shot in an unnecessary war even while revealing how such wars hurt ordinary people. The working class is hereby acknowledged and their concerns validated even though they are gently, sympathetically, and affectionately depicted humorously.

The unnecessary war between Freedonia and Sylvania is also not averted, and Harpo brings to Freedonia's war the same trickster irreverence he brought to football in *Horse Feathers*. For a moment, peace seems possible: Mrs. Teasdale and Trentino summon Firefly; they reconcile; they even reminisce good-naturedly about their fight. But doing so is a bad idea: remembering the insult rekindles the affront, and their meeting ends with Firefly's statement, "This means war!" It follows that Trentino schemes to get Firefly's war plans just as Darwin schemed to get Huxley's game plan. Vera, this film's Connie Baily, is enlisted in the scheme, and the spies Chicolini and Pinky are sent to join her in the effort to steal the plans.

As the espionage element of the plot heats up, so do the manifestations of Harpo's trickster nature, especially his buffoonery. When told to ring the doorbell, he rings a bell from his coat pocket, then Chico's belly button, satirizing language even while making more relevant though not necessarily sane gestures like ringing the actual doorbell, hiding in the bushes like a child, locking himself out, leaping on Vera when she answers the door, and dancing her back in. Once inside, Harpo tries to control time, setting all the clocks to midnight. This turns out to be an example of trickster self-sabotage, for when all of the clocks start chiming, he loses both anonymity and control.

At one point Pinky reaches under the lid of the grand piano and plucks the strings as if they were a harp's. But Chicolini closes the lid on his hands, never touching the piano keys himself, a meta-cinematic gesture telling us that there will be neither harp nor piano solo in this film. We may have trickster but we don't have his harp, the means by which Harpo intimates the divine. And perhaps this is appropriate, for the divine seems mostly on the lam in times of war.

We see trickster's capacity for magic though, and in one of the Marx Brothers' most famous scenes, Harpo, in shape-shifting mode, leads the charge against fixed and stable identity, becoming Firefly's double. When Mrs. Teasdale calls Firefly from his bed to take Freedonia's war plans off of her nervous hands, Pinky hears her on an extension, the mute guy adept on a telephone when all he has to do is listen. Pinky sends Chicolini to retrieve the plans; Chicolini takes it upon himself to lock Firefly in a closet and become the first to impersonate Firefly by donning nightgown, nightcap, mustache, plus a cigar. When Pinky puts on the same disguise, the hyperbole actually takes us one beyond doppelgängers.

This tripling of Firefly, made possible by distilling the essential elements of his appearance, makes for a magical scene. It is absurdly amusing when Mrs. Teasdale doesn't suspect that her Firefly is really Chicolini, especially when she hears the Italian accent: In this case, the inflexibility of an assumption based on appearance blocks true perception. When Pinky changes places with Chicolini and Mrs. Teasdale gives him the plans, she asks if he "has lost his voice," but she still does not suspect an imposter, blinded again by the superficial aspects of what she sees. Meanwhile, Chicolini is back in the room, and because he and Pinky both look exactly like Firefly, we too are becoming confused.

More trickster magic occurs when Pinky escapes with the plans and tries to hide them in a safe. He is either turning dials on a radio that looks like a safe, or the safe is fulfilling its own fantasy of being a radio. Whichever it is, the box blasts Sousa music that Pinky can't turn off. Here we have a parallel to what happens when trickster of myth and legend, in an attempt to get what he wants, sometimes sets forces in motion that he can't control. Here the humor in the scene is based on out-of-control technology. Ordinary physical laws don't govern here, for when Pinky unplugs the radio, sits on it, stuffs it in a closet, smashes it, hacks it into pieces, and throws it out the window, the band, insistently surreal, plays on.

It is amusing that when Firefly goes to Mrs. Teasdale's room to call headquarters, we see Chicolini's version of Groucho under her bed. But it is more amusing when Harpo breaks the hall mirror, then has to pretend to be Groucho's reflection when, investigating the noise, Groucho passes what used to be the mirror. Like Harpo, the scene itself is completely silent. And its enduring status offers evidence of how well Harpo's silence stands up to Groucho and Chico's verbal repartee as exemplified in the next scene, the trial of Chicolini. Here Harpo's impersonation of Groucho's mirror image is almost perfect, and the slight imperfections — the different hats they are holding, one white and one black (another echo of the trickster Eshu with his half-black, half-white hat), the occasionally delayed or altered gesture — heighten the effect by letting us know that these two really *are* Harpo and Groucho and not Groucho and his own reflection. They even change places; after they do, their hats are the same color: more trickster magic. However, when Chicolini appears on the scene, making Firefly's identity not double but triple, the strange phenomenon crumbles under its own weight.

Pinky and Chicolini flee. Apparently Pinky escapes, but Chicolini is caught, so before we see Pinky again, we must suffer, with pleasure of course, Chicolini's trial for high treason. Firefly seems to be rooting for him, apparently moved by Chicolini's inability to bribe anyone to testify on his behalf as well as by his nonsensical defense made up of malapropisms, non sequiturs, and puns. Chicolini seems pleased to be making hash of all arguments against him, though his word play is not as vivid and literally three-dimensional as Harpo's. Ironically, Chicolini is saved by war. His trial is interrupted by the news that Sylvanian troops are about to land, Mrs. Teasdale's "final effort to prevent war" having failed because Firefly again slaps Trentino with a glove and repeats, "This means war!"

Harpo reappears to participate in the extravagant and frenzied musical scene, "We're going to war." Whereas in a Busby Berkeley musical number the camera angles enhance the kaleidoscopic order, in *Duck Soup* the camera angles accentuate the madness and disintegrating effect of war fever. Harpo marches in like a drum major with a baton, knocking down the chandelier. Zeppo, Groucho, and Chico play on soldiers' helmets as if they were notes on a xylophone while Harpo castrates their tassels. *Horse Feathers* may have deconstructed surrogate war, but *Duck Soup* is after the bigger game of war itself.

Harpo romps through the choreographed chaos of this fevered scene that borrows from various aspects of American musical culture, starting with a spiritual, "All God's Children," who in this case "got guns" instead of "shoes," and "Oh Freedonia" sung to the tune of "Oh Susanna" with banjo, square dancing, and Harpo playing the fiddle. The brothers are dancing all over the place, high and low, forwards and backwards, turning their backsides inelegantly to the mooned-but-for-their-trousers camera. As depicted, this war fever is simultaneously comical and, for those who have experienced the likes of it — which is just about everyone, considering America's involvement in a new war every twenty years throughout the twentieth century and on into the twenty-first, not to mention the rest of the world's various wars — deeply disturbing.

Harpo and his cohorts furthermore develop allusions to a myriad of wars via the retrospective medley of costumes that they wear, especially hats, both American and European, seventeenth to twentieth century, until the satire on war ceases to apply only to America and becomes universal in its scope. The Marx Brothers' uniforms are constantly changing, shape-shifting from war to war to war.

But no allusion is as vivid and iconic and then again revisionist as Harpo's ride through the streets of Freedonia to rouse the troops. Brief allusions to the American Revolutionary War have occurred in each film so far, but in *Duck Soup* they are multiple and manifest. Like Paul Revere, Harpo mounts a sturdy horse, in this case white for nighttime visibility, and he sets forth to deliver warnings of the impending battle to Freedonia's *hoi polloi.*

Yet almost immediately Pinky's interest turns from war to sex. From the back of his white horse, he sees a pretty woman in a window. She happens to be running a bath for her husband, and while historical record does not mention Paul Revere's pausing in his legendary ride for a dalliance or two, we do know the appeal to some women of a man in uniform. At any rate, Pinky hangs a feedbag on his white horse, mounts the stairs, chases the woman around the room, and then hides in the bathtub when her husband comes home. The husband turns out to be none other than the lemonade vendor, Pinky's old enemy, who prefers to have a nice bath instead of going to battle. Dramatic irony results, for he gets into the tub while Pinky is hiding and honking underwater.

Pinky resumes his ride, only to be seduced again. A woman in another house summons him from an upstairs window, and instead of pausing to hang a feedbag on his horse, he rides his horse into the house and up the stairs. The ensuing scene may represent the only time we see Harpo's character score in any of the films, the nuptial tackle at the end of *Horse Feathers* notwithstanding. Nevertheless, the nature of this *Duck Soup* dalliance remains ambiguous. For the next thing we see reinforces either trickster's lust or his deep connection to animals depending upon interpretation. The camera first lingers on three pairs of shoes lined up next to the bed, metonymic signs of the sleepers within: Pinky's shoes, the woman's more dainty pumps, and horse-shoes. When the camera's eye, which is also our own, rises from floor to bed, we see that Pinky and his horse are sleeping in one bed and the woman is sleeping in the other.

The shot has ribald implications. Is this a *ménage a trois?* Is the horse Harpo's lover? Is the horse a voyeur? Or does the scene lack prurience, instead merely showing us two people and a horse taking a nap? We may never know, but the fact that Pinky lands in bed in proximity to a woman in the midst of war helps *Duck Soup*, via Harpo's trickster essence, prioritize *eros*, or at least affection, or at the very least repose, over war.

In fact, neither Pinky nor his trickster cohorts are committed to this war. When Freedonia needs more soldiers, Pinky is out recruiting in the midst of a battle, but he looks punchy and oblivious while wearing a sandwich board that says, "Join the Army to see the Navy." The message appears to make little sense. Yet if we consider how, in the Iraq and Afghanistan wars, various branches including the National Guard — the latter according to some opaque logic — served and are serving side by side, it seems insightful. His recruiting efforts also reflect the logic by which men and women enlist in the military in order to secure a job, a paycheck, and benefits like health insurance. This incentive that America's currently all-volunteer army is predicated upon makes the rest of the logic clear. And Pinky also hangs a "Help Wanted" sign on the door of their Freedonia bunker, implying, again, that deep in its very nature, war makes mercenaries of men.

Yet the bottom line of the film, echoing trickster's life-affirming message so relevant in times of war when humanity literally turns against itself, is that men and women feel a natural inclination to avoid the violence and insanity of war and to care more about the pleasures of living. For example, Firefly has so little interest in the war that he shoots at his own men in the same addled spirit in which Wagstaff pep-talked the wrong team in *Horse Feathers*. Moreover, Chicolini, Freedonia's secretary of War, turns out to be Sylvanian, but he is fighting, sort of, for Freedonia because he likes the food better on that side. Pinky's patriotic ride takes him only as far as women's houses, and then it's delight and lights out. Trickster's irreverence for the protocols of war runs rampant in this film.

The satire on war closes with verbal wit and physical gags, and again, Harpo's contributions are over the top in terms of trickster essence. Chicolini puns on "tanks," but Pinky's Revolutionary War hat that looks suspiciously Napoleonic gets spun around by bullets like in a carnival game. When Firefly, Chicolini, and Pinky go to Mrs. Teasdale's home to eat her food, Firefly radios for reinforcements. He adds "send two more women," but Pinky gestures for him to make that three. Because they need a brave volunteer to deliver a message in battle, Chicolini has them play the hand game rimspot to choose. In other words, not one of them is endowed with foolhardy courage to volunteer. Because Chicolini's finger keeps landing on himself, he repeats the game until his finger lands on Pinky, who is complimented for his reluctant willingness to go by being called "a sucker."

Before he leaves, though, Pinky snips Firefly's raccoon tail from his current hat, then mistakes the closet door for the back door. So he doesn't go on the dangerous mission after all, but is locked in the closet by the others who don't know the difference between the doors either. As in *The Cocoanuts,* doorways are liminal spaces, thresholds to the unexpected, in this case to the supply of ammunition. Meanwhile the others, thinking Harpo is on his way to battle, barricade the door with all the furniture available to keep him from chickening out and trying to return, never mind that he is really locked up on the premises. And with trickster's capacity for bumbling, he manages to ignite the ammunition by lighting a match.

The resulting explosion frees him, just as trickster's buffooneries in myth and legend sometimes win the day for him. Harpo is blasted out of the closet in time to hear, "Help is on the way," accompanied by a montage of fire trucks, runners, and stampeding jungle animals. When Groucho loses his helmet, Harpo tries to substitute the water jug, another more peculiar hat gag. When the jug slips down, trapping Groucho's head inside, Harpo paints a graffiti caricature of the iconic mustached face of Groucho on it before blowing it off with dynamite. As Mrs. Teasdale is pushing against the door to resist Sylvanian invaders, Pinky helps her, copping a feel by pushing on her bum.

So, with strategies from trickster's arsenal, Harpo and his cohorts defeat Sylvania. Trentino's head stuck in the door, they pelt him with fruit, strangely anticipating the pelting of another dictator, the hanged Mussolini, with tomatoes. When Mrs. Teasdale, looking Wagnerian in her headgear, sings "Hail, Hail, Freedonia" from an elevated corner behind a railing, they pelt her too. Harpo and company may lack enthusiasm for war, but they are definitely against upstart dictators, and they are especially opposed to pompous singing.

6

A Night at the Opera (1935)
CLEANING WITH DIRT

"Tricksters begin by muddying the gods on high."
— Lewis Hyde, *Trickster Makes This World*[1]

In this extraordinary Marx Brothers film that satirizes pretentiousness in the arts via one of its most grand manifestations, high opera, Harpo debases, as does trickster of myth, in order to cleanse and renew. And while he's at it, he fights for love and unrecognized talent by battling against predatory insincerity and undeserved fame. Harpo, a trickster at work in the service of love and against pretentiousness, allies himself with the underdog Ricardo Baroni, played by Allan Jones, who happens to be the more talented tenor with greater heart. While he's assisting Ricardo and Rosa, Harpo also manages to interrogate the false division between high and low art, a theme that the Marx Brothers returned to in *At the Circus*. This theme is introduced here by mixing the popular pastime of baseball with opera, the epitome of sophisticated cultural entertainment and one that has grown inaccessible to ordinary people though it was once rooted in and drew inspiration from their lives.

In *A Night at the Opera,* Harpo plays Tomasso, mute dresser of Lassparri, a cruel and abusive employer, a celebrated tenor but one who lacks the soul of art. In the usual pattern, Harpo enters after the nature and shortcomings of the film's milieu have been established, in this case in an opening scene in an elegant restaurant where the shadow world of culture is revealed. Wealthy widow, (Margaret Dumont) Mrs. Claypool, is attempting to purchase social status by making a large donation to the New York Opera Company, but Groucho's Otis P. Driftwood, her contact with that institution, stands her up for dinner, then alternately insults and woos her before he finally introduces her to Mr. Gottlieb (Sig Ruman), the head of the opera company. She is eager to exchange a generous donation for an introduction into society.

After we understand the entanglement of high art with social climbing, the film cuts to Harpo's Tomasso. He is in Lassparri's dressing room, wearing a clown costume from *Pagliacci*. Because it is on Harpo, it also hints at trickster's buffoon tendencies. Opening his mouth wide to belt out a song, Harpo riffs on his own muteness, for naturally, he makes no sound. Then he sprays his throat as opera singers do and tries again, but it improves the timbre only of his silence.

Harpo's shape-shifting capability is introduced here too, for when Lassparri returns to discover Harpo wearing his costume, he beats him and orders him to take it off. In a gag that will rhyme with the series of absurd scrim changes in the performance of *Il Trovatore* near the end of the film, he strips off costumes, alluding to various operas Lassparri has apparently starred in while also commenting silently on art, artifice, acting, and suspension of disbelief. When he strips off the clown costume, an admiral's costume is revealed, and under it, a woman's dress. Tomasso strips down to the woman's dress — we might wonder why this is in Lassparri's wardrobe — but no further, suggesting not only that gender identity is malleable but also that the *anima* resides on the innermost and hidden layer of Harpo-Tomasso's being.

Furthermore, this first Harpo-as-Tomasso scene aligns our sympathies with him, for he tries on Lassparri's costumes in the spirit of playfulness. His mischief is essentially harmless, so the whipping he gets establishes Lassparri as the enemy of play. And the abuse has a witness, Rosa, played by Kitty Carlisle, who steps out of her dressing room across the hall just as Lassparri is beating and throwing Tomasso out of his own. Thus, in a violent twinkling, Lassparri wins our dislike, and Tomasso and his comforter, the lovely Rosa, win our sympathy.

It is also a good thing that Tomasso has a life beyond being Lassparri's servant. We see this when he and Fiorello (Chico) embrace as old friends. Because Tomasso and Fiorello seem ecstatic to be reunited, we know they are deeply connected by a shared past even though their exploits and prior relationship isn't revealed in this scene. They even exchange identical gifts: giant salamis whose phallic shapes, hard to ignore, are reminiscent of trickster's autonomous penis that goes about its business on its own in trickster's early inchoate stage in the Winnebago Trickster Cycle. When Tomasso brandishes a cleaver, we think castration; when instead he whacks off the salami's tip, we see he has made instead a Jewish joke on circumcision. But it is also true that sometimes a salami is just a salami: Harpo eats from both pieces because he's hungry and salamis are food.

Backstage at the opera, the relationship between trickster and his cohorts, the opera, and the plot of the young lovers coalesce when it is revealed that Ricardo Baroni, Rosa's sweetheart, knew Fiorello at the music conservatory. Moreover, his accepting Fiorello's offer to manage his career asserts another value in the film: friendship over ambition, for it is hard to imagine the good-natured, impoverished, and illiterate Fiorello being able to promote the talented Baroni in the competitive and connected opera world. Because Fiorello is trying to help Ricardo Baroni succeed, not only to share his talent with the world but also to unite him with Rosa, this scene places both Fiorello and Tomasso squarely on the side of love. These virtues (talent, but only when combined with love, friendship, and loyalty) become enmeshed with trickster's mischief and mayhem in the film, ultimately to triumph over heartless ambition and social climbing.

The plot thickens on an important question: Who is the best male tenor? It is a question that involves both ethics and aesthetics. Groucho's Driftwood, despite his connections, is so little interested in opera that he tries to arrive late enough to miss the performance entirely. He almost succeeds, joining Mrs. Claypool and Gottlieb in their box just as the curtain is falling. He does arrive in time, however, to learn that Gottlieb wants to sign "the greatest tenor," whom to Gottlieb means Lassparri.

Tomasso delivers Gottlieb's handwritten offer to sing with the New York Opera Company in a covered dish as if it were food. And in a way it is. Work, especially in the arts, translates into sustenance, feeding both body and soul. *Room Service* takes this theme and runs with it, as does *Love Happy*. One must eat, but human beings also need either to sing or hear others sing; to dance or watch others dance; to make music or hear others do so; to paint, sculpt, draw, photograph, film, or behold the results of these efforts; to write or to read. In other words, the human spirit needs the sustenance that comes from making or experiencing art. And trickster is about satisfying needs.

Lassparri, resentful of Tomasso's intrusion during his moment of adulation, chases him away, unable to appreciate the proffered feast: a coveted place in the New York Opera Company. Later, when the stowaways Ricardo, Tomasso, and Fiorello enjoy the generously bestowed and opulent Italian dinner in steerage, followed by joyous singing and dancing, we get the metaphor and thus understand how stinted is Lassparri's artistic soul.

This time when Lassparri threatens Tomasso, Driftwood is a witness, calling him a "big bully" but also calling Tomasso a "little bully." We know who the underdog is, but significantly that doesn't make him morally superior: They are both bullies. For Tomasso, like trickster of myth and legend, doesn't fit into tidy moral categories but exists in his own wild, mischievous, and sympathetic (because ultimately life-sustaining) zone. Moreover, if Lassparri and Tomasso are both bullies, Tomasso is a little one, but Lassparri is a big and dangerous bully who uses his force against both playfulness and love. He has power to do much damage. So when, without vehemence but rather with logical nonchalance, Tomasso clubs Lassparri on the head, knocks him out, then revives him with smelling salts, nodding proudly when Driftwood says that shows "a nice spirit," Tomasso doesn't hesitate to knock Lassparri out again.

We want to, and do, laugh, amused instead of troubled because we've seen enough to know that Lassparri deserves what he gets, because of his cruelty and because he is Ricardo Baroni's rival for both Rosa's affection and tenor career. With Lassparri reduced to a prop, Driftwood flicking his cigar on him and he and Fiorello resting their feet on him as if he were a railing, a hinged space opens for Ricardo's career to be advanced. When Driftwood, Gottlieb's representative, says he wants to sign "the greatest tenor in the world," Fiorello offers him Ricardo, noting absurdly that Ricardo "could sail yesterday" for enough money. And when Driftwood and he sign their duplicate contracts, the "sanity clause" interchange suggests that *sanity* in their negotiations may be as relative as time.

Tomasso is in the background, a non-contender in these dialogues, but not for long. When Gottlieb finds Lassparri reviving, Tomasso drops a sandbag on his head. So he is rendered unconscious yet again, and the opera company now has two aspiring tenors, though Lassparri remains the official one. Driftwood and Fiorello's agreement is reduced to a thin strip of paper, unsigned because neither has a pen and Fiorello can't write anyway.

Harpo's manic romp in the scene of the ship's departure from Italy, bound for New York, provides background as Rosa sings "Alone" in a farewell duet with Ricardo for the crowd, her clever way of auditioning him for Gottlieb, when, conveniently, the miserly Lassparri refuses to sing because he's not being paid. Meanwhile, Tomasso leaps onto Fiorello's back while he is giving Rosa a farewell hug, and then, as if drunk from human touch,[2] goes through the crowd on a rampage, jumping on passengers, both male and female, to hug and kiss them. Harpo doesn't chase blondes in the film (though he does grope women in the stateroom scene), nor does he offer his leg to anyone. He seems to be after something greater in this scene though: rambunctiously indiscriminate physical contact: trickster's appetite.

Tomasso, along with Fiorello, and Ricardo Baroni become stowaways, stealing their passage to New York on the ship. Driftwood, although he skipped out on his hotel bill, is the only legitimate passenger among the trickster cohorts. There is an interlude before we see Tomasso again, a brief scene in which Driftwood recapitulates the film's major characters and plot lines as well as predicts a few as he rides his trunk to his stateroom on the ship that is meanwhile translating the film's setting from Europe to America. He passes the three bearded men, heroic aviators we later learn. He passes Gottlieb "beating around the bush" of his beard. He delivers a love letter from Ricardo to Rosa as she weeps in her stateroom. He invades Mrs. Claypool's space, lounging on her bed and threatening to embarrass her unless she agrees to a rendezvous in his stateroom. He sings "Ho to the Open Road," a metaphor for the unpaved ocean that expresses the picaresque aspect of trickster lore. He even tries to sell "insurance" to the porter, slipping his unpaid hotel bill instead of a policy into the porter's pocket. At the end of this montage-like reprisal and foreshadowing of events to come, Driftwood discovers how extremely small his stateroom is. Booked by Gottlieb, it reflects Gottlieb's opinion of him. For all we know, Tomasso, Fiorelli, and Ricardo Baroni are in still in Italy, waving goodbye to the departed ship.

But they're not. And the stateroom scene develops two dimensions of Harpo's trickster essence only hinted at in prior films: his hyperbolic ability to sleep and his hyperbolic flatulence. When Driftwood opens his trunk, he finds the three stowaways inside. Tomasso is asleep in the shirt drawer, prompting Driftwood to quip that he couldn't be his shirt because his shirt "doesn't snore." Fiorello says Tomasso is "trying to sleep off his insomnia," and having, we notice, great success. In fact, Tomasso sleeps through the entire scene, contributing his slack somnambulant posture to the scene's legendary hilarity. Even while asleep, Tomasso expresses his trickster nature. In the films preceding *A Night at the Opera,* we learned of Harpo's appetites for food and women, his sympathy for young lovers, his talents for theft and for playing his harp. This scene demonstrates not only his huge capacity for sleep but also his ability to dive onto food and grope women *while asleep.* In other words, he is so essentially who he is (hungry, mischievous, chaotic, and lustful) that his trickster essence is the same whether he is asleep or awake.

Another of Harpo's hyperbolic trickster traits is developed in this scene as well, one hinted at in earlier films: flatulence, suggested here via the auditory metonymy of his honking horn combined with the olfactory metonymy of hardboiled eggs. When Driftwood orders food so the stowaways will leave him alone for his assignation with Mrs. Claypool, summoning "Stew," the steward, and ordering everything on the menu, Fiorello repeatedly throws in requests for "two hardboiled eggs." With a honk from the sleeping Tomasso, Driftwood says, "Make that three hardboiled eggs." And this repeats. Granted, Harpo's horn contributes a repertoire of meanings in the films, for it is often his mouthpiece. Yet here it is clearly his *tuchus* piece. Conflating the sulfurous

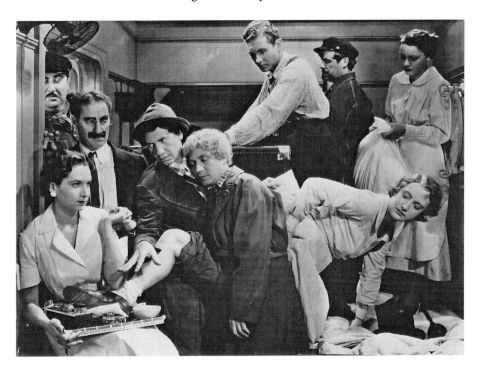

Although asleep, Harpo expresses his trickster nature in the small and crowded stateroom. Left to right: Jack "Tiny" Lipson as engineer's assistant, unknown actress as manicurist, Groucho Marx as Otis B. Driftwood, Chico Marx as Fiorello, Harpo Marx as Tomasso, Allan Jones as Ricardo Baroni, Frank Yaconelli as engineer, Edna Bennett as maid and Inez Palange (kneeling) as maid. *A Night at the Opera*, MGM, 1935.

odor of hardboiled eggs with the sound of the horn indeed suggests farting. Driftwood translates each of Tomasso's honks as an additional "hardboiled egg," and a short honk as "a duck egg," thereby adding the auditory similarity of the distressed quack of a duck to a fart, as in the euphemism: "Who stepped on the duck?" When Tomasso emits a whole series of honks while fast asleep, Driftwood orders "twelve more hardboiled eggs." It is as difficult to ignore the implication of flatulence in this scene as it is to ignore an actual fart, especially in a small crowded stateroom where flatulence would be particularly unwelcome, though from a certain point of view quite amusing.

For every moment the stateroom is becoming more and more crowded, and the comedy is exacerbated because some of those who drop in are exceptionally large. A giant of a woman comes in to "mop up," a hefty engineer with his assistant to turn off the heat, two not small maids to make the bed, a slight woman looking for her "Aunt Minnie," in addition to a manicurist, the steward and waiters and food. All the while, Tomasso sleeps, leaning on, being passed by, and climbing over others, putting one shod foot on a food tray and another on the manicurist's tray, groping and wrestling women, and generally being shifted, pushed, and passed around like a prop. When Mrs. Claypool finally opens the door (Driftwood is far from alone so the assignation is foiled), they all tumble out, Tomasso having slept, farted, and groped women through it all.

Tomasso is clearly among the "riff raff" Mrs. Claypool objects to at the elegant banquet on the final night of the voyage in a scene intercut with an opulent meal generously and democratically served in steerage, a meal that provokes an expression of ecstatic wonder on Tomasso's face. The intercutting shows us that the ocean liner itself reflects the culture's social class stratifications and their relationships to art. Ironically, this ship's steerage is full of immigrants from Italy, birthplace of opera. And there is great musicality there. Furthermore, its many children take a shine to Tomasso, and no wonder, with his mischief and his wide eyes. As his plate is heaped with food (spaghetti, a chunk of meat, bread, fruit, and antipasto), he has the same mutely awed expression we have seen in other films when he beholds either sorrow or kindness. He always seems stunned by human excess.

Tomasso returns to central focus after the three finish eating, mop up their plates, and Ricardo sings "Cosi Cosa," the steerage passengers singing and dancing with him in a huge musical number. Fiorello plays the melody on the piano, then other tunes while the children gather around. When Tomasso replaces him on the keys, the children laugh with joy. He plays a wild, out-of-control piece, sizzles his bum by spinning the stool, slams his hands in the piano, then pretends they are loose and out of control, painting the piano with limp fingers and palm, then painting the children too. Again we see the connection between his humor and his willingness to ignore physical boundaries between people, one kind of border crossing. When his mania on piano subsides, he calmly plays "Alone" on the harp, looking serious and angelic even while jazzing it up and whistling the melody. And as if they instantly understand and appreciate everything he stands for, the children, like the children in *Monkey Business,* cheer for him.

Tomasso's antics are at the heart of the next scene too, wherein the stowaways are imprisoned and must escape deportation. Lassparri alerts the authorities that they are on the ship, and following a chase, they are locked in a detention cabin. Luckily it's a cabin with a view. Unperturbed, Tomasso plays "Cosi Cosa" on a comb, becoming louder and more raucous, providing a musical transition from the gala steerage scene while reminding us of trickster's diverse musicality. But his tune annoys Fiorello, who throws the improvised instrument out of the porthole. When Tomasso opens it, water rushes in. Undeterred and unable to resist the temptation to explore and perhaps escape, Harpo leans out the porthole, a liminal space indeed, and Driftwood, from a neighboring porthole, throws him a rope. Like the scene in *Duck Soup* where Harpo is the dupe chosen to go on a dangerous mission, Fiorello and Ricardo vote to send Tomasso out the porthole on the rope "to see if it's safe." Is it? Tomasso is alternately dunked in the water and reeled to the top of the mast, dizzyingly up, then down, high, then low. In spite of his repertoire of tricks and props, and his ability to seize opportunity, Tomasso is not, as trickster in tales is sometimes not, in control.

Then suddenly Tomasso takes control, with mischief and outlandish imagination. He uses the rope to climb into the porthole of the three bearded celebrity aviators — a wonderful irony that aviators are on this slow ocean liner — who are sleeping side by side by side in one wide bed, an uncanny apparition with their beards outside the covers. There is something archetypal about these bearded men, a Smith Brothers cough-dropian doppelganger-plus-one reminiscent of the mirror scene in *Duck Soup* wonder of nature, and this is confirmed when a butterfly flutters from under a lifted beard. Tomasso wears an enchanted and amused expression as he gazes on them, though we can see he is also hatching a plan. Out come scissors, a prop he began to wield with dexterous mischief in *Duck Soup*. And the rest of the scene works by implication. We see him snip the air and lean towards a beard: We don't see but surmise his theft.

We may not understand at first why Tomasso is stealing the aviators' beards, especially because we know he is capable of gratuitous cutting. But we begin to suspect the method to the madness when we see the three aviators bound and beardless in their bed. And our suspicions are confirmed when Fiorello, Tomasso, and Ricardo emerge from the stateroom wearing uniforms and beards. They are costumed and playing the roles of the heroic aviators, a bit of theater within the film before it houses an opera within itself too. This is a desperate scheme, Tomasso's stratagem to get them from the ship and into New York without being arrested as stowaways. Yet it actually works better than the Maurice Chevalier imitations in *Monkey Business* and even though it threatens to unravel when they are placed before a radio microphone to speak at a reception in their honor.

This is surreal stuff. When Tomasso is introduced at the microphone, what follows is a memorable gag based on his silence. Fiorello goes first, stalling by taking a drink, then talking nonsense about their trans–Atlantic flight: running out of gasoline, going back for more even when inches from landing in America, and once forgetting the airplane and having to return

Harpo and his cohorts exit the ship disguised as celebrity aviators, replete with beards stolen by Harpo. It's a desperate scheme that soon goes out of control. Left to right: Groucho Marx as Driftwood, Harpo Marx as Tomasso, Allan Jones as Ricardo Baroni, and Chico Marx as Fiorello, *A Night at the Opera*, MGM, 1935.

for it. When it is Tomasso's turn, we wonder how a mute guy will make a radio speech. The answer is by stalling, by drinking outlandish quantities of water, and by slopping water onto his beard until the glue washes away and his beard leaves his face and cleaves to the face of the suspicious bulldog of a cop whom Tomasso, in a burst of affection, embraces. So the chase begins.

Tomasso's antics are also central to the breakfast scene in Driftwood's hotel room where the stowaways are hiding next. Tomasso entertains his cohorts as he exhibits his outlandish appetite for food along with his capacity for gender-bending, twice imitating a woman in this sequence. And he and his cohorts even shift the shape of the rooms. The stowaways' crime of imper-sonation, a meta-joke because this is essentially the actor's craft, has made the morning papers. But neither Driftwood nor the others are concerned; they are far more interested in breakfast.

Harpo, in what seems like unscripted gags eliciting genuine laughter from his brothers, plays with most of the food on the table so that in the end no one else gets much to eat. He combines the edible and inedible like in *The Cocoanuts,* making a sandwich with pancakes, coffee cup, cigar, and a snipped-off piece of Chico's tie. Chico proclaims him "half-goat," the film's first allusion to trickster's animal nature. Then Harpo impersonates a woman putting on lipstick using ketchup on his pinkie finger and powdering his face with a pancake as puff and sugar as powder. Finally he blows up a rubber glove from deep in one of his pockets and milks the improvised udders into everyone's coffee.

This one-man show with some deadpan commentary by Groucho is interrupted by the arrival of their nemesis, the bulldog cop, whom they manage to foil in an expansion of the shape-shifting trope: They change the semblance of the suite of rooms right under his nose and behind his back, moving the beds from one room to the other via door or balcony until the cop's suspicions evolve into complete confusion. Unable to trust the input of his senses to determine what is real, he stumbles into the bedroom, now looking like a parlor. In it, Driftwood plays an elderly man of the house reading the newspaper while Tomasso, dressed as an old woman and making the Gookie face, sews and rocks in a chair. It happens to be a human chair, improvised by Fiorello and Ricardo covered with a sheet.

The next two brief scenes may lack Harpo but they establish the need for his cleansing chaos. Rosa's debut is cancelled when Lassparri intrudes upon her and Ricardo's reunion, bitterly maligning Rosa, hence sincere love, and earning a punch from Ricardo. Meanwhile, Gottlieb fires Driftwood and takes charge of Mrs. Claypool's affairs. Driftwood withdraws his offer of marriage to her, and, with an echo of Harpo's gender-play, withdraws his offer of marriage to Lassparri too. The scene ends with Driftwood getting kicked down the stairs. Tomasso reappears only in the aftermath of these firings, when all four (Driftwood, Fiorello, Tomasso, and Ricardo) sulk on a park bench. As usual in the films, Harpo willingly shares their troubles yet seems detached, perhaps a result of his tendency to drop in and out of situations.

Because circumstances for the young lovers are desperate and none have anything to lose, the cohorts hatch a plan with Tomasso's capacity for mania at the heart of it. First Driftwood, Fiorello, and Tomasso take over Gottlieb's office, Tomasso enjoying a cigar even as Driftwood criticizes its quality. Tomasso tosses the cigar box up in the air so that it lands on Gottlieb's head, accidentally on purpose knocking him out. With Gottlieb's tuxedo on Driftwood, and other formal attire on Tomasso and Fiorello — again, they are costumed to play roles — they return to the opera house and the cleansing-by-debasing high opera begins in comic earnest.

Tomasso's contributions can be summed up as wildly inappropriate behavior both in the orchestra pit and on the opera stage. He sword-fights using the conductor's baton and a violin bow, substitutes the musical score of "Take Me Out to the Ballgame" for the score of *Il Trovatore*, seizes an audience member's hat to mute his trombone, sticks his musical score to the back of another musician's head with chewing gum, and plays catch with Fiorello, both somehow in possession of baseball mitts and a ball. When Tomasso grabs a violin to bat with, we are aghast.

But our disapproval would land us on the side of the snob contingency headed by Lassparri and Gottlieb. And Gottlieb, wearing Driftwood's suit badly for it barely covers his paunch, has been rendered foolish and is sputtering with outrage. So though we are gasping — a violin!— we are also laughing. And we are contemplating the unusual mix of popular culture: baseball and peanuts with high art (opera).

Suddenly we get it: Opera *was* popular culture and perhaps should remain so, or at least be more accessible to ordinary working people like those who used to sing arias on the street in opera's early days.[3] Hijacked from its plebian roots, opera needs to be reunited with them. Lassparri, Gottlieb, Mrs. Claypool, and the wealthy members of the audience are not opera's rightful inheritors, the film suggests. So Tomasso's assault is not meant to destroy the art form, though for a while he helps turn it inside out, but to return it to the people cleansed of pomposity, which includes replacing the singers in the starring roles in this performance of *Il Trovatore*.

Once we understand this — and the musical extravaganza in steerage offered a strong hint — we can relax and enjoy the chaos. The confused performers stalwartly endure the absurdly rising and falling scrims and try to ignore the invasion of the chorus by Fiorello and Tomasso as well as the authorities pursuing them. They try to disregard distractions like wigs airlifted from one head and dropped onto another, Tomasso's trapeze and gymnastics stunts transpiring over the stage, not to mention police chases across it. The performance is held together, barely, until the right tenor and soprano, Rosa and Ricardo, make their triumphant debut.

Tomasso begins his role in *Il Trovatore* in the chorus. Like trickster, he embeds himself in an exalted situation and behaves inappropriately, in this case making the Gookie face. He is accompanied by Fiorello in the ironic task of luring the authorities onto the stage in full view of the audience. Gottlieb, foiled and knowing it, is beside himself until the cop sees him aiming a skillet in defense of his opera. Mistaking him for Driftwood — it must be the suit — the cop knocks Gottlieb out. Fiorello returns the favor, knocking the cop out. Tomasso whips Lassparri, reprising Lassparri's whipping of him, in a

Hiding from the police in Groucho's hotel suite, Harpo plays with the breakfast food, impersonating a woman, then eating like a goat. Chico Marx as Fiorello, Harpo Marx as Tomasso, Groucho Marx as Driftwood, and Allan Jones as Ricardo. *A Night at the Opera*, MGM, 1935.

scene on stage. And with trickster's lustful mischief, Tomasso whips off a female performer's skirt, tickles her torso, and whistles.

About to be nabbed, for the cop and Gottlieb are making their way toward him from both wings also in gypsy costumes, Tomasso, with no other exit from center stage, summons trickster's capacity for magic and the surreal to run *up* the curtain. At this point the opera morphs into a circus, for Tomasso climbs curtains, balances on sets, swings on ropes and bars, and when he falls, slices through a curtain with his legs as he descends. He has become a human scissors, a meta-cinematic gag on his favorite tool. He also manipulates weights and levers, changing the scrims and turning *Il Trovatore* into a collage of many operas with humor especially for opera lovers who can identify the various allusions and unpack the absurdity of their juxtapositions.

Eventually Tomasso turns out the lights, giving Fiorello the opportunity to kidnap Lassparri, whose screech completes the cleansing of opera, returning it to its rightful participants. Gottlieb has no choice but to hire Ricardo to replace the missing Lassparri, and Ricardo insists upon singing with Rosa. Moreover, the opera-loving audience recognizes their worth, cheering them through a joyous encore and booing Lassparri who tries to return to the stage. This success wins amnesty for the stowaways, defeats Lassparri, unites Rosa and Ricardo, establishes their careers, lands Tomasso in Gottlieb's arms, and gets Driftwood rehired. New contracts are made and torn up, and Tomasso closes the film by ripping the back of Gottlieb's tuxedo, vestiary marker of wealth, from tails to head while managing to wear a beatific expression.

7

A Day at the Races (1937)
IT'S GABRIEL

"Trickster is a boundary-crossing figure."
— Lewis Hyde, *Trickster Makes This World*[1]

In *A Day at the Races*, some of Harpo's trickster traits are reiterated, like lust, appetite, and thievery. Others evolve, especially the supernatural dimension of his character along with his alliance with the marginalized. Reinforcing his angelic nature when he plays the harp, Harpo as Stuffy is specifically identified in this film as the angel Gabriel, messenger from God to humans. Although Groucho's Hugo Hackenbush (a character Groucho identified with) may seem like the film's central character, and both Groucho and Chico's Tony partake of greater trickster essence than in prior films, Harpo continues to evolve as a more multidimensional trickster than his brothers. He also continues to lead them in advancing his trickster agenda. In this film, Harpo eats like a goat, lusts after nurses, shape-shifts, plays variations on the theme of identity, and creates a mud-splattered chaos that in the end helps the sympathetic and struggling characters who include not only his trickster cohorts and the sweethearts Judy (Maureen O'Sullivan) and Gil (Alan Jones) but also the cast of African American track workers and their families. All of these underdogs become top dogs in the end due to Stuffy's efforts.

Some changes occur in *A Day at the Races* in how Harpo and his cohorts are depicted. Speaking the language of gesture, for example, seems more arduous for Stuffy, who actually faints after an attempt to tell Tony about an overheard plan to frame Hackenbush, in spite of the fact that Chico is usually his most intuitive translator. And interestingly, Hackenbush exhibits the kind of rapport with animals usually reserved for Harpo in the films. For example, in Groucho's first scene introducing Hackenbush in his clinic as a veterinarian who will be posing as a physician, we are charmed by his bedside manner with a horse, then behold a puppy napping in the sleeve of his coat. These are reminiscent of Harpo's characteristic rapport with animals, his blurring of the distinction between animal and human, between four-legged and two. Of course Harpo continues to infuse his own enthusiasm for animals into his affectionate interactions with the horse High Hat in this film, and he carries the theme throughout, unlike Groucho.

Extending the trope of the equine beloved introduced in *Animal Crackers* and repeated in *Duck Soup* when Harpo took a horse to bed with him, in *A Day at the Races,* Harpo's Stuffy is Gil's racehorse High Hat's jockey and trainer as well as his chef and his friend. And while Harpo remains a thief, though stealing somewhat less compulsively in this film, he has honor when it comes to horses: He is too honest to throw a race. In this way and others, Harpo continues to develop a theme that runs through the films: that *mischief* and *evil* differ. This is an important distinction, given trickster's penchant for rule-breaking, and it offers a key to reconciling his rebellion with his wild celebration of life. It also trains us in the art of developing a nuanced understanding; that is, a hinged mind.

Beyond familiar trickster traits developed in prior films, in *A Day at the Races,* Harpo ascends to what can only be called the inner circle of the divine. In an extended jazz sequence unique in Marx Brothers films so far, Harpo is identified by the African American track workers as an Old Testament angel and messenger of God when they translate the musical phrase he pipes in response to the question, "Who Dat Man?" as "It's Gabriel." Moreover, Harpo has a unique relationship with this community: He is the only Marx brother to cross the racial divide to enter and be accepted in their world. Being a border-crosser like trickster, Harpo draws the camera lens to a people who were underrepresented in film or were often behind the scenes in their pursuit of life, liberty, and happiness.

The object of trickster's satire in *A Day at the Races* is not a formidable institution or social class: not land speculation, the upper class, art, collegiate sports, politics and war, or opera, as in previous Marx Brothers films. This film targets, instead, malevolent schemers and social inequality. The setting itself, a sanitarium, is not under attack, though hypochondria and medical indulgence of the wealthy provide sources of humor. In fact, keeping the sanitarium afloat financially is the goal, for its solvency is scaffolding for the future happiness of young lovers Judy and Gil.

The sanitarium must, then, get the money it needs. The underdogs (Judy, Gil, Chico, Harpo, Groucho, and the African American community who appear briefly but memorably) need a windfall. Redistribution of wealth is necessary to set things right and to thwart the greed and dirty tricks that often reinforce class divisions, represented in the film by the characters J.D. Morgan and Whitmore. To the extent that the wealthy widow Mrs. Upjohn (Margaret Dumont) can be parted from her money, she is on the side of social justice and love.

As in every film so far, this one's milieu, the sanitarium and its discontents, is introduced before Harpo appears as Stuffy. First we get an opening shot of a train arriving at the Florida resort that offers horse racing, casinos, and rest and relaxation at the sanitarium. The problem is clear: No one wants to go to the sanitarium, even though Tony is offering a "free bus." His apparent loyalty to Judy — he assures her that while she may not be able to pay him, she cannot fire him — places him squarely on the side of love.

Tony's solution to the scarcity of patients is to summon Dr. Hackenbush, a favorite of the wealthy hypochondriac patient Mrs. Upjohn. Gil's solution, a rather desperate one, is to invest all of his money in the racehorse High Hat, a get-rich-quick scheme that his singing gigs can't deliver. Judy's response is anger at Gil for "gambling away our happiness." But she acquiesces to Tony's plan, the secondary problem, the separation of the lovers, evolving from the first, the financial instability of the sanitarium, and inducing Tony to lie to Mrs. Upjohn, telling her that Dr. Hackenbush is coming, then trick her into revealing his whereabouts so he can summon him. So far, Harpo hasn't entered the film, but when he does he will lighten, scramble, and diffuse the desperation.

First, so we fully understand he is a veterinarian, we get that initial glimpse of Hackenbush in his clinic where he feeds a horse a large pill, the same pill he later attempts to feed to Mrs. Upjohn while reassuring her that his last patient "won the Kentucky Derby," and where he pulls that puppy from the sleeve of his coat. Before he leaves, he counsels the horse as if it were human. After this, he arrives at the sanitarium as the specialist Dr. Hackenbush at the very moment Judy's accountant, Whitmore, is pressuring her to sell the place to J.D. Morgan, who secretly wants to turn it into a casino. Because we know her deep attachment to the sanitarium — it's her family's legacy — we hope, with hinged minds, for the success of the Hackenbush scheme even though we know he is not really a medical doctor.

In that context Harpo enters the film as Stuffy. This time he doesn't arrive from elsewhere but is working as a jockey at the racetrack and is on affectionate terms with Gil's horse High Hat. Through his bond with the horse, he is allied with Gil, and therefore Judy, and therefore Tony, and therefore Hackenbush. When Morgan attempts to beat Stuffy for not throwing the race, we recognize him as the same schemer who wants to turn the sanitarium into a casino. His name even hints at the film's critique of wealth, power, and dubiously gotten gains. Morgan's violence makes us sympathize with Stuffy, as does our trust in horse sense, for High Hat goes berserk when he sees Morgan or hears his voice, an effect Stuffy will later exploit to win the race. In contrast, High Hat lets Stuffy kiss him. Stuffy hides from Morgan in the hay while Gil brushes High Hat, but he manages a swift kick at Morgan, who thinks the blow came from the horse.

Stuffy, speaking the language of props and gestures, tells Tony he has been "fired" by lighting a match. Tony, a prior relationship between them implied here as in nearly every film, alludes to Harpo's trickster complexity when he says that Stuffy is too honest to throw a race but you have to watch him or he'll steal the ice cream. The threat is ironic because the ice cream wagon, we soon discover, is full of books. The tricks come when the sheriff, the law being on the side of the antagonists in this film, demands money for High Hat to qualify for the race, money neither Gil nor Tony has. So Stuffy adroitly picks the sheriff's trouser pocket and slips the money back to Tony. They give the sheriff the same five-dollar bill three times, multiplying the payment to fifteen. But when the sheriff, unbeknownst to Stuffy, pockets the bill in his vest pocket instead, Stuffy gropes so deeply in his pants pocket that he retrieves the sheriff's socks. The problem of raising money to keep High Hat in the race has been postponed but not solved.

Because it is loaded with the kind of verbal repartee that Harpo's silence competes against, he is not present during Hackenbush and Tony's famous Tootsie-Fruitsie Ice Cream sequence, Tony selling Hackenbush a tip on a horse in code, then tome after tome to decipher the code, meanwhile betting and winning on Sun-Up, the horse Hackenbush intended betting on in the first place. The scene is full of trickster nuance on Tony's part, to be followed by Hackenbush's vocal shape-shifting on the telephone in the next scene. The crisis of Judy and Gil's separation has been pre-empted by the threat of Hackenbush's exposure by Whitmore, whom we have just overheard scheming with Morgan. So Hackenbush takes matters into his own hands, or mouth that is, intercepting the call Whitmore is placing to the Florida medical board by playing operator, colonel–records keeper, and himself. He accomplishes this right after he almost confessed that he is really a veterinarian to Judy. Until Harpo surpasses them, becoming the angel Gabriel, his brothers are trickster runners-up. But who's keeping score?

Stuffy and his cohorts are together for the first time after this scene, when Stuffy and Tony climb into Whitmore's window. It is not clear how much they overheard, but Tony bribes Stuffy to see the doctor by offering him a steak. When he adds spinach to the description, Stuffy heads for the window again, and Tony offers nurses to lure him back. In this first scene with the three together, we see their multiplied potential for mayhem. Stuffy plays a small flute to divert Hackenbush's attention from his racing form. Hackenbush examines Stuffy, using stereotypical doctor phrases like, "Say Ah." When he says "Louder," Stuffy gapes wider though still silently. When Hackenbush takes his temperature, Stuffy eats the thermometer. When Hackenbush palpates his stomach, Harpo blows bubbles. With the mirror turned on himself, Hackenbush describes the dubious health of the patient. When Tony points out the error, they clown and laugh. Then Stuffy jabs Hackenbush's leg with Novocain, so when Hackenbush says he doesn't have a leg to stand on, he really doesn't and falls to the floor.

From this point on, Stuffy helps diffuse and effervesce the mounting difficulties. At the end of the examination, Tony reads the inscription on the back of Hackenbush's watch. It states explicitly that he is a veterinarian. So in the next brief scene at the track where Gil is timing High Hat, Gil must swallow two disappointments: the first, that Hackenbush isn't a medical doctor, and the second, that his horse isn't fast enough to win. Their most pressing problem, however, is the sheriff's sudden appearance, for he tries to take possession of High Hat. To avert that, Tony slips the harness onto Stuffy, who is willing to be an animal again. He imitates the horse's gait as the sheriff leads him off. When discovered, he mounts High Hat and rides away, one of several scenes in which Harpo did much of his own riding. Note that Harpo always collaborates with the horse against authority.

Stuffy appears in the next sequence in disheveled upper class garb, simultaneously exhibiting and deconstructing the vestiary markers of wealth. In a musical extravaganza featuring Gil singing, a chorus dancing, fountains spraying water, and a ballerina twirling, Stuffy's top hat is flattened and his cummerbund is not tucked in, so we can see his working man's flannel shirt underneath. In fact, his entire outfit is a nice signifier of social strata *fermished* in one being.

Hackenbush steals the scene for a while, dancing back and forth between Mrs. Upjohn and the blonde Flo, twirling Upjohn away, dancing with Flo, returning to Upjohn, and in general wooing them simultaneously while arranging an assignation with Flo. Meanwhile Stuffy and Tony, sitting on a diving board, watch Judy and Gil reconcile. When Morgan sees Tony and Stuffy, they escape through the musicians' portal, and that establishes the premise for the film's next musical interlude, first Tony on the piano, then Stuffy, who plays it so violently that keys fly up, the piano falls apart, and he extracts a harp from it: a musical instrument begetting a musical instrument and a memorable moment indeed.

This is the surreal premise for Harpo's harp solo, with a minor bump in continuity when the piano's soundboard morphs into an actual harp. As in every film, Harpo's demeanor changes: He becomes angelic while he plays the harp. Moreover, his and Chico's performances secure reprieves, for the sheriff and Morgan must wait until they are finished playing their solos to arrest them. To escape, Stuffy enacts more magic. By spinning the piano stool, he catapults himself into the pond and swims away.

But he remains in the vicinity. Meanwhile, lust, an aspect of Harpo's trickster persona in this film, serves the additional purpose of saving the sanitarium, for while chasing chorus girls, Stuffy overhears Morgan and Flo scheming to frame Hackenbush in his room at the sanitarium so as to expose him to Mrs. Upjohn. Stuffy interrupts Tony's game of blind man's bluff with more chorus girls to communicate the scheme they need to thwart. For the first time in the films, however, Chico does not easily translate Harpo's gestures into words. Unlike Harpo's mute eloquence in *Horse Feathers*, his *A Day at the Races* miming of Morgan's scheme to entrap Hackenbush is arduous; he keeps starting over with "Hackenbush," "a woman," "come to his room," "frame him," until Chico almost gives up. Although Stuffy at last succeeds in making Tony understand, he faints from the effort.

All three trickster cohorts have active roles in the scene in Hackenbush's room at the sanitarium after Flo arrives, but Harpo ups the ante, making it almost as chaotic as he does the scene of the examination of Mrs. Upjohn. Hackenbush and Flo's excessively polite but ultimately sleazy assignation doesn't last long because Tony and Stuffy barge in, pile up on Flo's lap, Stuffy gestures for Hackenbush to join them, and they even have a tug of war over her. Groucho gets rid of them, but they return disguised as detectives, Stuffy in Sherlock Holmes regalia seemingly recycled from *Duck Soup*, but with French bulldogs instead of bloodhounds on a leash. While Flo is powdering her face, she tells Stuffy to "blow," meaning, "scram." Ever the literalist, he blows the powder all over her: delightful homonym humor from a mute performer. More interested in Flo than the sanitarium, and resisting Tony's loud warnings well within her earshot, Hackenbush puts a steak down Tony's pants. The dogs jump on him, entangling Stuffy, who is holding their leashes. Harpo is the last to go out the door, as if on a dogsled minus the sled.

Tony and Stuffy gain their ultimate reentry by breaking down the locked door, this time to paper the walls. They wallpaper over Hackenbush and Flo, yet by the time Whitmore and Mrs. Upjohn arrive, Flo is buried under the sofa cushions, and Hackenbush, under layers of wallpaper, is reading a book. Stuffy and Tony have thus successfully foiled the scheme to discredit Hackenbush. Whitmore and Upjohn leave, Flo emerges from deep in the couch

To rescue Hackenbush (Groucho, seated)from a plot to discredit him, Harpo and Chico crash his assignation and wallpaper over the blonde (Esther Muir). *A Day at the Races,* MGM, 1937.

in a serious huff, and Stuffy punctuates her exit by smacking a piece of wall-paper onto her bottom, rhyming with the newspaper he glued to Trentino's bottom in *Duck Soup* as well as with his surreptitious and irreverent parting kick at Morgan at the end of his first stable scene.

Harpo brings chaos, climax, and closure to the next scene too, featuring all three Marx brothers in the anarchic medical examination of Mrs. Upjohn. Wooing her in the garden, Hackenbush convinces her to help Judy financially. But Whitmore interrupts her signing the papers that would transfer some of her wealth to the sanitarium when he introduces Dr. Steinberg, played by Sig Ruman (Gottlieb in *A Night at the Opera* and Stubel in *A Night in Casablanca*), here reintroducing the sputtering and pompous persona, this time as an old-school professor of medicine hired to expose Hackenbush.

Hackenbush insults him in various ways, but he can't derail the proposed examination of Mrs. Upjohn that is really an examination of his medical credentials, so he runs to his room to pack his bag, an escapist impulse like the one to come in *At the Circus* and similarly quelled by his sympathy for the female part of the young lovebird's equation. He discovers he isn't alone in his room: Tony and Stuffy have High Hat stabled in the closet. Stuffy is even harvesting straw from the mattress to feed him — trickster is always one to root around for feeding opportunities — while Tony convinces Hackenbush to stay at the sanitarium for Judy's sake.

Hackenbush is in big trouble in the examining room until Stuffy and Tony arrive. Of course, he is in more trouble *after* they arrive, but the trouble is such good fun. At first Hackenbush is the only quack attending Mrs. Upjohn while Steinberg and Whitmore observe. Hackenbush stalls by taking a long time to scrub up, meanwhile insinuating that Dr. Steinberg is unwashed and furthermore may steal his watch. But unable to postpone the inevitable, he asks Mrs. Upjohn to flap her arms like a bird (a logical request from a veterinarian); she happily complies. Tony and Stuffy arrive to assist him, the backs of their white coats stenciled with "Joe's Service Station" and "brakes relined," thus deconstructing the distinction between white and blue collar work as well as between doctors and mechanics. Groucho alludes to the magic

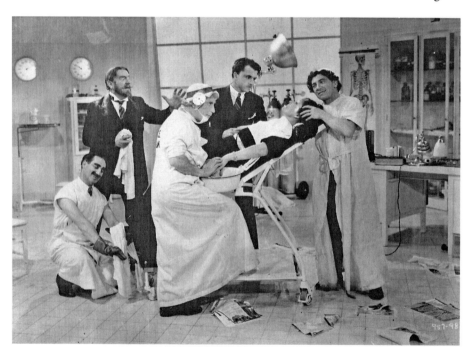

Mrs. Upjohn gets a medical examination that includes a shave, manicure, and shoeshine. Left to right: Groucho Marx as Hugo Hackenbush, Sig Ruman as Dr. Steinberg, Harpo Marx as Stuffy, Leonard Ceeley as Whitmore, Margaret Dumont as Mrs. Upjohn, and Chico Marx as Tony. *A Day at the Races*, MGM, 1937.

of trickster, saying "Just rub a lamp and they'll appear," then introduces them both as "Doctors Steinberg." Harpo surprises and delights us by bowing backwards to accommodate Dr. Steinberg's forward bow. Then all three wash their hands while singing "Down by the Old Mill Stream," a barbershop quartet standard and thus a meta-gag like in *Monkey Business*. But Zeppo bailed from the act, and one remaining Marx is mute, so there are only two voices, unless Harpo is singing too. Is he? The jury, at least in my living room, is out.

They wipe their hands on each other's coats, moving in a circle like circus elephants. They scrub and scrub, but Hackenbush can't stall any more. When he is told to take Mrs. Upjohn's pulse, he defers to Stuffy, who takes her purse, an immigrant's misapprehension of English recycled from *Monkey Business*. With trickster's impulsive desire, Stuffy grabs a nurse — Tony does too, but with more subtlety than Stuffy's wrestling hold — interpreting her attempt to secure his hospital gown as a hug and tearing her uniform off as she escapes screaming in petticoat and socks, a projection of his own penchant for stripping down to underwear.

Stuffy attacks the pretensions of both doctors and the wealthy in this scene. He hangs a MEN AT WORK sign on the ankles of Mrs. Upjohn, who is completely helpless in the reclining chair while he pumps her legs up and down, gives her a manicure and helps give her a shave while Groucho shines her shoes, sells an "extra" edition newspaper when Dr. Steinberg calls for x-rays, wipes his hands on Dr. Steinberg's coat, scrolls down a picture of a horse and kisses it, and finally turns on the fire alarm and overhead sprinklers. In the midst of the chaos that is mostly of Stuffy's making though enhanced with contributions from Hackenbush and Tony, High Hat arrives with a pigeon on his back. All three brothers jump on him and ride out of the examining room to escape the downpour. Now Harpo is associated with the element of water in addition to the wind and fire from prior films.

Stuffy also provides transition to the next scene when we see him, unruffled, drying his wet socks over a campfire in the barn. Hackenbush, Tony, and Gil who all look dejected, flank him, while High Hat eats hay from the top of Stuffy's flattened hat. Judy, sad but appreciative of their efforts, offers them blankets. When Gil sings "Tomorrow Is Another Day" to cheer her up, Stuffy's eyes are big and round, for he is stunned by her tears. We have seen him wear this expression in the face of human sorrow before.

But soon Stuffy becomes a real angel, infusing hope in the entire cast of protagonists. He accompanies Gil's song on a small flute that introduces the next musical number, a jazz extravaganza featuring the African American racetrack workers and their family members. Stuffy crosses the racial divide, taking the camera with him, into a cabin, a juke joint, and a courtyard to mingle with these working people who keep things running behind the scenes. We see and hear a chorus of singers, dancers, and musicians, including Ivie Anderson, the Crinoline Choir, some members of the Duke Ellington Orchestra, and Whitey's Lindy Hoppers,[2] not identified in the original credits. When children, then a young man ask, "Who dat man?" Stuffy responds with a musical phrase. They translate the notes: "It's Gabriel," Old Testament messenger of God who in this film dances with children who cling to his coat, makes bad times pass by fluttering calendar pages away, and eventually brings those who need a windfall a new and improved tomorrow with High Hat's victory in the race.

As Gil's song suggests, the theme of this jazz sequence is hope. The everyday lives of the track workers and their families are fraught with financial anxieties. We see this in the crowded, multi-generational, and sparely furnished cabin. For different reasons, Judy and Gil's lives share financial anxiety too, so a parallel is drawn between them. Ivie Anderson sings, "All God's children got frowns" and "trouble," acknowledging the difficulty of life. But she adds that "All God's Children" also have "swing" and "rhythm," alluding to the process of sublimation from which art arises, and signaling a welcome contrast to the values satirized in *Duck Soup* wherein "all god's children got guns." Whitey's Lindey Hoppers follow her song with a dance, young couples introducing fashion and swing-dance styles to a wider American audience. When the Crinoline Choir sings, Stuffy conducts, then leads the entire entourage on a march as if he were a drum major, but with a pitchfork instead of a baton, which is appropriate since he works in a stable.

Harpo is the only Marx brother to enter the working class African American world. He is also the only one to leave half of his face unblackened in the next scene, which ends this sequence with an evocation of blackface. While "The humanity and subjectivity of African Americans have often been staged by white people performing blackness,"[3] in *A Day at the Races,* African Americans represent themselves. Their dignity, crowded living conditions, melancholy, and fear of the biased law result in sublimation of these anxieties into art, particularly instrumental music, song, and dance that provide catharsis and hope for the future. Blackface in this scene, though likely to make contemporary viewers wince, is not enacted in the spirit of degrading minstrelsy but as a disguise, for the law is on the side of the white antagonists. And they are crooks and exploiters of the financially needy, as we see when Morgan tries to pressure Judy into selling the sanitarium and when the sheriff demands money Gil can't pay to keep High Hat stabled and eligible for the race. Gil and the Marxes oppose them. So when representatives of the law invade the barn where the Marxes, Gil and Judy, and the African American cast of characters are singing and dancing, Groucho, Chico, and Harpo, and Gil darken

"It's Gabriel!" Harpo pipes when asked who he is, an angel even though he's not playing the harp. Harpo Marx as Stuffy, unidentified members of crowd. *A Day at the Races,* MGM, 1937.

their faces with axle grease in order to blend in and escape. Indeed, the African American characters also fear the law and try to flee. The lighter skinned though not necessarily pale Marxes are trying to pass as black to escape arrest.

But leave it to Harpo to put a trickster spin on this unfortunate evocation of blackface: He blackens only half of his face. Like the Afro-Caribbean trickster Eshu, he creates ambiguity that has profound implications about racial identity. Harpo is like Eshu and his hat, one side white and one side black, potentially undermining the testimony of witnesses, for seen from one side, Harpo is white; seen from the other side, he is black. Yet he is the same man, and this suggests that the perception of racial identity, indeed racial categories, depend upon point of view. So Harpo's half black, half white face signifies the instability of racial dichotomies. He interrogates racial divisions by donning a mask that unmasks premises running deep in the culture. And there may be more to this. For Harpo is a Jew, and the Jew is off-white in American culture, neither suffering the full weight of discrimination of blackness nor experiencing complete acceptance in white-dominated culture. The Jew partakes of both identities, abiding somewhere in between.

Race isn't Harpo's only unmasking in this scene. He also unmasks High Hat's talent. This begins at the end of the blackface sequence when High Hat, predictably, goes berserk seeing and hearing Morgan in the barn. When Harpo escapes on the back of this agitated horse, High Hat leaps over the barn door, then over nearby hedges. In this way Gil and company discover that the horse Gil spent his last money on in desperation is actually a steeplechase horse, and a fine one at that. To punctuate the significance of this discovery, Stuffy is thrown from High Hat right through a billboard announcing a steeplechase race. Hope returns.

Stuffy plays a trickster role in the long final triumph-of-the-underdogs sequence, the steeplechase race. In fact, all three Marxes function as a well-oiled trickster machine in this sequence. The race is announced musically by "Cosi Cosa," Allan Jones' optimistic song in steerage from *A Night at the Opera*. Here it ultimately champions the marginalized too. Always interested in expanding capabilities and overcoming limitations, Stuffy mooches Hackenbush's binoculars to see the track; Hackenbush splits them in two, giving Stuffy and Tony each one monocle. Although Stuffy doesn't hear Morgan coaching his jockey to ride dirty to the extent he can get away with, we hear him, and we are thus reminded of how bad the bad guys can be. At this point, of course, all hope is riding, pun intended, on the outcome of the race: for Judy and Gil, the sanitarium, Hackenbush and his pursuit of Mrs. Upjohn, for Tony, for Stuffy, and for the African American track workers and their kin, who have all bet on High Horse to win.

Trickster must go for the joint to make that happen. First, unfortunately, the sheriff seizes High Hat right before the steeplechase race begins, so the Marxes, Gill, and Judy have to cause the race to be delayed while they figure out how to get High Hat back onto the track. Stuffy lends more than a hand in coming up with tactics: He soaps saddles so jockeys fall off, and he soaps the bugle so it blows bubbles instead of notes to start the race. When the race begins in spite of their efforts, Tony and Stuffy open the fence so the horses run off the track into a field and must be rounded up again. Then Stuffy turns on a huge fan that blows the hats of all the men in the stands onto the track, an intensifying of the hat gags in *Duck Soup* with the humor of instable identities as men scramble for their hats and sometimes put on wrong and ill-fitting ones. And again, the track must be cleared. Meanwhile, Tony and Hackenbush direct cars onto the racetrack with FREE PARKING signs, the police chasing them over the resulting traffic jam of cars. Again and again the track must be cleared.

After Gil and Judy steal High Hat back from the sheriff, Stuffy, as a jockey with trickster's versatility, adapts to challenges in the race, which begin with getting High Hat back into the line-up. They hook High Hat to the fire wagon, Stuffy sprays the firemen off with hoses, and he's off to the races.

In the race itself, Harpo shows High Hat Morgan's picture to make him run faster, a truly amusing pragmatic predicated on the horse's ability not only to perceive a photographic likeness but also to confuse that picture for the man himself. When Stuffy loses the photograph of Morgan, Groucho and Chico must substitute Morgan's actual voice to spur High Hat, pun intended, on to victory. Here the mischief of the three Marx brothers coalesces into one united effort and in some ways one trickster essence. They invent various ways to provoke Morgan so that he hollers into a microphone plugged into the public address system, at one point even attaching the microphone to a dog and getting it to jump on Morgan.

Harpo may play tricks, but he doesn't play dirty ones like Morgan's jockey does during the race, kicking, spurring, and whipping Stuffy and High Hat. But luck or grace is on Harpo's side as it is often on trickster's. After the horses go down in the mud, and Harpo and the crooked jockey remount to finish the race, High Hat appears to have lost in a close finish. Yet it turns out that the horses actually got mixed up in the mud that hid their numbers, and it was High Hat, ridden by the bad jockey, who won the race. When the error is discovered, Harpo kisses High Hat for the second time in the film.

High Hat's triumph dominates the film's conclusion. But *A Day at the Races* also has a denouement, a big musical number that closes the film with almost the entire cast: Judy and Gil, Hackenbush and Mrs. Upjohn, Tony, Stuffy, and the African American track workers, families, and friends. Theirs is a triumphantly ebullient march toward the camera and better times, because "all god's children," "got a letter from the man in the moon," foiled the enemies of love, loyalty, and social justice, and won big. What has trickster to do with this? He foretells it, facilitates it, and celebrates it, Hermes-like, with harp, then flute.

8

Room Service (1938)
GIMME SHELTER, FOOD AND ART

"Coyote and his kin represent ... the pure creative spark that is our
birthright as human beings."
— Erdoes and Ortiz, *American Indian Myths and Legends*[1]

Although *Room Service* is somewhat off the Marx Brothers trajectory,
being filmed at RKO and based entirely on a stage play originally starring
other actors, it does remain faithful to developing Harpo's trickster essence,
the most distilled of his brothers. Here his innovative capacities are emphasized
over his angelic nature. He plays no divine harp solo in this film, and he is
over his lust: He chases no women, though he does ogle one woman when
he is playing dead in a late scene. Even so, this film focuses on a motif common
in trickster lore: the sometimes convoluted and necessarily incessant effort it
takes to satisfy the basic needs for food and shelter. In addition, Harpo is
deeply involved in the satisfaction of a third basic need, one some might not
consider essential though it is: the need for the sustenance of art.

Room Service cleaves close to the classical unities of place and time while
braiding together these three essential human needs: for food, shelter, and
artistic expression. The entire film takes place in the hotel, much of it in one
hotel room, in the few weeks prior to the premiere of the play within the
film, its title *Hail and Farewell*, a meta-echo of Groucho's "Hello, I must be
going" song from *Animal Crackers*. The trickster cohorts struggle on behalf
of artistic expression, attempting to shepherd through to opening night the
production of an underfunded play. And that struggle is enmeshed with meeting
the other two needs, for food and shelter.

The lack of funding for the play results in the bodily hunger of director,
writer, cast, and crew for food, and threatens to result in loss of shelter when

100

they face eviction, also from lack of funds. While food and shelter must be secured first, the need for artistic expression, *Room Service* argues, eventually must be satisfied as well. Harpo's role in all of this, though at times peripheral, is memorable.

Harpo has only a slightly delayed entrance. The three unsatisfied needs are established before he appears. The opening scene in the hotel dining room, instead of being focused on food, highlights the predicament of a frustrated artist, the immigrant waiter Sasha Smirnoff (Alexander Asro), an established actor in Russia who, having come to America, is reduced to waiting tables and begging Gordon Miller (Groucho) for an audition. Sasha, serving food while suffering a deep and frustrated hunger for the stage, embodies the conflations of the three hungers, especially working where he does, in a hotel dining room. The first scene also introduces the threat to food and shelter: Without a backer for the play, Miller can't pay the hotel bill. The playwright Leo Davis (Frank Albertson) even stands to lose his typewriter, his tool for creating and editing his art. And the entire cast and crew, harbored by Miller, face both hunger and eviction. In comparison, the waiter Sasha might seem better off, but he probably wouldn't agree.

Once the problem needing trickster's remediation is clarified, Harpo as Faker Englund appears, already swimming against the current because he has been evicted from, of all places, a shelter. This makes him worse off than the others. In the unified space of Miller's hotel room, where various characters enter, complicate the plot, then leave, Faker is one of the entourage. But rather than exit, he decides to move in, quickly becoming involved in the triple dilemmas of eviction, hunger, and an underfunded play when Gribble (Cliff Dunstan), hotel manager and Miller's brother-in-law, asks Miller and Binelli (Chico) to move out before Wagner (Donald McBride), the hotel's efficiency consultant, suspects that the cast and crew are being harbored there.

With trickster's attraction to liminal spaces, Faker moves in while Miller and Binelli are moving out and, to do so, donning layers of clothes instead of packing them, all the better to skip out on their unpaid hotel bill. Faker helps, putting on only coats because he "doesn't believe in shirts" according to Binelli, shirts apparently subject to belief or disbelief, a little like Gatsby[2] or God. Faker is indeed bare under his coat for the third time in the films, so apparently Chico means something more literal. With trickster's hyperbolic thirst, Faker drinks a bottle of something on the dresser, it's either cologne or booze, and with trickster's appetite for chaos and his talent for the absurd, he puts on layers of coats and a stack of hats, echoing hat gags in *Duck Soup* and *A Day at the Races*.

But when the legitimacy of their occupation of the hotel room stabilizes,

When the playwright Leo excuses himself to use the bathroom, Harpo rummages in his bag for items to pawn. Groucho Marx as Gordon Miller, Harpo Marx as Faker Englund, and Chico Marx as Harry Binelli. *Room Service*, RKO, 1938.

they peel the layers down with alacrity. Christine (Lucille Ball), enters with news that she has found a backer for the play. Next Leo Davis, the playwright, , enters, having, so he says, left home for good. When he adds that he has "burned his bridges," Harpo lifts Leo's coat to look at his britches, still hearing English with an immigrant's accent, or wanting to check out Leo's bum. When Miller introduces Faker to him, calling him "the brains of the organization," Faker responds with a vapid expression, one more addled and empty than the Gookie. Charmed by their hospitality, Leo inherits their debt.

A thief because he is trickster, or *vice versa*, Faker rummages through Leo's bag seeking items to fence. He kisses a picture of Leo's mother out of affection for its silver frame, making off with the frame and a pair of roller skates. Binelli steals Leo's typewriter and pawns it to pay a ticket on his illegally parked moose head, an absurd ticket but a more absurd action, and one that seems counterproductive because Davis will need the typewriter to revise scenes. But in the logic of dire straits, the typewriter, the playwright's tool, is actually better off in a pawnshop than repossessed. Only with an advance from a backer will Miller be able to pay the hotel bill and keep the cast and crew, his cohorts, and the playwright sheltered, fed, and equipped. Though Faker is not central to securing a backer, and in fact threatens the success of acquiring one with his bumbling, his stratagems do help provide shelter until a backer is found.

Wagner, the antagonist who aspires to be the hotel company vice-president, calls them all "chiselers," but we know that's not the right epithet when Binelli comes in with the moose head, an apparent *non sequitur* that is nevertheless relevant because it suggests hunting, a basic way of procuring food. Unfortunately, the moose head represents only a memory of food, for it is inedible, and the moose it belonged to has long since been digested, perhaps by Binelli himself.

Luckily, a man named Jenkins has agreed to back the play on behalf of a wealthy and powerful client who prefers to remain anonymous. But because Wagner evicts them anyway, refusing to wait for them to secure the check, he becomes the triple enemy: of food, shelter, and art. Moreover, he prohibits the cast and crew from using either room service or the dining room, he evicts them all from the hotel, and he threatens to close down the production of the play. He's starving them on three levels.

Yet Wagner also inspires Faker's fresh and original solution. Reversing the momentum of eviction, Faker sets up his cot and hangs up his birdcage. He's poorer than poor, and if possible worse off than the others, having been evicted from a shelter, yet he helps devise a plan to forestall the eviction: faking the dreaded measles. And he presses, literally with a sort of half nelson, the innocent newcomer Leo into the role of the sick guy, wrestling him into bed and giving him "a contagious disease" by spitting Mercurochrome onto his face, neck, and chest through a colander until both Leo and his pillowcase have measles. Binelli pronounces Faker a "second Michelangelo," and the stratagem works. The thugs whom Wagner has summoned to carry out the eviction see the measles quarantine sign — perhaps all the cohorts needed to do was hang a sign — and they skedaddle.

With the problem of shelter solved, albeit temporarily, Miller, Binelli, Faker, and Leo must contend with their intense craving for food, a constant motif in trickster stories perhaps because that's how it is: Everything alive needs to eat, and the job is never done; we must keep ingesting food, meal after meal, day after day. With room service denied to them, the cohorts gaze hungrily at a catering truck on the street below the window. They have nothing to pawn besides the moose head, and Chico won't allow that, so in desperation they convince the Russian waiter Sasha to bring them food in exchange for an audition.

Throughout the film, we are distracted by the intermittent appearances of the repo man who tries to collect Leo's typewriter. He's like a fly at a picnic without food but that nevertheless needs swatting. Faker contributes nothing to the conversations in which the cohorts tell the repo man he'll find Leo at a maternity hospital, and then at a mental hospital, but he does assist on a more physical level, by shoving him out the door. Then Faker vanishes for a while and returns, having poached game like American Indian tricksters, in this case the prize in a contest he was judging, a turkey: neither fresh, frozen, nor roasted, but an impractically alive turkey. Again we are struck, as in other films, by Harpo's relaxed and familiar handling of living props. Appearing from inside of Faker's coat, the turkey, or at times, we suspect, the turkey's mechanical double, flies around and around the room like a bat. Faker chases it until it escapes out the very window through which they gazed with longing at the food delivery truck.

When Sasha, true to his word, brings them food, they descend on it hungrily, but none as hyperbolically so as Faker. They all eat ravenously, but Faker more ravenously. He becomes a veritable eating machine, rhythmically stoking his own mouth, pausing only to kiss his kewpie doll when asked if he has ever been in love, perhaps the closest thing to lust in this film until near the end when Faker, pretending to be dead, comes alive to ogle a woman. Faker, in fact, consumes more than anyone else at the table. He intercepts food headed for others' mouths, biting Binelli's toast, catching the salt he throws over his shoulder, and successfully spearing food from Miller's plate. He not only continues the automatic fork-to-mouth movement until every scrap of food is gone, but he also eats several bananas after the meal, taking one from his coat and thus ironically revealing that he had a private stash all along and didn't share it.

Room Service, like the other Marx Brothers films, has a subplot involving young lovers, here threatened by society's lack of support for the arts since one half of the couple is the playwright Leo whose play's success is scaffolding for their future. Faker observes them with sympathy. Yet he can pivot them toward union only by helping the play succeed on opening night. When Leo abandons his role as quarantined guy with measles because love trumps art, Faker approvingly watches from a window as Leo and Hilda, a hotel employee and the other half of the love equation played by Ann Miller, meet on a bench outside and kiss.

His spying turns out to be serendipitous because while he's at the window, his turkey flies past, having remained in the vicinity, perhaps out of attachment to Faker. This small scene offers an example of how Harpo, though not the center of the plot, is pivotal, here braiding the film's triple-needs theme and hinting at a fourth one, the need for love.

Despite the quantity of food he has recently motored into his mouth, when Christine arrives with sandwiches, Faker eats one, paper and all. And when Wagner and the doctor come in to check the condition of the measles patient, Faker rises to the occasion, diving into bed as Leo's understudy, his measles having evolved into a tapeworm. Christine tends him wearing a nurse's cap improvised from a folded napkin, and Binelli pretends to be a doctor, dropping bits of food into his mouth "to feed the tapeworm." Although they insult the hotel physician, Dr. Glass, he takes the patient seriously. During his lengthy "say ahhh" examination of Faker and his tapeworm, Binelli provides the sound by squeezing the kewpie doll. Then Binelli takes the doctor's medical bag and locks him in the bathroom. In spite of this treatment, the doctor ends up expressing sympathy for their cause, having overheard Wagner's obstructionism.

Faker takes a few steps backwards even as he promotes their hopes, like the legendary trickster who sometimes plays the buffoon and sabotages his

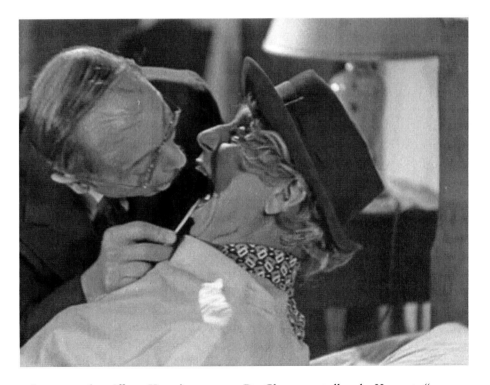

In a scene that riffs on Harpo's muteness, Dr. Glass repeatedly asks Harpo to "say *ahhh*," and Chico provides the sound by squeezing Harpo's kewpie doll. Charles Halton as Dr. Glass, and Harpo Marx as Faker Englund. *Room Service,* RKO, 1938.

own efforts. His turkey having returned to him, it is now flying around in the adjoining room of their suite. Chasing it, Faker manages to disrupt and perhaps thwart the bestowal of the much needed advance from the wealthy anonymous backer: When Jenkins returns, ready to sign the check, not only does Wagner interrupt the proceedings, and not only does the disheveled kidnapped doctor stumble out of the bathroom, but also Faker chases his homing turkey through the room, swinging a bat, thwacking Jenkins on the head, and knocking him out.

When he revives, Jenkins signs the check solely to escape what he considers a madhouse. Miller signs the check over to Wagner. Faker takes it from Wager, who doesn't notice, then whistles and gives it back — stealing, again, for the fun of it, no harm intended, while slapping Wagner on the back a little too forcefully with a foolish but deeply satisfying gesture. And although Jenkins stops payment the next day, Wagner doesn't know, so he cancels the evictions, moves Miller, Binelli, Faker, and Leo to a more elegant suite, and reinstates their access to the restaurant and room service. Again, though precariously, the needs for food, shelter, and artistic expression seem on their way to being satisfied, with help from Faker and even without necessitating the sacrifice of the turkey.

Faker's trickster antics especially illuminate the film's conclusion and denouement. He begins packing again, this time from the more elegant suite they moved into so full of hope, when they learn that Jenkins has stopped payment on the check and moreover never actually signed the contract. Nevertheless, Christine begs them not to cancel the opening, and Miller agrees, deciding to gamble on the three days it will take the check to bounce, forging Wagner's name as the play's new backer. So they continue to get ready for opening night. Faker becomes instrumental, perhaps central, to the desperate measures they take when the bank tells Wagner the truth about the bounced check and he again becomes, with intensified vigor, the antagonist of art, not to mention food and shelter.

This happens on opening night when everyone is dressed for the debut, Binelli in a spiffy suit, Miller and Leo in tuxes, and Faker in his costume for his part in the play, his usual scruffy clothes and a hat with a burning candle reflecting his role as coal miner but also an apt symbol of his enlightenment, his association with fire, and his daring pragmatics. For Faker plays the same role twice, adapting it at once to the drama unfolding in the hotel room before he plays it later, as Leo intended, on stage. The ploy works because, in ignorance arising from his antagonism to art, Wagner is utterly unfamiliar with Leo's play. He fails, therefore, to recognize that both Leo and Harpo's suicides are concocted with lines from the play.

Wagner locks Miller, Faker, Leo, and Binelli in the hotel room, preventing them from attending this first performance, a predicament not unlike the kidnapping scene in *Horse Feathers* that threatens to keep Harpo and Chico from the Darwin-Huxley game. Throughout this scene, the candle on Faker's hat burns in readiness for his part in the play. Meanwhile, he uses it to start a fire, a trick to get them out of the room that seems too extreme to the others who conceive of a more reasonable albeit crazy plan. Instead, Leo will fake his suicide, a ruse, he tells them, he once pulled off successfully in college. So Leo "takes poison," and Faker tries to revive him by giving him more. Wagner and Gribble, fearful of bad publicity for the hotel, try to restore Leo with ipecac and eggnogs instead of calling an ambulance.

Leo must play his dying scene for two and a half hours to allow *Hail and Farewell* to run, a sacrifice he makes for the sake of his play. And Faker peppers the dying scene with multiple trickster maneuvers. For example, Wagner, feeling guilty and afraid, passes the eggnogs distractedly to Faker to give to Leo, but Faker drinks them down, one after the other, dozens of eggs and quarts of milk, returning the empty glasses for more, while poor Leo drinks nothing but ipecac.

So Faker costars in Leo's suicide drama while Miller and Binelli forestall Wagner, who wishes Leo had died "at the Astor," from calling the police. They beg to "Say a few words" and they sing "Swing Low Sweet Chariot," homage in spite of Groucho's later excesses, to African American musical culture, while Faker accompanies them on the harmonica, the candle on his miner's hat's candle still burning. The scene is interrupted by the repo man's final appearance, but this time the interchange is distilled, with no dialogue and the action simplified: He runs in, they salute him, say "Hail and farewell," the title of Leo's play, and he salutes them and runs out.

Faker multiplies the challenges Leo's bogus suicide creates for Wagner by adding his own histrionics. He fakes weeping, and while Miller continues to stall by not letting Wagner use the "same phone" Leo used to call his mother, Faker slips out so that when Wagner opens the door, he falls into the room, a knife in his chest securing a note that blames Wagner for both his and Leo's suicides. We don't get the fullness of the humor until the final scene of the film, when Faker plays a corpse on stage with the same knife in his chest and the candle burning on his miner's hat.

One of the best and most trickster-esque gags in the film occurs when Wagner and Miller carry the playing-dead Faker out, each holding one of his rigor-mortised arms. Amusingly, Wagner doesn't see Faker turn to ogle an

Harpo turns his head to ogle a woman even though he's supposed to be dead. Left to right: Donald MacBride as Gregory Wagner, Harpo Marx as Faker Englund, and Groucho Marx as Gordon Miller. *Room Service,* **RKO, 1938.**

attractive woman because Faker's synchronizes the turning of his head with Wagner and Groucho's turning heads. This is the second muted allusion to Harpo's lust for women so prevalent in other films. The first was his kewpie doll. Only his stiff hands remain in corpse character. When Miller convinces Wagner to deposit Faker by the stage door in the alley, the humor of the scene is predicated on two ironies: Wagner is unhinged with fear of a living dead man, and Faker is right where he needs to be in order to get back to the stage to perform his part in the play.

So Wagner and Miller leave Faker conveniently where he ought to be, and Miller, Binelli, and Leo sneak into the play right before Faker's death scene on stage. The now fulfilled Russian waiter Sasha is delivering his lines with panache when Harpo is carried on stage on a stretcher. Seeing him in the play causes Wagner to become agitated. And when Leo, the other dead man who is also very much alive and in the theater watching the triumphant conclusion of his play, speaks to him, he faints. Just deserts, we think. The film closes with Miller, Binelli, and Leo reprising "Swing Low, Sweet Chariot" while Faker dies again, but not really, on stage.

9

At the Circus (1939)
SWINGALI'S SNEEZE

"He calls us to join him in the frenzy."
— Erdoes and Ortiz, *American Indian Myths and Legends*[1]

It comes as no surprise in such a setting that trickster's *simpatico* with animals is a huge part of Harpo's characterization in *At the Circus*. Even the film's theme song, "Two Blind Loves," evokes familiar mice. Harpo as Punchy takes it beyond the usual relationship of circus worker to circus animal, though, for he collaborates with a gorilla, sleeps with a sheep, fights a battle from the back of an ostrich, and is coached by a seal while playing a game of checkers. He even gets spanked by that seal when he is quadruple-jumped after making a move the seal told him not to make. Granted, it is sad that circuses tame magnificent animals to entertain people, but such exploitation is almost never Punchy's shtick, for he is at home with animals and is sometimes treated like one himself, for example by Goliath the Strongman. Also in this film, like in *A Day at the Races,* Harpo shares a special bond with African Americans, here cast as circus workers. And as usual, he is prone to his own kind of excess; his magic, musicality, border crossing, and mischief reflect his trickster essence.

In addition to exotic animals, circuses feature extreme human attributes to entertain people. While Punchy aspires to be the strongman, he actually has other esoteric powers to be proud of. Punchy's surreal powers are on display in his very first scene. His entrance is not delayed as much as in many Marx Brothers films, though we first get a quick sketch of the film's circus milieu before Punchy appears. We meet Jeff Wilson, the sympathetic circus proprietor played by Kenny Baker, and Julie, played by Florence Rice, Jeff's betrothed, who sings and prances with horses. We also meet the gorilla Gibral-

tar, Jeff's banker and friend. When we see Punchy performing as the strongman Goliath's sidekick, he is dressed in a leopard skin like Goliath, and
Goliath's wig is so much like Punchy's that Punchy seems like a diminutive
mirror image of him.

Although he doesn't match Goliath in size and strength, Punchy's costume harbors an uncanny power that surpasses Goliath's: the leopard's head
hanging in the vicinity of Harpo's crotch rises, with phallic intimations, to
growl back at the caged and growling lions that they pass. Later in the film,
in a scene with Eve Arden as Pauline, Groucho as Loophole makes a joke
about getting around the Hays Code, but Harpo has already done an end run
around it in this suggestive animation of his responsive and autonomous dangling animal, a buried evocation of trickster's autonomous penis, and this
time a more vital one than a salami.

Before we get the rest of the exposition — Jeff's having chosen the circus
over social class privilege, Jeff's debt to Carter, his future marriage to Julie

The leopard on Harpo's costume comes alive to growl at a caged lion, the surreal
implications extending to Harpo's crotch. Harpo Marx as Punchy. *At the Circus,*
MGM, 1939.

shakily predicated on the success of the circus — we learn that Punchy, essentially a buffoon, aspires to be the circus strongman. As Goliath's assistant, Punchy has to light the cannon so Goliath can demonstrate his strength by catching the fired cannonballs. But when Punchy deliberately mistimes it, or goofs, so that one cannon ball hits Goliath's bum when he bends over, Goliath throws the ball back at him. Punchy catches it, but the force sinks him into the ground. Clearly he has a long way to go.

We also meet Punchy's trickster cohort, Antonio (Chico), the somewhat unintelligent but generous circus worker who tells Jeff, "I don't have nothin,' but you can have half," then sends for the lawyer Loophole, to help Jeff navigate his bankruptcy problems. We don't actually meet Mrs. Dukesbury, played by Margaret Dumont, until halfway through the film, but we get a glimpse of her airs in a newspaper article about Jeff's choosing the circus over his inheritance. In this way the social class lines are drawn, the social class conflict is established, and our sympathies are aligned with Jeff.

Punchy is clearly on the pop culture side in this conflict, the dichotomy of high and low art interrogated in this film as it was in *A Night at the Opera*. Interestingly, this is a distinction that has become passé in our post-postmodern disinclination to separate high and low aspects of culture but simply to experience, study, and learn from them. Harpo as Punchy takes up figurative arms to level the art and culture field for all, again by deflating the inflated, elevating the marginalized, and ultimately helping us see beyond the high art versus pop culture dichotomy and learn to embrace what we enjoy.

Harpo's trickster nature is ascendant in the first scene that unites the three Marxes involving the rain-drenched boarding of the circus train. Loophole (Groucho) arrives in a taxi, stiffs the driver, and then is prevented from boarding the train by Antonio, the very man who has summoned him, because he lacks an official badge. Loophole calls Antonio "an old badger," a pun connecting the Marxes to the film's numerous animals. In the midst of their absurd conversation whose logic is reminiscent of the "Why a Duck?" dialogue in *The Cocoanuts*, the contract-signing in *A Night at the Opera,* and the Tutsi Frutsi-ing Groucho gets in *A Day at the Races,* Punchy arrives in a taxi with a seal. When they get out, he holds an umbrella over the seal, never mind that its habitat is water, as they make their way to the train.

Harpo shows more badges than needed inside his overcoat, reminiscent of the numerous badges he flashed at the cop in *Horse Feathers.* And the seal also shows his badge under his lifted tail, mooning the viewer in the process. To resolve Loophole's badge dilemma, Antonio gives him his own badge, then won't let him on the train because it is "last year's badge." We leave Loophole in a puddle, but somehow he ends up on the train, where Harpo and his

Harpo's pal, a seal, coaches him at checkers, then spanks him when he gets quadruple jumped. Buck Mack as checkers player, Harpo Marx as Punchy. *At the Circus,* MGM, 1939.

trickster cohorts are quickly united in serving the cause of Jeff, Julie, and the circus.

On the circus train, in a sequence with musical interludes for Antonio and Loophole but not yet Punchy, Antonio plays the piano in the club car while Punchy plays checkers. Again the depth of his relationship with animals distinguishes Harpo's fuller trickster essence. In this scene, for example, his seal friend coaches him through the game, whispering advice in his ear and kissing him, though when Punchy ignores the advice and gets quadruple-jumped, the seal spanks him with his flippers. We have two eyes on Punchy and the seal, but one eventually drifts to Pauline because she is conspiring with Carter to steal Jeff's box office receipts in an effort to gain control of the circus. The midget Professor leaves with Goliath to do the dastardly deed. But mostly our eyes are on the seal, Punchy's comrade and perhaps his superior, but at the least an affectionate coach capable of meting out discipline.

Punchy's ascendency is simultaneously reinforced and undermined when Loophole mistakes him for the circus boss. Groucho stands corrected, pulling a rabbit from his borrowed magician's suit and punning that he is "splitting hairs." But Harpo, far more at ease with the likes of that coat, picks Loophole's pocket, retrieving a dove. Like trickster, Punchy is a thief, though stealing is not the aspect of his trickster nature emphasized in this film. In fact, he works with the others to remedy the damage of Carter's theft. It is significant in this scene that unlike Punchy, whose coat is always full of props, both animate and inanimate, Loophole does not wear the borrowed magician's coat easily. He refers to it as "haunted," is clearly wary of it, and thus stands very much in contrast to Punchy's confident and delighted discovery of endless surprises in the inventory of his own pockets throughout the films. Moreover, Punchy is spontaneous with props; they are his language. Here he pretends to march military-style with a toy rifle over his shoulder, a visual pun on the battle they are engaging in on Jeff's behalf, a vague allusion to the Revolutionary War iconography aped, pun intended in this ape-proximal context, in earlier films, and maybe even an acknowledgment of the impending World War. One can't help thinking of W.H. Auden's poem "September 1, 1939," written on the eve of World War II, the same year of this film's release. It follows that Harpo, making Auden's plea literal in the midget's car with enormous matches, offers his own "affirming flame."[2]

In *At the Circus,* again, it isn't thievery or lust or hunger or flatulence that defines Harpo's trickster nature but his friendship with animals, his alliance with young lovers, and his efforts to cleanse high culture of pomposity, recalibrate it with popular culture, play music on a stringed instrument and a trombone, and contribute mayhem and magic to several scenes. For example, back in the club car, when Loophole is singing "Lydia the Tattooed Lady" with Antonio at the piano, everyone in the car joins in to sing the chorus and dance around. Even though they are even dancing with lifted tables, Punchy's cavorting is more extreme. He skips back and forth from background to foreground, leaping, dancing with a woman while seated on her partner's shoulders, and ultimately swinging, like a monkey, from the chandelier.

Punchy moves to the center of the action in the scene in the Gorilla Gibraltar's car when he and Antonio try to figure out who knocked out Jeff and stole his cash receipts. Punchy, in convoluted trickster-buffoon style, takes them many steps backwards and wide of the goal in the course of the film before they succeed in recovering the money. For example, when they attempt to recreate the crime, Punchy, told to "act," kisses Antonio all the way up his arm to this face, then lifts him and lays him down to continue, as if *acting* necessarily means *performing a love scene*, another twit of the Hays Code and another example in the films of gender-bending. Punchy asserts his credentials to play the part of the crook by displaying a jaywalker-wanted poster featuring himself. Then, in their re-enactment of the assault on Jeff, he derives humor from repetition: Punchy keeps hitting Antonio on the head because Jeff was hit on the head. Then Gibraltar the gorilla, the only witness to the actual mugging but unable to say what he saw because, like Punchy, he is mute, proceeds to speak Punchy's language of gesture, hitting Antonio on the head as well. Punchy and Gibraltar should not be sent to the *punitentiary*, because Antonio is also being hit over the head with the truth about the assault.

As in previous films, Harpo and his cohorts in *At the Circus* become unlikely heroes. In addition to being inept, they aren't brave: Although they suspect Goliath, they fear confronting him. And they have conflicting priorities: Loophole, for example, wants to take a "detour" to grill Pauline "'til she's tender," and is actually inclined to bail on them all until Julie, whom he meets on a platform car, appeals to his sentimental nature. But in spite of their ineptitude, Punchy finds a real clue at the scene of the mugging: a cigar. He mimes the crime, he and Antonio pace in circles trying to decipher the clue, then Punchy marches with his pretend rifle, reminding us that this means war: between innocence and corruption, young love and the forces that thwart it, high and low culture, the deserving and the undeserving, and maybe even between animals and humans, or certain animals and certain humans.

The cigar leads Punchy and his cohorts to the midget's car where Punchy contributes the ultimate chaos, evoking the last of the four elements, wind, via his hyperbolic sneeze. It happens twice. The scene's humor in part arises from absurd size distortions and silly repetitions. Loophole and Antonio keep bumping their heads on the light fixture, as does Punchy, for they are too large for the car that is built perfectly to scale for the Little Professor, the only one who is comfortable, as well he should be, in his living room. Humor also results from the repetition of Antonio's passing Loophole a cigar each time he tries to collect one from the Little Professor to compare to their cigar-evidence. Loophole has to keep disposing of Antonio's cigars, and where else but in the bowl of the ceiling light fixture that he can easily reach. Each time he asks the Little Professor for another cigar, Antonio intervenes, offering one of his own, then Punchy offers to light them with a match from a box that would be oversized in a normal room and is outlandish here. Of course, each time the midget starts to give Loophole a cigar, Antonio finds yet another one in a pocket of his jacket. We see that he is still having difficulty holding contradictory ideas in his mind simultaneously, as he did in the circus badge–train scene or even in the bidding-up scheme in *The Cocoanuts*.

So Loophole and the Little Professor enact the lighting-up ritual, then shake hands, again and again. Punchy varies the ritual by offering a light between his legs and from a match attached to his shoe. The gesture's awkwardness is intensified in the cramped car even while reminding us of Punchy's connection to the fire, echoing trickster's giving fire to humans. In *Horse Feathers* he burned books and had a candle lit at both ends, in *Duck Soup* he used a blowtorch to light a cigar and had two hat bonfires, in *Room Service* a lit candle burned on his miner's hat, and in *Love Happy* his lapel flower was a lighter. This time — and why not?—fire comes from his shoe.

The repetitions involved in Loophole's disposing of Antonio's cigar, asking the midget for a fresh one, Antonio's foiling the attempt to get incriminating evidence, the lighting of the cigars, then the formal handshakes are interrupted, as if the proceedings were as annoying as a nose full of pepper, by Punchy's hyperbolic sneeze. It blows through the scaled-down room like a hurricane, upsetting the furniture and leaving everything in a heap on one side of the room, upending even the piano. Just as they are setting everything right, and the Little Professor threatens to sue, and Loophole gives him his lawyer's card in case he needs a lawyer to pursue it, Punchy sneezes, producing the same results again.

Following this scene, its redundancy so satisfying yet so satisfyingly disrupted by Punchy's redundant sneezes, is a scene in which Loophole tries to find the stolen money in Pauline's tent, Punchy supplying liberation at its end. Pauline, Carter's moll, is actually hiding the stolen money there, but when Loophole, suspicious of Carter, finds it, she picks his pocket during an embrace and hides it in her bodice, inspiring a bit of meta-cinema from Loophole when he says, "There must be some way of getting the money without getting into trouble with the Hays Office!" directly to the camera. Then, in a fresh take on the standard movie chase scene, he asks Pauline to demonstrate how she walks upside down on the ceiling. But Pauline, no slouch, insists that Loophole walk there with her, so he dons a froufrou circus outfit and suction shoes. Though the wallet inevitably falls out of her upside-down bodice as he hoped, Pauline, more adept than Loophole at righting her position, escapes with it. What does all this have to do with Punchy? He rescues Loophole, whom she left hanging upside-down, stuck. Punchy terminates the nonsense abruptly by supplying more: He unties Loophole's suction shoes, precipitating his sudden liberation from the ceiling.

Harpo and his cohorts flop in their mission to help the young lovers when they fail to recoup Jeff's money. So, fearful of losing the circus, Jeff encourages Julie to accept an offer from a competing circus, Miracle Shows. Even if Jeff is just playing at being self-supporting — rich kids generally have other options — he is nevertheless taking an admirable stand in opting for what he loves, the circus and Julie, instead of his inheritance. But without his inheritance, Julie, like Rosa in *A Night at the Opera*, is a better breadwinner than her guy, and in the retro world of these films, that is not an acceptable imbalance. So Punchy and his cohorts resolve again to remedy Jeff's financial woes. Loophole paces like the monkeys in the cage he walks back and forth in front of until he comes up with a plan. It involves parting Jeff's aunt, Mrs. Dukesbury, from some of her money.

Intercut with Loophole's conceiving this plan is the most important Punchy-as-trickster sequence in the film. It suggests his magical nature even as it evolves into a musical number that employs a large cast of talented African American singers, dancers, and musicians, many of them children. Punchy's trickster essence comes to the fore at the beginning of the sequence, right after lions scare away the custodian picking up trash, when Punchy tames them with his trumpet, inducing them to lie down, hush up, face forward, and go to sleep. Meanwhile children, weaving among the elephants' legs to spy on him while he skips around, now playing the stick of his horn like a flute, say he "doesn't belong to the human race," he's "got voodoo in his stick," so he must be "Swingali," a pun on "Svengali" that suggests Punchy's conflation of music with magic. They are joined by adults singing "Boogie Boo" and casting their own spell on Punchy, making him lean backwards, oddly suspended in air in defiance of gravity. So they have their magic too.

Dudley Dickerson, also dancing in this scene, sings a beautiful rendition of "Why Be Melancholy When We've Got Swingali?" Then children in the chorus hop aboard a circus-wagon bandstand to play an instrumental number that ends with two trumpet solos, one on a trumpet played by a little boy while Punchy mimes and contributes the bulb of his horn as a mute, using the rest like a conductor's baton.

The interaction between Punchy and these extraordinary workers and their children attached somehow to the circus tells us pretty clearly whose corner he is in. Harpo again draws the camera lens to African American talent under-represented in film at the time as well as to the workers in the story, as in life, who keep things running behind the scenes. Here this cast is brought forward and celebrated in a sequence that also serves to emphasize Harpo's border-crossing nature along with his mysterious other-worldly powers.

In it Harpo plays perhaps the most beautiful and nuanced of all his harp solos in the films so far. Members of the African American chorus lift him up and carry him to his harp, telling him to "make it a blues." And this he does, while we see him and the chorus through a variety of stylized camera angles. His melody is "Blue Moon" with a little "Swing Low, Sweet Chariot" mixed in. The chorus hums an accompaniment to the decidedly blues quality of his harp rendition, infusing it with melancholy, release, and even transcendence, for music refreshes the soul, something the neon "Refreshment" sign in the background of the scene reminds us of.

While Harpo plays his harp solo enhanced by human voices, the camera lingers on various faces, often in close-up, including a stunning shot of an older woman who suddenly appears in the light behind the harp strings, and a beautiful serious and shy young woman who sings to the right of Harpo, and the spunky little girl who earlier called him "Swingali" and now contemplates each note he plays as the camera, from a low angle, reveals her through the strings of the harp. Although some members of the chorus are standing to the sides, most are behind the harp. When Harpo finishes playing, he swings himself to their side of the harp, symbolically casting his lot with the members of his chorus, and together they look through the harp strings at us.[3]

This scene dramatizes a principle of art: its sublimation of human suffering and joy. Harpo's is a world distinct from the one his brothers-cohorts find themselves in. If he is an angel on the harp, Swingali notwithstanding, then the members of the chorus are also angels co-habiting his sphere, a status suggested by the camera's reverential treatment of faces, especially the gazing child's. Harpo's interlude combines his essence with the blues while revealing people who work, sing, and celebrate their children's gifts until everyone, Harpo-Punchy included, applauds at the end.

Harpo, the only Marx brother to cross the racial divide in the films and find acceptance, does so while Loophole is busy invading the world of Dukesbury and her ilk, the white upper-crust mansion world. While Dumont's Mrs. Dukesbury is reclined on her chaise lounge, talking on the telephone about party arrangements, especially her special guest Jardinet, Loophole barges in, outrages the butler, invades her room, and woos her with nonsense, puns, and insults. He pretends to be Fontaine, Chardonnay's impresario. Dukesbury swallows it all, writing Loophole a check for $10,000. Punchy isn't in this scamming-of-Dukesbury scene wherein Loophole injects trickster's spirit of irreverence for the wealthy and powerful. Loophole lobs the critique squarely at upper class society without him and begins to up the manic ante.

But Punchy frontloads the very next scene with the same, including buffoonery. Here Antonio and Punchy invade Goliath's bedroom in a scene filled with trickster mischief and mayhem. Its prelude begins on the circus train where Punchy and Antonio are sleeping in stacked births. Antonio, worried about the circus, can't sleep, so wakes up Punchy to ask how he can. Punchy answers by pulling a lamb out of his bed, miming that he needs to count only one to fall asleep. Punchy also pulls out a gun, again suggesting their cause is a battle of sorts. Yet though it may look dangerous, it turns out to be a squirt gun, a kind of shape-shifting of the inanimate. He drinks from it several times.

Both now awake, they plan to look for the stolen money in Goliath's room while he sleeps, which sounds like a recipe for mayhem. It's a small room, they are making a lot of noise, and there is the constant danger of waking up Goliath, who could bend them in half (we've seen him bend steel). Nevertheless, it is a scene Punchy pumps full of fun. Goliath, with his Harpo-like hair, "sleeps like a baby," an amusing description because he is anything but a baby, so big and mean is he when awake. In addition, whenever the noise they make, and they make plenty, starts to rouse him, Antonio sings "Rock-a-Bye Baby" to put him back to sleep, and Punchy, ever inspired by music, extemporizes on harmonica or flute. Once when they awaken Goliath, they must turn off the lights. When the lights come back on, Punchy is hanging inside Goliath's coat on the door and Antonio is in the upper bunk.

Harpo's antics in this scene make even Chico laugh. For example, when Chico steps on Harpo's hand, Harpo puts Mercurochrome on it, then paints the door red, using his hand like a paint brush as he did in *A Night at the Opera* when he pretended to paint the children in steerage. And Harpo again brandishes scissors, his favorite tool in many of the films, giving them his typical warm-up snips in the air. In this scene he cuts in half the blanket tucked around Goliath so he can look under it for the money, carefully rolling the top up and the bottom down. Then he slices open the pillow. When feathers fly as a result of his turning on the fan, he dresses up like a Salvation Army Santa Claus with pail and bell and a white feather beard. Chico laughs at this too.

But their antics are making Goliath restless, so Antonio dissolves a sleeping pill in water for him. Punchy, buffoon that he is, drinks it, then passes out. Antonio tries to revive him with water, but throws it in Goliath's face instead. And this truly rouses him. To hide from the wakened giant, Punchy cuts open the mattress and crawls into it. Now the mattress honks, this wakes up Goliath again, he throws it up to where Antonio is hiding in the top bunk, Punchy inside, and climbs up after it to sleep. Antonio sings "Rock-a-bye Baby," Harpo honks in time, and Goliath, thinking his room is haunted, flees. This would be a felicitous conclusion to the scene except that they haven't found the stolen money.

In order for Punchy and Antonio to save the circus and comically punish the gods on high who scorn it, here represented by Mrs. Dukesbury and her ilk, pompous upper class consumers of high art, they must set up the circus on Mrs. Dukesbury's front lawn. Loophole shares this "great scheme" with Jeff, who approves, then Loophole sabotages Jardinet's arrival by telling officials on the steamship *Normandy* that their illustrious passenger is the head of a dope ring. The classic conflict in trickster legend between the powerful and

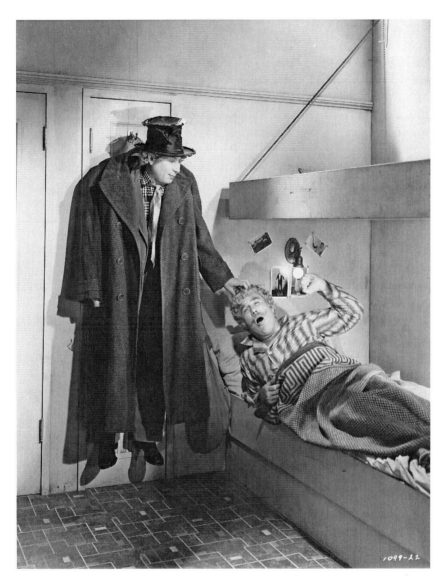

While trying to find the stolen money, Harpo wakes up the sleeping giant and has to conceal himself while putting Goliath back to sleep. Harpo Marx as Punchy and Nat Pendleton as Goliath. *At the Circus,* MGM, 1939.

the powerless is heating up, to be played out in the contrast between high and low culture: the planned concert featuring classical music on a specially designed floating stage versus Jeff's circus.

Loophole fights on the Dukesbury interior front, fastening her buttons with a tool while making a joke about having been a riveter, then prolonging dinner while Antonio, Stuffy, Jeff, and the crew set up the tents and get the

circus ready. This scene contains amusing juxtapositions of high and low culture: elephants braying at the moment Mrs. Dukesbury opens her mouth to
make a dinner table speech, Loophole's wooing her at the table while she mistakes a giraffe's long tongue slurping her back through the open window for
his caress, giggling, "Not here, monsieur."

Outside, the battle continues. Punchy is on the front line of the circus'
defense. Carter and Goliath have hired thugs to trash the show, but Antonio
and Punchy fight, Punchy leading the charge from the back of an ostrich and
knocking out the bad guys with his horn, which quadruples, having been a
mute and a flute and a horn and now a hose to put out the fires the antagonists
start. He is the ostrich's intimate, hiding his head in a hole in the ground side
by side with her. In recognition of their bond, perhaps, she presents him with
an egg that becomes a weapon in his hands. When he hurls it at Goliath, it
covers his face with glop.

The battle scene is intercut with Loophole at the banquet, delaying the
start of the concert with requests for more coffee. When the outraged Jardinet
arrives, Antonio takes him to the bandstand for a good "send-off," accomplished, of course, by Punchy who is wielding really big scissors, more like
gargantuan garden shears capable of cutting through the thick rope that moors
the stage to the dock. He sets it free to drift on the ocean with an oblivious
Jardinet and his oblivious orchestra playing music to the waves.

So thanks to Punchy, high culture is floating, unbeknownst to anyone,
out to sea on Mrs. Dukesbury's special stage even while indoors she is introducing what she thinks will be Jardinet's first symphony piece. To her aston-
ishment and horror, circus music replaces it. But when she sees that her guests
are charmed by the surprise — and this reminds us how such cleansing and
deflation can ultimately refresh and restore — Mrs. Dukesbury is happy. Or
rather, she is skeptically willing to suspend disapproval. This she does, and
all is copasetic, until Carter lets the gorilla Gibraltar out of his cage. And here
we get a nuanced view of evil, for when Goliath sees the danger in what Carter
is doing, he withdraws his support from the scheme, saying, "I want no part
of this."

As a result of Gibraltar's entering the ring in pursuit of Carter, the circus
goes completely out of control, chaos and mayhem reaching a crescendo
as Loophole is catapulted into the act by Antonio. And he joins Goliath,
Gibraltar, Punchy, Carter, and Mrs. Dukesbury, who was fired from the
canon after her bum accidentally got stuck in it. They all become part of a
high wire trapeze act. And at the center of the act is Gibraltar pursuing Carter.
Gibraltar, it should be emphasized, is allied with the good guys: He witnessed
the theft, he is loyal to Jeff, and he is a competent banker to boot. He counts

the stolen and recovered money at the end, his thumbs-up certifying that it is all there.

Punchy contributes to the act, springing up the pole against the laws of gravity, pun intended, when Gibraltar enters the ring. When the gorilla grabs the rope and starts to climb, causing Punchy to descend, Punchy smiles and tips his hat to him. The two of them are an act unto themselves for a while, Punchy pursued by the gorilla, who seems to be competing with him to reach the high wire. Punchy lounges nonchalantly sideways on a rope for a spell, relaxed in the midst of the chaos. Then he becomes part of a trapeze act, seeming to enjoy participating in the show. At one point Punchy hangs from Carter's legs, while Mrs. Dukesbury, shot from the cannon, hangs from Punchy's, then Antonio from hers. She is stripped down to her pantaloons, for Antonio takes her skirt with him as he falls. But he hits a seesaw with Loophole on the other end of, and this is what catapults Loophole into the act. Gibraltar, on his own trapeze, catches Loophole's legs, making a bridge of them all to walk across to reach Carter. Punchy is amused throughout, never afraid of Gibraltar as he was, sort of, fearful of the sleeping Goliath.

So the circus is saved, Jeff can marry Julie, the crook Carter is punished, and the upper class is cleansed of affectations, especially Mrs. Dukesbury, who has been shot from a cannon, swung on a trapeze, liberated from her formal gown, and thus forced to appear before her refined guests and the rest of us in her bloomers, while Jardinet's symphony plays under the darkening sky to the ocean waves.

Punchy didn't make all this happen and he didn't accomplish it all alone, but he injected magic into the proceedings, helped whip events to a chaotic froth, he collaborated with animals more deeply than his cohorts, he displayed his varied musical gifts, he sneezed a hurricane, and perhaps most memorably, he crossed a border, inspiring a memorable musical interlude while paying tribute to the talent and dignity of a population not often well-served in film.

10

Go West (1940)

FEEDING THE TRAIN THE TRAIN

"He is the character in myth who threatens to take the myth apart."
— Lewis Hyde, *Trickster Makes This World*[1]

If anything is satirized here, it is the genre of Westerns itself. For in *Go West*, we don't have to wait for an imbalance in the culture to be clarified before Harpo appears. The film's setting, the Old West, is too open, unsettled, loosely governed, wild, and free of rigidified institutions to need trickster's recalibrating chaos. It provides its own. Even though Harpo as Rusty Panello says he wants to go back to the East, the West is trickster's kind of place. As if to emphasize this, the Indian chief, rejecting S. Quentin Quale (Groucho) because he "talks too much," embraces Rusty. Rusty is also referred to as "the redhead" several times in this black and white film, an example of the deconstructive impact of his trickster persona upon the medium that accommodates him, though none is finer or more resonant in implication than Rusty's feeding the train to itself in the penultimate scene.

In the film's opening scene, Rusty displays both lust and a penchant for stealing, and will eventually reveal other trickster traits too, like creating chaos, allying himself with the procreant urge by helping young lovers, bumbling his way to successes even while playing the fool, and animating the inanimate when he encounters a roll-top desk with a mind of its own. He also drinks from a horse trough as if that were a natural thing for him to do as an animal, and he goes from beast to divine, soaring to the sublime in his jazz duet (the Indian chief on flute and Rusty on harp). Plus he keeps the train running toward its destination by surreal and deeply philosophical means.

The opening scene sends Rusty, in picaresque style, on his way west. He

122

strolls into a somewhere-in-the-East train station holding hands with Joe Panello (Chico), his fictional brother. Given the Marxes' aging—Harpo is fifty-two, Chico is fifty-three, and Groucho is fifty in this film—it is moving to see them holding hands. They appear right after Quale has failed to bamboozle the agent for a train ticket. Because Quale needs money and Rusty is wearing the vestiary markers of a bumpkin (big plaid pants, holey shoes, a checked jacket, and a derby hat, all ill-fitting), Quale attempts to fleece Rusty and Joe. But looks are deceiving. They turn out to be more adept than Quale at his own game. Like him, they need money to go west. Harpo makes curves in the air to let Joe know that he spent his train fare on a woman. They need more money for the ticket.

This opening scene reiterates in new incarnations several trickster motifs familiar in Marx Brothers films. The life of facial hair and the identities that hats signify will be major sources of humor in this film. Quale, insisting that Rusty must be properly garbed to travel west, sells him a beaver cap to replace his derby. Negotiating the price, Joe says that Rusty's cost a lot of money even though it was stolen. Later, Rusty will play upon the hat motif, orchestrating manic confusion with hats on the stagecoach. And later still, Quale will call the Indian chief's feathered headdress a "chicken." But in this first scene, Quale inspires his mark with the immigrant's own myth that in the West the streets are paved with gold, something Rusty apparently already believes, for he takes a shovel from his bag with alacrity and mimes scooping imaginary gold.

Rusty endures jokes made at his expense with good-natured obliviousness. When Quale says, "Don't you love your brother?" Joe answers, "No, but I'm used to him." Then Quale puts the beaver hat on backwards so the tail covers Rusty's face, saying it's not on backwards on him. After all three of them stroke its fur, Rusty pays Quale for the hat with a coin purse he hauls up on a string from deep in his trousers. It spews dust. Apparently he has been living by means other than money.

Rusty does have a ten dollar bill on a string, and every time he passes it to Quale to pay one dollar for some purchase like the hat or the coat, he collects nine dollars change, then retrieves his ten-spot by tugging on the string, once even swinging it around as it escapes Quale's pocket, and once sneaking the nine dollars change into his own hand so that Joe's remains empty and Quale has to pay out the change again. This is the football trick from *Horse Feathers* and the fleecing of the sheriff trick from *A Day at the Races*, simultaneously familiar yet refreshed here. Throughout the scene, Quale keeps getting more fleeced. Rusty also picks his pocket, and when the string breaks, his ubiquitous scissors appear and he cuts his way into Quale's pocket. Indeed,

With a ten-spot on a string and scissors as a back-up, Harpo fleeces the fleecer Groucho in order to buy a train ticket west. Chico Marx as Joe Panello, Groucho Marx as S. Quentin Quale, and Harpo Marx as Rusty Panello. *Go West,* **MGM, 1940. Photofest.**

he cuts all around one leg of Quale's pants while Joe distracts him. In these ways they manage to fleece Quale out of his money, their last ploy their insistence on paying the sales tax and needing, of course, change for a ten. They also riff on Rusty's muteness, for when Quale begs not to bother with the tax, Joe says he won't say anything but that Rusty might, and when Quale asks what he wants to keep quiet, Joe says, "Nothing." In addition, Rusty finesses a quick swap of their hats after Quale tucks the little money he has left inside of his.

In the beginning of the scene, Rusty's brother is sending him west, but the premise disintegrates, and who cares? Both apparently acquire train tickets because when we next see them, they are in Dead Man's Gulch digging for gold, Rusty undoing Joe's efforts by dumping each shovelful of dirt he scoops into the hole that Joe, puzzled by his lack of progress, is digging. Quale, fleeced of his money for a train ticket, hitchhikes west.

A brief railroad company board meeting scene gives us most of the exposition we need to understand the conflict. The company is laying tracks through the mountains and needs stations. The locations are economically charged decisions. Terry Turner promotes a route through Dead Man's Gulch because, as he openly admits, he wants to get married, and his beloved's grandfather, old Wilson, owns the deed to the land, a source of bitterness between the families and thus an impediment to his marriage because Turner's grandfather duped Wilson into buying the worthless land. If Terry can convince the railroad company to buy it, and thus make it valuable, he stands to end the feud by compensating old Wilson. Then he can marry Eve. These are just and pure motives that contrast with the cynical and mercenary motives of the antagonists, Red Baxter and Beecher.

We get the last nugget of exposition when Rusty and Joe meet old Wilson while they are prospecting for gold. They happily lend him $10, "no strings attached," a delightful pun on the fleecing of Quale that also tells us in a twinkling that Rusty doesn't really care about money. He is, in fact, generous, and that furthermore, he has an instinct for character and casts his lot willingly and wholeheartedly with this particular underdog, which ultimately connects him to the sweethearts. Here again are trickster's ethical layers and twists like we've seen in prior films: Though he gleefully fleeces the fleecer Groucho, Harpo has an essentially benevolent nature.

So Wilson, an honest man, gives them what he thinks is a worthless deed to Dead Man's Gulch for security, alluding to the basis of the Wilson-Turner feud. He also expresses his devotion to his granddaughter Eve. It's now clear that Rusty and his trickster cohorts will to have to restore the deed to Wilson, its value renewed by the deal with the railroad company, thereby helping the lovebirds by ending the feud. The worthiness of their cause is reinforced in the next scene when Eve, alone at her log house waiting for her grandfather, receives a visit from her sweetheart Harry Turner, who shares the wonderful news that he has sold Dead Man's Gulch for $10,000.

Helping them seems like a tall order for a buffoon like Rusty. (At the end of the prospecting scene, an arrow stuck in his *tuchus* is holding up his pants.) Nor have Rusty and his cohorts met Eve yet. First Rusty and Joe go to town and, with typical trickster indirection and self-sabotage, lose the now-valuable deed. Parched with thirst, Rusty drinks from the horse trough, going beyond what his cohorts would do, and drinking from it naturally. But Joe stops him, saying, "that's a no good," before they enter the saloon. So Joe is still thirsty. And his thirst leads to mischief that leads to the loss of the deed.

We hear the first hint of Beecher and Baxter's conspiracy against Turner's deal with the railroad company to buy Dead Man's Gulch. Intercut, Rusty demonstrates his hyperbolic thirst with a surreal gesture, lighting a match on his sandpaper tongue. But problems begin when he steals a beer sliding down the bar toward a paying customer. Red Baxter, owner of the saloon, catches him. So Joe gives him an I.O.U. to cover the cost of the beer written on the back of Wilson's "worthless," but of course not worthless, deed. Baxter places it in the cash register, unaware at the moment that it is the coveted deed. We have layers of dramatic irony here.

As they leave the saloon, Rusty and Joe are asked to deliver a telegram to Wilson, and this affords another opportunity to parse the relative ethics of their trickster behaviors. Joe says, "We don't open it." Then he says, "We open it but don't read it." Finally he says, "We read it but don't listen," and tells Rusty to block his ears. Their ethical breach, however, turns out to be a good thing because by reading the telegram, they learn the value of the deed, and furthermore that John Beecher wants old Wilson to meet him at the rail-road station, most likely so he can steal the deed. So their nosy behavior turns out to be a good thing.

When Joe and Rusty go to the station instead of Wilson to meet Beecher, they pepper the encounter with more buffoonery. Before they will accept Beecher as Beecher, Joe insists on placing a carnation in his lapel by means of which they will know him. Then, certain now that Beecher is Beecher, Rusty leaps into his arms with that affectionate and unrestrained violation of personal space that we have seen in prior films. The scene closes acknowledging that Rusty's silence is a speech act, for Joe tells Rusty he "talks too much" and needs to "keep his hands shut," mainly because he mimed that the deed to Dead Man's Gulch is in Baxter's safe.

Unlike in other Marx Brothers films, Harpo has been present almost continuously from the first scene of *Go West*, and Groucho, who in other films is often omnipresent, has been absent since the first scene. This change in Marxian balance in *Go West* indicates Harpo's centrality to the film. When at last we see Groucho again, he is hitchhiking for a ride at the side of the road, an anachronism considering the lack of traffic on Old West roads, and one on par with Chico's later telephone reference.

Quale does score a ride though: He is picked up by the very stagecoach Rusty and Joe happen to be on, escorting Beecher to town. Although Rusty and Joe were working against Quale in the first scene, here the three unite against Beecher. It takes one — make that three — to know one, and the three of them smell a crook. They do good work in collaboration, preventing the sale of the deed without projecting sanctimonious images of themselves. In fact, they do the opposite. When a passenger says her baby is crying because of "the jerks in the coach" — and indeed it is a bumpy ride, sometimes taking bends on two wheels — Rusty and Joe assume that they are the "jerks," and in an abashed and humble gesture try to exit the moving coach.

The stagecoach scene turns hilarious. Rusty laughs with silent hysterics — the loudness of his silent laughter indicated by the diameter of his mouth — at Quale's jokes. He flops and sprawls over everyone, in addition to laying his feet and head on other passengers, transgressing the boundaries of polite behavior in such a crowded place and surpassing even his earlier leap into Beecher's arms. This is one way Rusty suggests the power of inhabiting the joint, for no one is physically looser than he is in this scene. He seems to be the only one on the coach utterly at ease, relaxed unto floppiness in the confined space. He also foments chaos in the coach, chaos necessary to prevent Beecher from gaining the title to Dead Man's Gulch, which would foil Turner's triple hopes: to end the feud, to do a good turn for old Wilson, and to marry Eve.

Rusty, like trickster, offers cleansing chaos in this scene. When Beecher, posing as Wilson's agent, tries to manipulate Joe into signing a bill of sale for Dead Man's Gulch, Rusty starts moving hats from head to head, snatching them off, replacing them, putting them in carpet bags, and taking others out until even the elegantly dressed Lulubelle's chiffon-draped bonnet ends up on Beecher's head, making him look mighty foolish as he struggles to maintain dignified control of the negotiations. His interjections of "give me back my hat," and "Where is my hat?" while bargaining for the deed against Quale's bidding-up scheme (reminiscent of the one in *The Cocoanuts* but this one more successful) don't further his cause. Meanwhile, Rusty is playing with other identity markers, turning the woman's bustle around and around, drinking from the baby's bottle, emptying Beecher's carpetbag, and ending up wearing the bustle himself.

At the saloon, Rusty continues to foment chaos. It is supposed to be where the deed for Dead Man's Gulch is delivered to Red Baxter for the agreed-upon $10,000. But it doesn't work out that way for this is the ungoverned West. Quale enters the saloon in grand meta-style, shooting for no reason other than that he is in a Western. Meanwhile, Lulubelle, Red Baxter's girlfriend, sings for the patrons, assisted theatrically by Quale, who also offers memorable advice to a drunk who looks suspiciously like he was transplanted from Degas' *A Glass of Absinthe,* telling him, "Fan the flames of love with the bellows of indifference," and "Time wounds all heels," his verbal dexterity providing an excellent contrast to the mute Rusty's physical dexterity.

Rusty retrieves the deed from the register while tossing money around as if money has no importance at all. This, and his later flinging of deeds and letters from the safe in Baxter's office, like his tossing and tearing of mail in *The Cocoanuts,* shows the same freewheeling and refreshing disregard for documents in a culture that over-values them. Rusty and Joe, believing they are about to profit enormously from the sale of the deed and intending to skim some off the top for themselves, are celebrating in the saloon. Rusty helps the drunk drink, wipes his face with his hat, then goes manic when Joe plays the piano: choking a woman, bouncing around, and eating a fruit that Joe confiscates to roll on the keys.

But the cause of their ebullience is meanwhile expiring upstairs. In Baxter's room, Quale hands over the deed, expecting the agreed-upon inflated price. But Baxter and Beecher turn on him, taking the deed but refusing to pay him anything at all. Baxter intimidates Quale by shooting corks out of bottles on the bar from upstairs, then trips him down the stairs, his empty briefcase falling open at the bottom.

Because they are afraid to do it themselves, Quale and Joe send Rusty to confront Baxter in a shootout, another iconic Western motif. Harpo seems destined in the films to be elected to perform these dangerous missions. Like in *Duck Soup* when he was chosen in the rimspot game to deliver a message in the midst of battle or in *A Night at the Opera* when he is elected to go out the porthole on a rope, Harpo is again chosen. And he repels danger. His first weapon is his mean expression as he paces toward Red Baxter for the showdown while the patrons in the saloon run for cover. He and Baxter approach each other until they get close. But Rusty spins the iconic scene twice, first, when about to shoot or be shot, he pulls not a gun but a whiskbroom out of his holster and dusts the lint off of Baxter's coat. Everyone laughs with relief, and that is when the second spin occurs: Harpo points and fires bullets from the broom.

Only Harpo of his brothers could pull off this surreal feat, validating, perhaps, Chico and Groucho's sending him into danger instead of themselves. For Harpo has that aspect of the trickster essence that goes beyond ordinary human capacity. The whiskbroom, by the way, will turn up later, minus its power, when it is swapped, in a dark tunnel on the train, for Baxter's gun.

After they lose the deed, Harpo and his cohorts meet the romantic lead, Eve Wilson, and their motives shift. They know that things are looking bad for her grandfather. As they approach her log cabin, they hear her singing "Beautiful Dreamer," because she believes that Dead Man's Gulch has been sold to the railroad company and that she and Terry Turner can marry. Rusty is carrying a huge rag doll, their gift to the little girl they imagine to be Wilson's granddaughter. They are surprised to see she is a woman. And the sad and dismayed eloquence of Rusty's mute face tips her off that something is wrong, so Quale tells her the truth. This scene provides the change in Rusty, Joe, and Quale's motivation away from monetary gain and towards helping Eve, Terry, and Old Wilson. It is now mostly unselfish. The cohorts are united in the cause of young love and clearly allied with the underdogs.

Rusty does most of the work of retrieving the deed in the next scene, and his methods reflect trickster's zaniness as well as his flair. When the saloon women find the three cohorts in Baxter's room, they send for him. But meanwhile, they ply Quale and Joe with mint juleps to waylay them for the ambush. When Lulabelle refers to Harpo as "a red-headed demon," he smiles with pride in the next room where he is trying to crack the safe. With a huge magnet, he pauses to steal the tiara from her head from behind the curtain dividing the rooms, and he has other equipment with him as well, though his holster is belting his big-pocketed coat in this film too tightly for us to believe in it as a repository of sometimes useful, sometimes gratuitous props. Meanwhile, on the populated other side of the curtain, everyone seems to be getting drunk on mint juleps, laughing and toasting various Southern states (the women are faking it, pouring their drinks into the wastebasket while Quale and Joe get more schnockered). Rusty gets his share by intercepting mint juleps with a pail in his hat on the wastebasket. But mostly he remains in Baxter's office on the other side of the curtain.

The taste of the drink gives him the idea to blow up the safe with TNT, an example of how potent non-verbal gestures and the resulting joke can be. And Rusty just so happens to have some TNT, as he happened to have a huge magnet and dynamite, a hammer, and a small cannon. First, though, he searches the roll-top desk for the deed to Dead Man's Gulch.

That is when the desk comes alive. This differs from the animation of the inanimate introduced in *Animal Crackers,* and the order reversed in *Monkey Business,* for here it isn't a representation of something not alive coming to life (or *vice versa*). Rather, we behold a desk, its drawers and rolling top opening and closing in response to Rusty's investigations as if it were being tickled. Perhaps the physical intimacy developing between Rusty and the desk is the basis of their friendship, for later in the scene the desk behaves as a good friend, hiding Rusty from Baxter and Beecher when they enter the room.

Eventually Rusty bungles his way to blowing up the safe, though his dynamite stick doesn't work, while the one that does work seems to be one of those party favors with a paper hat inside. He puts the hat on and stands still while the safe unaccountably explodes open. Then he flings everything out of the safe until he finds — and kisses — the deed.

The scene concludes with a hyperbolic rendition of another iconic moment in Westerns, when the good guy pulls a gun on the bad guy, but in this scene the good guys lose and gain, lose and gain power. Baxter and Beecher are holding the Marxes at gunpoint until Harpo pokes his cannon into Beecher's back. That would seem to settle it except that the barrel of the cannon goes limp, an amusing riff on the phallic nature of guns, so Harpo slinks away. Then the Pony Express messenger working for Baxter holds them hostage at gunpoint again until Eve and Terry Turner arrive and make the bad guys drop their weapons. Terry also shoots out the lights and locks Baxter and Beecher in the room. So with Rusty's help, they have recovered the deed.

Riding to the train station to travel east and deliver the deed to the railroad company affords a Western genre–style interlude during which Rusty plays a harmonica while casually riding his horse. The others sing "Riding the Range," Quale's voice harmonizing oddly with Terry Turner's tenor. And after the range-singing, only one Western motif remains to deconstruct.

And far be it from the Marxes to avoid the challenge of dealing with the representation of American Indians in Westerns. What seems like cultural insensitivity in the next scene probably should be understood as satire. Groucho calls the chief "no Indian" because he is likely a white actor cast and costumed as an Indian. These "friendly Indians" have a totem pole bearing an image of Quale, who remarks on his likeness with self-deprecating humor and riffs ironically on the white man's treatment of Indians before he offers Rusty's Gookie face as an addition to the pole.

But the chief, enacting his own critique, rejects Quale and his offers, saying, "White man talk too much." It is rather Rusty whom he approves of and feels connected to. If we suspend disbelief for a moment, imagining that "no Indian" is indeed an Indian chief, then Harpo is again the Marx who crosses borders, like in *A Day at the Races* and *At the Circus*. Again he doesn't stand apart from minority Americans, seeing them as others, but instead meets them in friendship, mutual appreciation, and communication, particularly via the universal language of music.

Being trickster, he doesn't forbear to honk his horn at the pretty daughter of the chief. In fact, when the chief talks to Rusty, Rusty honks responses. Rusty is the only one the Indians like, though he is frightened at first by the medicine man, leaping into the chief's arms as he leaped into Beecher's, and this time his cohorts do the same. Moreover, when Joe and Rusty blow into the medicine man's horns, we have, as we did with the circumcised salami, another Jewish joke, this one alluding to blowing the *shofar*, the ram's horn, on Rosh Hashanah. Then Quale adds more seasoning to the cultural stew, singing "My Bonny Lies Over the Ocean," a Scottish ballad, to their raucous tune.

The chief offers his daughter to Rusty, and then shares a musical interlude

With the chief (actor unidentified) on flute, Rusty Panello (Harpo) plays on a harp improvised from a blanket loom, somewhat redeeming an otherwise freighted scene. *Go West*, MGM, 1940. From the collections of the Margaret Herrick Library.

with him, a beautiful duet. First the chief plays the flute while Rusty whistles a tune, then Rusty plays a harp improvised from a blanket loom, the warp threads becoming the strings while an unfinished Navajo blanket remains on the bottom third. They play a rendition of "From the Land of the Sky-Blue-Water, a piece written by Charles Wakefield Cadman based on an Omaha love song, first Rusty, then the chief, who continue to pause for each other's musical phrases. The others calm down and approach to listen as Harpo and the chief jazz up the melody. As if aware that their collaboration may have resulted in one of the loveliest musical performances in all of the Marx Brothers films, when they finish playing, the chief pats Rusty on his shoulder, a gesture of approval and affection that ultimately redeems the scene.

Rusty also remains central in the next stupendous sequence, the train sequence. In it he almost single-handedly assures that the deed to Dead Man's Gulch is delivered to the railroad company back east, and this in spite of his many blunders. Eve and Terry have agreed to board with the deed at the next station to avoid Baxter and Beecher, who are boarding at their station. Meanwhile, Rusty and Joe take over driving the train, fencing with the engineer and conductor with the long spouts of oil cans, winning the match, then tying their prisoners up. Quale and Joe's confrontations with Baxter and Beecher contribute to the antics, but Rusty is the major buffoon-deliverer in this sequence, simultaneously creating and solving problems, sometimes with surreal panache.

First he "breaks the brake," and because of that, the train can't stop for Eve and Terry to board, and they must race in their buggy to keep up with it. He also dumps the wood needed to stoke the engine, thinking that he is lightening the load and thus making the train go faster. When the train is finally slowing to a stop for lack of fuel, and Eve and Terry are about to board, Rusty pours kerosene into the engine thinking it is water because part of the label, Waterbury Kerosene, is obscured (like the WO syllable of WOMEN was hidden in the bathroom gender gag in *Monkey Business*). The fired-up train zooms smoking mightily past them again.

Yet Rusty also manages to take Baxter's gun from him in a dark tunnel, so that when Baxter goes to shoot at the cohorts, he is holding instead the ubiquitous whiskbroom. Rusty has that gun in his possession for only a

A trickster-buffoon, Harpo uncouples the wrong car, then must become the coupling. Chico Marx as Joe, Groucho Marx as Quale, and Harpo Marx as Rusty. *Go West*, MGM, 1940.

moment, then he accidentally drops it between cars as they hurtle on. But Rusty doesn't like guns anyway. And when Baxter and Beecher uncouple the car that Quale, Joe and Rusty are on, hoping to get rid of them, Rusty and Joe do the same to get rid of them, but they uncouple the wrong car. At that point, Rusty must use his very body to keep their car coupled to the train. As he hangs onto both cars with his hands and feet, stretching between them, the bottoms of the legs of his pants rise, suggesting that his legs are stretching surreally as the train jolts and rolls.

During a chase on top on the moving train, Rusty and his cohorts get waylaid by the mail pole, the U.S. mail's revenge, perhaps, for Harpo's mischief in *The Cocoanuts, Duck Soup,* and this film. It swings them around before depositing them back on the train. Several times Quale and Joe club Baxter and Beecher and shove them into a closet only for them to be freed by Lulubelle, who is also on the train. And all this time, Eve and Terry are pursuing the train in their horse-drawn wagon, stalwart and determined but unable to catch up until the train eventually stops when it truly runs out of fuel. Finally then Eve and Terry board, but Baxter and Beecher get off the train and jump into their wagon, believing they have a better chance of getting to the company office that way because they assume that there's not a scrap of fuel on the train.

And there isn't, unless you consider the options with a hinged mind. As Quale says and Rusty demonstrates, "There's plenty of wood on the train." Of course, much of that wood *is* the train. So Quale and Joe but mostly Rusty dismantle the train to stoke its own engine: They feed the train to itself to keep it running. At one point, Rusty falls into the furnace, but he comes out looking fine, an amused Shadrach-Meshach-Abednego whose essential goodness is reinforced by the allusion. The three throw everything they find without discrimination into the engine. One of Rusty's contributions is a crate of popcorn that pops berserkly, burying Quale and Joe in its "snow." Quale mans the engine, repeatedly calling for "timber," a multi-faceted pun. And Rusty scours the train for wood, taking it apart, pulling down its very walls, going down the aisles in the direction of the engine with wooden luggage crates, stacks of chairs, and boards. At least once he drops all but one plank of wood by the time he reaches the engine. He is a Mudhead indeed. But he's keeping the train running.

One surreal sequence features mostly Rusty but has the stamp of Buster Keaton. Baxter and Beecher, annoyed to find that the train is still running, remove part of the track, causing it to detour through a farm. It chugs around and around "like a merry-go-round," says Joe happily. It is said that Keaton was an unacknowledged writer of *Go West,* and some of the stunts in this sequence surely suggest his choreography. For the train even runs through the farmhouse while the oblivious farmer is fixing his roof. And when Rusty falls off the train, a bull eying him ominously, Rusty goes through the front door of the house and out the back just by standing still while the house, pushed by the train, swallows him and spits him back out. Eventually Rusty repairs the track and hops back on the train, now on its proper way again. Of the three Marx brothers, only Harpo could have survived the vicissitudes of that scene.

And we know that, because we have been conditioned from watching these films to expect Harpo to push the perimeters of the possible and add a splash of the surreal. By now we accept his preposterous powers. Harpo continues to dismantle the train to keep it running until eventually the passengers are riding *al fresco*. He's on a roll, pun intended, even leaning through a gap in the floor to sharpen his axe on the metal wheels of the train. Baxter and Beecher, attempting to cross the tracks in front of the train, have to dive off the bridge into the river below to avoid being hit. And that puts the ultimate kibosh on their scheme.

With the last impediments removed, the film is rushed, mostly by Rusty's efforts, to a conclusion: The deed is delivered, the feud is ended, the lovebirds are united, old Wilson is enriched. In the denouement (the ceremonial hammering of the spike to connect East and West at the Dead Man's Gulch station), Rusty strikes a blow so hard that his hammer rebounds, hitting the president of the railroad on the head and hammering him into ground, a symbol even Thoreau[2] might have appreciated. It's all in a day's work for Harpo, this film's veritable savior-buffoon.

11

The Big Store (1941)
MERCANTILE MAYHEM

"Some scholars, notably Eliade, have seen the trickster as a descendent of the shaman, downgraded in myth as shamans became less important but still surviving as troublemakers."
— Voth, *Myth in Human History*[1]

In *The Big Store*, Harpo is Wacky, and the label is apt. He is also the lost and found brother of Ravelli (Chico), and they are Italian immigrants though nothing audible indicates that Wacky is: He could be anyone from anywhere, just like an archetype can, with his good-natured demeanor, his wanderer's rags, and his universal language of props and mime. As in prior films, Harpo, far more than his trickster cohorts Groucho and Chico, is associated with magic, musical diversity, thievery, and lust, Flywheel's (Groucho) interest in Martha Phelps (Margaret Dumont) being more about money and even affection, than lust. Harpo is also the main provocateur of chaos in this film, though of course his brothers contribute mightily. In addition, the film's material setting, the sometimes exotic, always opulent array of merchandise in a large department store, is ripe both for cinematic exploitation and trickster mischief.

Harpo doesn't appear until the third scene of *The Big Store*, and interestingly, Groucho doesn't either. Instead, the causes that the three — Harpo, Chico, and Groucho — end up fighting for in their dysfunctional though ultimately successful collaboration are first introduced. They are the interwoven causes of music and love. And it is greed that is satirized in this film, though not that of big commercial enterprises like the department store itself. Instead, the film takes advantage of the wonders the department store brims with, to celebrate American cultural diversity, its central theme, a diversity resulting largely, though not entirely, from immigration. A large American Indian family gets mixed in the hopper of the bed department scene, for example, along with Italian, Chinese, and Swedish families, while African Americans, their claim to a place in the cultural landscape touched upon in *A Day at the Races* and *At the Circus*, appear here only in the big musical number "Sing While You Sell." Yet while the store itself is not an object of satire but a place of wonder in the film, department store executives consumed by greed and willing to commit crimes, even murder, to get what they want, are under attack, as are their greedy counterparts in whatever their enterprise may be in other Marx Brothers films. And again, Harpo is central to exposing them.

One of the counterforces to evil in the film is music, a greatly humanizing form of artistic expression. Harpo's diverse musicality combined with Tony Martin's tenor are important in developing this theme. Harpo's cohorts are musical too: Groucho sings and dances and Chico plays the piano and passes on his inimitable trigger-finger style to the students at the music school. But only Harpo takes music into the realm of the surreal, playing in a trio with

Harpo wears many hats in this film, here as Flywheel's office chicken farmer and cook. Harpo Marx as Wacky. *The Big Store*, MGM, 1941.

his own mirror images who insist on making their own distinct musical contributions, first on the harp, as proper mirror reflections would do, then on cello and violin, as trickster mirror reflections would. Meanwhile, the romantic lead, Tony Martin playing Tommy Rogers, unites the cause of love with the cause of music because he is engaged to Joan (Virginia Grey), a clerk in the store's music department. He sings love songs to her, and furthermore, plans to endow a music conservatory to replace the hardscrabble music school he and Ravelli are associated with once he sells his share of the department store inheritance.

The first two scenes also establish the link between the Marxes and the worthwhile causes of music and love. In the first scene, the music school is threatened. The men trying to repossess the piano from under Ravelli's fingers are stopped only because of Tommy's celebrity status and not his shared roots in the music school with Ravelli. And because Wacky is Ravelli's brother and also works for Flywheel, the three trickster cohorts end up on the side of music, a force associated with trickster Hermes, who impressed Apollo with his lyre. And the scene in which Tommy is attacked in the Phelps Department Store elevator unites Flywheel, Ravelli and Wacky to the cause of young love. This cause goes beyond the implied continuation of life via the procreant urge. Rather, here Tommy's life is actually threatened, making the life-and-death issue more immediate. Grover is plotting to murder Tommy, marry Mrs. Phelps, and then murder her so he can marry his voluptuous blonde partner in crime, Peggy Arden (Marion Martin). The danger to Tommy, who is slugged on the head and knocked out in the second scene, obviously impacts his affianced Joan.

Wacky enters the film along with Flywheel when, as a result of the attack, Tommy's aunt, Mrs. Phelps seeks a detective to protect Tommy. Her finger lands on Wolf Flywheel's ad in the telephone book. And Wacky is detective Flywheel's assistant. Clearly the two are down and out, for they are living in the office, cooking, making toast, even harboring a chicken in a cage to lay their breakfast eggs.

Wacky is adept at hiding all the trappings of domesticity when clients appear. In the middle of preparing Flywheel's breakfast (cracking eggs on his elbow, throwing the shells in the coffee pot, frying the eggs in a skillet on a hot plate, making toast with a hyperkinetic toaster that catapults the bread into the air), Wacky quickly hides the hot plate, eggs sizzling, in Flywheel's desk drawer when Mrs. Phelps arrives. In fact, much humor results from the dramatic irony of that breakfast cooking volubly on the burner during her interview. Shots of her talking are intercut with shots of coffee boiling over and eggs crackling furiously in the pan inside the desk. When Flywheel greets

Mrs. Phelps, he withdraws his own hand from his hot desk, but Mrs. Phelps sits down on it, fanning herself and remarking on the heat while we are left to imagine her buttocks burning.

Wacky exaggerates Flywheel's importance by means of a fake hand reaching intermittently from a closet door to deliver telegrams. This seems to convince Mrs. Phelps that she has chosen a sought-after detective. Then throughout her interview, Wacky takes down her story on a typewriter as he was told to do, but is instead and ironically drowning out her voice with the noisy clacking of the keys. Flywheel asks her to repeat her story three times yet still fails to hear it because of Wacky's vigorous typing, the implication being that Flywheel takes the job in ignorance. But in truth he takes the case because, as we see, he needs the money, and for that very reason he also woos Mrs. Phelps in his charmingly insulting way. All the while, Wacky's typing contributes surreal absurdity to the scene. We wonder what he could possibly be typing so vigorously because neither he nor Flywheel can hear what Mrs. Phelps is saying. But does it matter? Trickster is more a buffoon than one who progresses logically from problem to solution. His cohorts are too. Furthermore, his typewriter, like its sibling, the toaster, challenges the laws of physics as the typist himself is prone to do, for the carriage travels beyond the typewriter, hovering in the air each time he needs to hit return.

Wacky contributes more bumbling excess when, like a good valet, he brushes lint from Flywheel's raccoon coat. It must be many decades old, for the rotten fur comes away with the lint. The bald coat is, however, well matched to the car. Wacky, now wearing a chauffeur's hat (his third hat in this scene, replacing the chef's hat and the clerk's visor), helps Flywheel and Mrs. Phelps in. The collapsing seat Mrs. Phelps drops into, along with the "Welcome Home, Admiral Dewey" sign on the trunk, date the car even earlier than its own invention, for Dewey returned to the United States a hero in 1899. This anachronism parallels the anachronism of the trickster archetype resurrected in the medium of film.

Wearing goggles, Wacky drives Flywheel and Mrs. Phelps to the department store, catches the car door as it falls off when he opens it to let them out, then continues the momentum of destruction, taking the car apart and piling pieces of it on the sidewalk. When a policeman approaches, Wacky goes into fast motion throwing the pieces back into the car. The cop might have repressed Wacky's chaotic impulse for the moment, but the encounter precipitates another of Wacky's guerrilla skirmishes with police in the films, reflecting trickster's perennial rebellion against power and authority. Here he outsmarts the cop by pointing out another car stopped in front of a fire hydrant, a fake hydrant from Wacky's arsenal of props. When the cop makes that driver move his car, Wacky pulls his own jalopy into the vacated space and tosses the hydrant back into the car. We have grown accustomed to assorted props appearing from the pockets and lining of Harpo's coat in earlier films. In *The Big Store* he is wearing that coat, and the jalopy is his coat's extension.

Intercut with Wacky's mischief on the street — which also involves his trying to keep his lucky find, the purse stuffed with money that Mrs. Phelps dropped in the backseat — are threats against Tommy and therefore Joan and the music conservatory. Joan's brother Fred is at first involved in advancing Grover's plot, but when Joan tells him she is going to marry Tommy, Fred changes sides and helps her and Tommy, risking his own safety. Then Tommy's virtue, along with his love for Joan, are confirmed in the music department where he courts Joan even while charming an elderly female customer by making her a personalized recording of "If It's You" because the record itself has sold out. The dialogue tells us that he and Joan were childhood friends in a tough neighborhood, one not unlike the neighborhood in which the Marxes, and perhaps Tony Martin himself, came of age. His story describes the hardscrabble immigrant ascent, both socially and economically.

Wacky's complex nature, good-guy and thief, is emphasized in the following scene in Grover's office. Called "a suspicious character," Wacky is hauled in with the evidence of his theft, Mrs. Phelps' purse, while Flywheel is simultaneously insulting Grover and making time with Mrs. Phelps. This flirtation, of course, threatens to undermine Grover's scheme to marry, then murder Martha Phelps. So in a way Flywheel's wooing has the potential to save her life. And perhaps Tommy intuits this, for he declares for no apparent reason that he heartily approves of Flywheel. In this way the plot inches closer to establishing Tommy's connection to Wacky.

Groucho's quick wit, puns, and sophisticated manipulation of language are always a foil to Harpo's silence in the films. In this scene, for example, Groucho quotes Byron, inspiring Dumont to quote Shelley, and he even cracks meta-cinematically on the screenwriters, saying, "There's no one writing stuff like that any more." But Harpo's silence in the films stands up to Groucho's loquacity because he has his own. In this film in particular he develops the celebration of the contribution of immigrants to America's cultural diversity while Groucho sleeps through the bed department scene. In that scene, as in all the films, Harpo's miming transcends the babble of tongues and goes straight to the heart, like music does. Because of the universal accessibility of Harpo's language of props and gestures, Harpo's silence functions as a speech act.

On the street, Wacky refuses to give Phelps' purse to the cop, and once brought into the store, he snatches it back, is chased, then falls into a display "of priceless antiques," breaking them and getting caught. That is how he ends up being taken to Grover's office. But once there, Ravelli recognizes him as his brother, and Wacky expresses his childlike and affectionate nature immediately when he turns around and hunches his back for a scratch. This warm moment between Harpo and Chico, like their entrance holding hands in *Go West,* suggests their deep affection for one another beyond the world of the film. It even smacks of mutual encouragement in making these films as they age. On that note, it is clear that Chico, Harpo, and Groucho, no longer spring chickens, do not perform their own stunts in the big chase scene near the end of this film.[2]

Wacky infuriates Grover in his office and steps on the floor detective's foot. Nevertheless, Tommy defends him, saying, "That man's no thief—just look at his face," while Wacky makes an innocent face: innocent, though not devoid of ironic mischief. Then Wacky gives up the purse while Flywheel digs Mrs. Phelps' cash that should be in it out of Wacky's fists. His trickster nature makes it impossible to judge Wacky by ordinary standards; we like him, we approve of him, he's funny, he loves his brother, he's Groucho's versatile jack-of-all-trades, and most important, he's on the better side, not Grover's greedy murderous side but the side of music and love. *And* he is a thief.

The big musical numbers in the film emphasize Harpo's diverse musicality. In one super-sized musical interlude, Groucho singing "Sing While you Sell, " Harpo sits in the oriental rug department, charming a snake with a flute and playing cards on an overturned basket with Groucho. He is positioned in the exact center of the scene where he also dances with a woman, something he rarely does in the films. That musical extravaganza, strange though it is, emphasizes the opulence of the setting and Harpo's magical nature.

A later musical scene expands Harpo's customary harp solo into a trio of Harpos, taking us well into trickster's realm of magic and the surreal and far beyond the trickster natures of Groucho and Chico. In a dream-like sequence, Wacky, abashed by Ravelli's remark that he can't come to the party dressed in his clothes that are like a "scared scarecrow," is alone, admiring baroque figurines. Then he is standing before full-sized mannequins who are dressed the same, and when he touches a mannequin's elegant period costume, magic happens: He is translated into the mannequin's attire, even his fancy wig. And *vice versa,* the mannequin is translated into his tramp's clothes. Wacky even takes a little snuff, almost sneezes, then shrugs, denying us a hurricane. Then he sits down at the harp in front of mirrors and begins his solo rendition of Mozart's Piano Sonata No. 15 in C major.

Who else but Harpo, musically diverse and magical, could finesse the skill of a snake charmer? Harpo Marx as Wacky, Groucho Marx as Wolf J. Flywheel. *The Big Store,* MGM, 1941. From the collections of the Margaret Herrick Library.

For a while he and his mirror reflections are one unified Wacky, but suddenly he hears notes he isn't playing. Startled, he looks suspiciously around. First he sees what we see: his own reflection in the two mirrors. He tries to outsmart the first reflection and catch it in the act of not reflecting, but it continues to reflect what he is doing. His viewers, however, educated by the mirror scene in *Duck Soup,* may not be as trusting of reality's surfaces as he is. He glances over his shoulder at the second mirror, confident now that he will see his own reflection. So it takes him a moment to realize that the second mirror's Wacky isn't reflecting him, that that Wacky doesn't likewise turn around. In fact, Wacky has to whistle to get his attention, though then they wave at each other good-naturedly.

In this way Wacky exhibits the capacity to accept with a hinged mind this altered reality. Then he gets another surprise: the first mirror's Wacky is now playing a cello. Fine, he seems to think, and fine again when the second

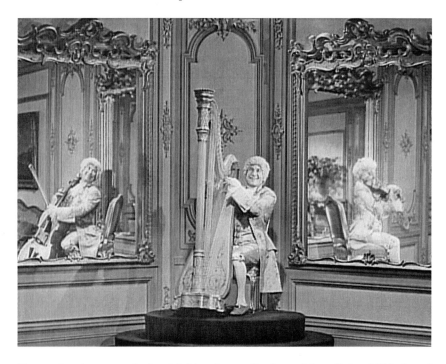

Harpo plays in a surreal trio with his mirror reflections, chips off the old block and therefore tricksters too. Harpo Marx as Wacky. *The Big Store,* MGM, 1941.

mirror's Wacky is playing a violin. They were performing Beethoven's Minuet in G major, but the second mirror's Wacky injects some wildness into the trio, jazzing up the score on violin. And Wacky, his face at first registering disapproval, quickly accepts the change and participates. The cello-playing Wacky reflection also catches the spirit and spins his cello enthusiastically.

By the end of their evolving trio, both reflections of Wacky are playing the harp again. The mirror images seem to coalesce into one Wacky. But not really. For now his reflection on the harp is multiplied in the first mirror, reflected unto infinity. This surreal scene reminds us that if Harpo is a trickster, his reflections must be tricksters too. Chips off the old block, they too are rebels, asserting their own autonomous ways of being. Thus they choose their own musical instruments and develop their own interpretations of the piece. That Harpo quickly accepts and embraces this, enjoying the musical enhancement and the multiplied effects, also educates us about the bounty inherent in diversity.

Right after this scene, Grover and Peggy plot to take control of the store by his marrying, then murdering Martha Phelps. Therefore we celebrate the next scene wherein Wacky and his cohorts dole out comic punishment to the blonde conspiratress. The Marxes are covering the music counter while Joan and Tommy go to lunch together. Initially attracted to Peggy, Flywheel and Ravelli scurry towards her, and Wacky actually follows her, ogling her intensely. But when she displays a supercilious attitude at the hat counter, criticizing Tommy for going to lunch with "the help," which "isn't done," calling Wacky "stupid," and responding rudely to a saleswoman, Wacky pulls his trusty scissors from the recesses of his coat, and with a couple of deft snips, renders her foolish.

For while Peggy is demanding a hat to match her dress, disregarding the saleswoman's insistence that they don't have that fabric in stock, Harpo cuts a big swatch from the back of Peggy's dress and hands it over the counter. Thinking that the saleswoman had the fabric all along and was withholding it from her, Peggy snatches it, tries it on a hat form, then changes her mind and huffs off, the missing chunk in the back of her skirt revealing her legs and thighs up to her panties. The ironic gap between her arrogance and her lack of awareness of her state — her shame covers are all but removed — make us gasp and laugh. Sometimes trickster's solutions are both breathless and breathlessly simple.

Harpo's contributions of mischief are also central to the comedy in the bed department, a sometimes surreal scene that reifies the American melting pot theme that will be the subject of Tommy's musical tribute, "Tenement Symphony." Tommy is sleeping in the bed department along with Flywheel, Ravelli, and Wacky. But their sleep is interrupted by a multicultural parade of customers enticed by the half-price sale in the bed department that Grover announces to get rid of them. The shtick in this scene in based on campy and flamboyant bed designs, lots of lounging for the Marxes, and entourages from the American cultural mix. First an immigrant Italian family (father, mother, and twelve children), press a button on the wall that raises a tall bed with Ravelli and Wacky sleeping in it. The Italian patriarch thinks Ravelli is mocking his accent — a meta-cinematic moment perhaps even more necessary today with our heightened awareness of cultural insensitivity. But when he realizes that Chico is an immigrant too, and moreover that they knew each other in the old country, he embraces him. They reminisce about pressing grapes, though the patriarch, whose off-kilter gait Wacky good-naturedly imitates, gets upset when Wacky presses his wife.

The implications of the immigrant's offense breaks the fourth wall, directly addressing Chico's use of an Italian immigrant persona. It *is* possible that an Italian immigrant might find it offensive. And Chico uses this identity, replete with accent, in every Marx Brothers film, a talent he developed as a kid navigating the streets of New York when, to avoid a beating, he learned to imitate the ethnic nuanced English of whatever block he happened to be on. This scene insists that Chico's intent is not mocking but affectionate, even while it obliges us to consider, as do scenes in other Marx Brothers films that depict racial or ethnic minorities, the extent and impact of the "foreign code of conscience,"[3] with which we judge older films and with which our own productions will be judged by future readers and viewers. For film art, like all art, "travels through time" and will be judged.

Wacky presses not only the Italian matriarch but also all the buttons on the wall, resulting in a confusion of ethnicities in beds of highly unusual designs — submarines, camping tents, bookcases — extreme metaphors for American ingenuity and consumerism. The many offspring of Italian, Swedish, Chinese, and American Indian parents intermittently appear and disappear into beds that vanish into floors and walls as Wacky pushes buttons.

And the chaos intensifies when Wacky tries to reunite parents and children, for he isn't particular and makes no distinctions. Children are children, all equal in the eyes of God and trickster. So he commandeers a cluster of Swedish kids and, laughing silently, returns them to the distraught Italian parents who are missing six of their children. Ravelli participates too, but when he tries to give them six Chinese children, the Italian matriarch faints. Chico and Wacky attempt to mollify the patriarch with "remember the grapes," Wacky wildly miming the grape-crushing motions, but they aren't successful. When Harpo tries to give them six American Indian children in traditional dress, the American Indian father chases Wacky across a bed to stop him.

Thus Wacky initiates chaos, whips it into peaks of frenzy, then resolves it by pressing the right buttons to return all the beds to the floor with all the missing children returned. The families are reunited, ethnicities intact. And perhaps this makes Wacky seem a little bit ahead of his time in suggesting that America's culture is not so much a melting pot — he and Ravelli tried solutions based on that assumption but they didn't work — but a salad or stew. Flywheel sleeps through it all.

Wacky intensifies chaos in another musical interlude, and then again when he and Ravelli attempt to entrap the murderers. At first the three are all sleeping so soundly in the bed department that Joan's brother Fred has a hard time waking them up to warn them about Grover's plot to kill Tommy. Then, while Flywheel continues to sleep, Wacky and Ravelli play a duet in the music department, hoping to lure the murderers. They have fun while they're at it, bumping their bottoms and slamming around on the piano. When they sit down to play, Ravelli says, "Remember when I used to give you lessons?"

and lo, we are beyond the fourth wall again: their mother Minnie paying for Chico's lessons, his being the oldest, and his coming home and teaching Harpo what he learned. Harpo grins a lot while they are playing this duet; he even lays his head on Chico's shoulder in a gesture of brotherly affection.

Their playing the piano together in this scene combines music and mime, for they play laughter with piano chords, Wacky's mouth wide with silent guffaws and the children in their audience supplying the laughter of human voices. A crowd gathers, but without men in gray suits. Wacky and Ravelli don't stay on task anyway but become increasingly rambunctious, Ravelli dominating the keyboard and Wacky trying various positions to access the keys, reaching between Ravelli's legs, then climbing on his back to get at them.

Wacky eventually helps catch the hired killers with a mix of buffoonery, setback, and indirection. Flywheel, having heard, though half-asleep, that the murderers are wearing gray suits, mistakenly handcuffs the gray-suited Hasting brothers, the legitimate buyers of the store, to a pole. But even when his error is revealed, he is unrepentant and keeps making eyes at Mrs. Phelps. Following an apology, they plan a contract-signing party with the Hastings brothers while Wacky tosses confetti.

Ravelli gives Wacky the disparaging critique of his clothes that precipitates his trio fantasy, but in spite of the well-dressed though out-of-date clothing he wears when he plays in the trio with his mirrored reflections, Wacky wears his plaid shirt and coat to the reception where he immediately gets slapped for pulling the hair of a woman he mistakes for a mannequin. And in this moment, like in the earlier translation of Harpo into the mannequin's clothing and wig, the animate versus inanimate theme from *Animal Crackers* and *Monkey Business* is resurrected. Sometimes Harpo seems to acknowledge a gray area between the two, to abide in a kind of intermediate reality, parallel to the one he inhabits between waking and dreams. In some ways he suggests that there is no such thing as inanimate matter.[4]

Wacky plays only a supporting role in Tommy Rogers' "Tenement Symphony," his musical tribute to American cultural diversity. Like the fictional Tommy (and Tony Martin, who plays him), Harpo is actually a performer who grew up in a tenement and in part, out of its influence, developed a language of props and mime. Tommy puns on the word "flats" in his lyrics, just as Harpo frequently puns with props and gestures. And Tommy's lyrics echo Harpo's identification with the less powerful in all of the films, which also reflects trickster's alliance with the marginalized in myth and legend. We hear this when he celebrates the inspiration of the ghetto in life and song. Moreover, the orchestra is comprised of children from the music school, and the chorus as well, the young singers' faces each illuminated by its own source of light. Ravelli accompanies them on the piano. But Wacky's harp accompaniment, which combines their innocence, hope, and glowing countenances with his sincere musical rapture, suggests the angelic.

This scene suggests two ways of seeing. One involves a transcendent vision of a place where angels dwell, with Harpo and the children inhabiting an otherworldly sphere not unlike the vision in Tom Dacre's comforting dream in William Blake's "The Chimney Sweeper" from *Songs of Innocence.* The second is a vision of tenement life in the actual gritty world where immigrants from diverse backgrounds somehow learn to live in harmony, symbolized here by the collaborative process of making music, and one interestingly not unlike Blake's insistence on real-world social justice voiced in his companion poem, "The Chimney Sweeper" from *Songs of Experience.*[5]

We are brought back to the mortal danger facing Tommy, when the film cuts to Grover loading a gun into a camera with the intention of tricking a reporter into shooting, pun apt, Tommy. But first Grover needs to get Joan out of the way. Fortunately, Wacky ends up in possession of the one piece of evidence, the photograph that Ravelli snapped the moment the lights went out at the party. It shows Grover kidnapping Joan. She had been standing next to Flywheel, but when the lights come back on, instead of Joan, Wacky is leaning obliviously against Flywheel. Those blackout moments during which crimes are committed, like the thwack on the head to Tommy in the elevator, constitute a minor motif in the film.

Realizing they must have important evidence, the cohorts hasten to a darkroom to develop the picture. Just as they complete the process, however, Grover barges in, demanding the negative, which he burns. But Wacky takes off with the picture itself, initiating a wild chase full of blunders and acrobatic feats throughout the varied and opulent setting of the department store. When the lights go off on the elevator, then come back on, the Marxes are pummeling each other, a regression in typical trickster style, yet Wacky shoots up through the opening at the top of the elevator in defiance of gravity, so manages to escape with the photograph again.

The chase scene is full of stunts and fast motion; we have to suspend our disbelief, imagining that those are really the Marxes and not stunt doubles. When Grover starts shooting at them, they escape on roller skates, gliding on the department store's numerous counters, floors, displays, ramps, and elevators. Once Flywheel and Ravelli join hands and scoop Wacky out of danger. Wacky (or his stunt double) makes long jumps, swings from hanging lights, and leaps onto the shoulders of Flywheel (or his stunt double) on a unicycle, his bicycle having gotten bisected. They knock down stacks of boxes and rolls of rugs to block their pursuers: Grover, the misguided policeman, and the duped janitor, the last two unaware that Grover is rotten to the core. Wacky ends up with a FRAGILE sign on his bum, then he gets attached to a bungee cord and twangs from pole to mirror and back, in the process knocking his pursuers down.

So far, Wacky still has the incriminating photograph. But barricaded in a storeroom, he carelessly puts it down, and in another step backward so typical of trickster's buffoonery, Wacky, Flywheel, and Ravelli mistake the light bulbs falling off a shelf and breaking when they hit the floor for gunshots. (There's similar confusion in *Duck Soup* when Harpo is likewise locked in a closet.) They open the door to Grover, who seizes the photograph and emerges from the room burning it.

All seems to be lost as far as photographic evidence goes, but when a journalist attempts to take a picture of the spuriously heroic Grover, Grover has to stop him, explaining that a gun is cocked and waiting inside in the camera. Thus he incriminates himself. And Wacky punches him, dropping him to the floor for good measure. Flywheel waltzes to his ancient car with Mrs. Phelps on his arm, and Wacky hops into the driver's seat, a chauffeur again. But when the camera pans back, giving us a wider shot, we see a collection agency tow truck, the front end of Admiral Dewey's welcome home car raised, and Wacky not driving at all. It's all about point of view, but we're satisfied because with trickster's help, love and music have been restored to this world.

12

A Night in Casablanca (1946)
META MARX

Trickster is "at the same time imp and hero."
— Erdoes and Ortiz, *American Indian Myths and Legends*[1]

This film offers more meta-cinematic commentary than other Marx Brothers films so far, from the allusion in its title, *A Night in Casablanca* to *Casablanca* (1942) starring Humphrey Bogart and Ingrid Bergman, to its references to iconic films like *The Blue Angel* (1930) along with its retrospective glance at the Marx Brothers films that precede it. Harpo's trickster essence unfolds in a highly liminal setting, a crossroads, and again surpasses that of his brothers. *A Night in Casablanca* accomplishes this self-and industry critique even as Harpo and his cohorts bumble their way to victory in a battle against the murder and greed of the film's villains and for the cause of young love. Harpo's role is both central and catalytic.

For the first time ever, Harpo appears before his brothers, right after a brief opening scene that portrays Casablanca as a crossroads of conspiracy. The film is set on Jewish-Arabic trickster Joha's turf, and stories about Joha span ancient to modern, through World War II and beyond. Like Joha, Harpo is first seen hanging out in the center of town. The war is over, but the Nazis aren't quite finished scheming yet. At an outdoor café, the manager of the Casablanca Hotel orders a drink, then keels over while two waiters exchange knowing looks. The Nazi Heinrich Stubel, played by Sig Ruman (Dr. Steinberg in *A Day at the* Races and Herman Gottlieb in *A Night at the Opera*), is passing himself off as Count Pfferman. With his sidekick Kurt, played by Frederick Giermann, he is murdering hotel managers in an attempt to position himself to take over hotel operations so that he can smuggle out of the country a stash of stolen art treasures hidden between floors at

148

the hotel, a Rembrandt painting among them. And he has a lover Beatrice, played by Lisette Verea.

The police, having been ordered to round up suspicious characters after this latest murder, arrest Harpo in the sweep while he is leaning on a wall, apparently loitering. When the policeman asks him sarcastically if he is "holding up the building," Harpo nods yes. He's dragged off anyway, but when he is removed, the building falls. In this way, Harpo's surreal nature becomes part of his entrance to the film. Furthermore, the metaphor suggests Harpo's importance to the architecture of this and the other films. Although Harpo is taken to headquarters, he is subsequently released with the other suspects, who are told there will be "no more questions." This sounds odd, of course, in Harpo's case. The phrase resounds absurdly, for how could this mute guy have responded to interrogation? It isn't the first meta-moment with an absurdist spin in the film either.

In addition, throughout, *A Night in Casablanca* references other films,

The cop sarcastically accuses Harpo of holding up the wall, and lo! When he lets go it falls down, a trope that suggests Harpo's importance to the architecture of the films. Harpo Marx as Rusty, and unidentified actor as the Prefect of Police. *A Night in Casablanca,* United Artists, 1946.

usually the Marx Brothers' own. For example, Harpo is a physically abused valet here, as he was in *A Night at the Opera,* only this time instead of working for a narcissistic tenor he is working for the bloodthirsty and bewigged Count Pfferman, who is really the Nazi Heinrich Stubel. And Ruman, with his thick belly, toupee, and pedantic posturing, not only reprises his own sputtering Dr. Steinberg in *A Day at the Races* but also recalls Professor Rath in *The Blue Angel*; he even loves, though not so deeply that he won't betray her in the end, a cabaret singer, though in this film her name is Beatrice, not Lola.

Harpo clowns in the scene in Stubel's suite, but there is method to his madness. For example, he has figured out ways to shine multiple pairs of shoes at once with an elaborate buffing mechanism strapped to his body, to dress and undress Stubel simultaneously, and to reveal Stubel's identifying scar by vacuuming the toupee from his head, though this last achievement may be the result of lucky bumbling. The theft of hair, of course, is reminiscent of stolen hair in *Monkey Business, Horse Feathers,* and *A Night at the Opera.* Even the recycling of hair as beards is reprised, for this is how Stubel's toupee last appears in the film's conclusion. No wonder Harpo laughs in this early scene with silent uproariousness.

Harpo is clearly a picaresque character turning up in Casablanca. We aren't sure how he got there or where he hails from or how he became Stubel's valet; a later scene suggests he works for the hotel and was assigned to him. But he eventually ends up allied with the causes of justice and love as in prior films. The next few scenes continue to develop these redux aspects of his characterization. We meet Beatrice, the chanteuse singing her rendition of "Who's Sorry Now?" and Annette, the hotel secretary who receives Stubel's toupee from the maid who found it in the vacuum cleaner. In fact, Annette along with Pierre, the French lieutenant tracking down Nazis and their stolen treasures, are the lovebirds the Marxes try to assist.

And as in other Marx Brothers films, Corbaccio (Chico) and Rusty (Harpo) greet each another as old friends, though again, we don't know where either comes from. We may suspect New York because of the names of Corbaccio's taxi companies, Yellow Camel and Checkered Camel, but we are sure only that they are happy to meet again. Back to back and *tuchus* to *tuchus,* they shake hands by reaching between each other's legs, complicating a simple gesture and showing their familiar and playful natures.

The focus drifts away from Rusty to reveal what his cohorts Kornblow (Groucho) and Corbaccio are doing in Casablanca. Corbaccio, wearing a too-small pointed felt hat and speaking with an Italian accent, is both a bodyguard and a taxi driver, running two taxi companies in Morocco. His camel may be yellow but is wearing a checkered cloth, so we know which he represents.

Corbaccio's stumping for passengers to the hotel reprises the opening of *A Day at the Races,* and when Kornblow arrives to assume responsibilities as hotel manager — or rather blow them off in his inimitable style — we are reminded of the similar role he plays as hotel manager in *The Cocoanuts.*

There is something more than suspicious about the set-up here, and given the serial murders of prior managers, only a sucker would take a job so likely to end his life. Kornblow is their man. The plot gets a twist when Annette shows Pierre the toupee while they are watched by a spy who tries to extort money from Pierre for information about its owner. But the film's focus returns to Rusty and his trickster magic once the atmosphere in which he will cavort has been thickened with conspiracy.

Rusty's second important scene plays out in Stubel's room where he mocks and angers Stubel by offering a frowsy replacement for his lost toupee — it looks like it could be a dead bird or a mop. As punishment, he is forced to fence with Kurt, Stubel's partner in crime, for Stubel really wants to shed Rusty's blood. However, with the unruffled nonchalance of one who knows he has eternity in his corner, Rusty clowns his way to victory in the match. To begin, Rusty dons baseball catcher's equipment to protect his body. Although it gets stripped from him with a few swipes of Kurt's sword, he doesn't fear. Rather, he sharpens his sword on Kurt's sword as if the latter exists to service his own. Then, as Kurt fences energetically and thrusts skillfully, Rusty steps hard on his foot, rolls dice when Kurt forces him to his knees, then leans on a wall, yawning, eating an apple, and warding off Kurt's sword thrusts in boxing gloves. Kurt with his fancy footwork eventually faints from exhaustion. Only Bugs Bunny, another trickster, faces peril on the big screen with similar nonchalance.

Rusty chases only one woman in this film, Beatrice, and not until the end, but he studies and imitates her style early on as she attempts to seduce Kornblow. In that scene she blows smoke rings — an allusion to "pucker up and blow" from *To Have and Have Not* (1944)? — and exchanges innuendoes to soften Kornblow up so that she can recoup Stubel's toupee. But Rusty has her number, sees the act, and matches it with his own female impersonation, imitating Beatrice with a hyperbolically long cigarette in a long holder like hers. He makes solid smoke, a gag from *Animal Crackers,* and he exchanges suspicious glances with Beatrice, each through a lorgnette, though Rusty ends up blowing bubbles with his, then tries to bite those bubbles just like a dog would. That gesture added to Stubel's calling him a "schweinhund," Corbaccio's calling him a "guinea pig," Rusty's own clapping like a seal, and his mad dog act in jail, all serve to remind us that he (not his cohorts) is like trickster of myth, part animal and sometimes barely distinguished from one.

Rusty (Harpo) impersonates Beatrice, chanteuse and Nazi moll, then gets silly, blowing bubbles with a lorgnette that matches hers. *A Night in Casablanca,* United Artists, 1946.

Rusty's insight penetrates Beatrice's facade. He knows she is not to be trusted with Kornblow, and the next scene validates his suspicions, for in the nightclub, after singing "Who's Sorry Now?" she plots Kornblow's murder with Stubel, now wearing his recovered toupee. It isn't clear how Rusty, or for that matter, Corbaccio came to be allied with Pierre. Corbacchio seems to have an already established friendship with him. Somehow, in the film's extra-diegetic world, they are allied. In the nightclub scene, Rusty and Corbaccio raise money for Pierre because he needs to pay the spy for information on the identity of the man who wears the toupee.

How would trickster get money fast? First Rusty tries to pick someone's pocket, then, noticing the queue of people waiting for tables in the nightclub, he takes the opportunity chance affords and runs with it, moving more and more tables into the dining room and collecting bountiful tips from patrons grateful to be seated. When Kornblow barges into the dining room and spills soup on Stubel, thus driving him away, then joins Beatrice at the table, Rusty is busy dragging in tables and seating more and more couples, as is Corbaccio, both of them to such excess that the dance floor ends up filled with tables, extra space left only for the orchestra and for one last couple to dance. That couple is Kornblow and Beatrice. He would dance anywhere.

Rusty and Corbaccio make a lot of money for Pierre this way, and we celebrate their generosity along with their mischief; no one gets hurt and a good man along with a good cause are promoted. Corbaccio plays the piano at the end of this scene, a classical piece that morphs into jazz, then into a ditty, his finger shooting, as it is wont to do, at the keys. But he adds a new trick: He bounces as he plays, and his bouncing is apparently contagious because members of the orchestra start bouncing too. We must wait a while yet for Harpo's harp solo. It will take place between floors, an interlude in the scene wherein he discovers, though is not fully aware of its significance, Stubel's stash of Nazi stolen art treasures.

Harpo is the catalyst for the ultimate unmasking and capture of Stubel, for in the next scene he overhears him plotting to murder Kornblow. And it's a complicated plot. Stubel intends to make the homicide seem justifiable: He'll shoot Kornblow seemingly to defend the honor of his affianced Beatrice. It is set to happen in her room, an entrapment scheme like that in *A Day at the Races* but more lethal in intention. While Rusty is overhearing Stubel's plot and Annette is telling Pierre that the toupee, their evidence, is missing, Kornblow comes stumbling back to the hotel in a disheveled state. He has been hit by a car that came at him three times, an attempt on his life that, amazingly, failed. When Pierre tells the battered Kornblow about Nazi loot hidden somewhere in Casablanca, and about the toupee and the scar it covers, they realize that Pfferman is the Nazi Stubel hiding stolen treasures, and that the murders of the previous hotel managers are part of a pattern.

Like in *Animal Crackers, A Day at the Races,* and *Love Happy,* Harpo, the mute guy, the one least able to tell others, is the one who overhears and must report the dire plot. And this he does, as in prior films, by miming the details to Chico, who is the films' most apt translator of Harpo's language of props and gestures into words. Harpo uses elaborate, eloquent, and exhausting gestures, acting out "Kornblow" by stomping on Chico's corns and blowing, then "soup" and "rise" for "surprise," next "Peek" and "knees" for Pekinese, the metonymic sign for Beatrice who carries a dog of that breed around with her. *Close* is good enough, and *sounds like* stands in for the word.

But when Chico takes Harpo to Groucho to warn him about the plot and offer himself as a bodyguard, instead of simply *telling* Groucho, he turns the task of communicating back over to Harpo, who must enact the entire charade again, though in an abbreviated version. This is typical trickster circumlocution on both Chico and Harpo's parts, a gratuitous complication that, in the long run, doesn't *not* work. In this case, Chico makes sure Groucho gets it, like a good editor but nothing more.

The warning scene is followed by an eating scene replete with a reprise of Harpo's hyperbolic trickster appetite evidenced in the earlier films *The Cocoanuts, Horse Feathers, A Night at the Opera* and *Room Service.* Chico, fearing Groucho's meal might be poisoned, suggests using Harpo as a guinea pig, the third animal reference applied to Harpo, who is already so hungry that he bites Chico's hand. Thus Harpo eats Groucho's lunch, taking the meal to a surreal level, transferring the candle's flame to his own finger, then taking a bite from the candle, salting the telephone when it rings, then munching a cup and saucer. When he uncorks the bottle, extracting an excessively long and dare we say phallic cork, the bottle is empty, which is logical, it turns out, because, according to Groucho, it holds "really dry" champagne.

Harpo's antics are also central to the next few scenes. In the hotel lobby, the sort of liminal space trickster likes to inhabit, he gives a strange woman his leg, that memorable gesture we haven't seen for a while and reminding us of the power of the hinge. This time, though, it has an additional rationale: Rusty is sweeping the lobby, using his shoe for the task because it opens like a dustpan. He is offering her his leg in order to raise his shoe higher for disposal of her cigarette. After she complies, he honks at her and she flees. Then he sweeps up the cigars and cigarettes on the floor, the toe of his shoes opening like a mouth to receive them.

Rusty saves Kornblow's life and discovers the Nazis' connection to the hotel in the next scene. While Kornblow is accusing an older married couple of trying to hide their tryst by registering at the hotel using the pseudonym Smythe, an outrageous accusation for Smythe is really their name, Beatrice calls to invite him to her room. This bit of hypocrisy on Kornblow's part — he willingly takes the bait — gets the murder plot against him rolling. So Rusty has to adapt. As the elevator operator, he prevents Kornblow from keeping the assignation by getting the elevator stuck between floors. Kornblow boosts Rusty out through the ceiling like in *The Big Store.* From there, Rusty accidentally discovers an opening in the wall between floors, and through that portal he enters a hidden room filled with art treasures. Could this be the inspiration for the absurd 7½th floor in *Being John Malkovich,* another film with meta-textual references?

This scene is important to the plot, for it reveals the stolen war treasures that Stubel intends to smuggle out of the country. But it also reprises Harpo's multi-faceted trickster essence. For in the room is a painting of a man making the Gookie face, perhaps a portrait of the original roller of cigars the real Harpo imitated from youth on. Maybe Arthur Marx even painted it, for he was a painter in addition to being a musician and comic actor. Or it could even be a portrait of Harpo himself making the Gookie face. Whichever it is, he makes the Gookie face back at the picture.

He also covers the portrait of the Gookie face with a painting of a beautiful woman with whom he is already smitten. Then he brushes a feather off of his sleeve, easily read as an allusion to wings, for he's now seated like an angel at the harp he has found among the room's treasures. The camera lingers on the slow descent of the feather and his catching it in his dustpan shoe. Then he plays a harp solo rendition of Franz Liszt's Hungarian Rhapsody No. 2, thus offering a nod to what was best in German culture, a generous and significant gesture in a film released one year after the end of World War II. He finishes his solo gazing at the woman in the painting coyly, as well he should, for it turns out to be a Rembrandt portrait.

All this while Kornblow has been trapped in the elevator and thereby saved from a lethal encounter with Beatrice and Stubel. But Rusty and Corbaccio can only delay and not prevent the inevitable assignation. After all,

Harpo, with the luck of trickster, breaks the bank at the casino. Chico Marx as Corbaccio, Harpo Marx as Rusty, and Groucho Marx as Kornblow. *A Night in Casablanca,* United Artists, 1946. Photofest.

she's "Beatrice," an inspiration. So instead they resolve to interrupt it. A series
of comic repetitions follow: Kornblow in Beatrice's room, Corbaccio telling
him to get out, Kornblow complying, Beatrice leaving a note for Stubel,
Stubel entering ready to shoot, reading the note, and going to find Kornblow
in his own room with Beatrice, but Corbaccio telling him to get out, so Kornblow obeying and lugging all their paraphernalia (champagne, flowers, food,
a table, even a record player) from room to room while Beatrice surreptitiously
leaves notes for Stubel. Somehow Corbaccio ends up with Beatrice and the
champagne, a peek beyond the fourth wall at his success with women, and
Kornblow and Stubel end up in the elevator, but with Stubel lacking a legally
defensible provocation to shoot him.

Interestingly, Rusty is not part of this chaos, but he is front and center
in the next scene, playing roulette in the hotel casino and demonstrating his
other-worldly luck such as we saw in the speakeasy scene in *Horse Feathers*:
the exceptional luck of trickster. He and Corbaccio find some money on the
floor and dive for it. Rusty gets it, and they head to the roulette wheel to
multiply it. Meanwhile, Rusty makes insulting faces and gestures at Stubel,
who can do nothing to retaliate. And he wins and wins, betting all of his
jackpots until the casino worker says he cannot continue to bet because if he
wins again, he will break the bank.

Kornblow, however, in his authority as hotel manager, overrides this
objection and approves Rusty's continued betting. And Rusty wins again,
indeed breaking the bank and going wild with joy, even kissing a nearby man
on the lips. While the affronted man tries to wipe the kiss off, a smiling Rusty
bathes himself in coins. This is not the first time Rusty leaps upon a stranger
regardless of gender and with unbridled affection and abandon in the films,
nor the first time he gambles and wins.

Unfortunately, Rusty's success at the roulette wheel allows Stubel to convince
the police that Kornblow, Corbaccio, and Rusty are involved in a conspiracy to
destroy the hotel. The police believe him, appointing Stubel to be the new hotel
manager and incarcerating Kornblow, Corbaccio, Rusty and also Annette, who
was working the roulette wheel in the casino. Harpo looks at her sadly as she
weeps; and he weeps himself, silently, when Chico blames him for placing that
last bet. Pierre too has been arrested and charged, to be tried in France. Yet he
tries to cheer up Annette by saying, "Maybe a miracle will happen."

And promptly, Rusty, with trickster's lucky timing, trickster's bumbling
into success, and trickster's intimations of the divine, delivers that miracle when
he tries to take another prisoner's pin-up picture, reminding us of his lust and
echoing his attachment to the Edwardian ballerina poster in *Horse Feathers*.
Rusty offers to exchange the portrait of the woman for the pin-up. It turns

out that he has stolen a stolen treasure, not because he knew Rembrandt painted the portrait but only because he was moved by its subject, in essence a tribute to Rembrandt's skill as a painter. But Annette recognizes it as a Rembrandt painting and therefore as evidence that the stolen Nazi treasures are hidden in the hotel. Thus Rusty tells them a whole lot without ever speaking, including clarifying the motive for the murders of the previous hotel managers. They break out of jail by tricking the jailor, calling "help" and "mad dog." Rusty's mouth is covered with soapsuds in yet another conflation of Harpo with animals, neither his first conflation with dogs nor his first jailbreak in the films.

Meanwhile Stubel and Kurt are packing for their getaway, a raucous scene stolen largely by Rusty. In fact, in a strange reversal of Jung's theory of the Shadow, the hidden or nefarious part of the personality, Rusty shadows Stubel the Nazi, stealthily walking behind him. Because Stubel as a Nazi represents the Shadow extant in the world, his hidden nature would have to be its opposite: hence Harpo as Rusty: sweet, fun-loving, and benign. This amounts to a kind of Jungian joke.

Beatrice, having overheard Stubel's intentions to abandon her, is there too, hiding in one of Stubel's trunks in his room where all three Marxes are concealed in closets and wardrobes and trunks while sabotaging Stubel's efforts to pack and abscond with the treasures. Sometimes Rusty is in a garment bag hoisted by Kurt to hang up in a wardrobe, then the bag animatedly runs off when Kurt turns his back. Throughout the scene, Rusty undermines and reverses Stubel's attempts to pack, more so even than his cohorts, the thrust similar to when he shovels dirt back into the hole Chico is digging in *Go West*, only much multiplied.

The frustration of his efforts to pack and the mystery of their undoing eventually drives Stubel to drink. Rusty slams Stubel's hand in the trunk while he hides in its lid. He empties drawers after Stubel fills them, unpacks what Stubel packs, even turns drawers upside down so when Stubel opens them, their contents fall out. Rusty opens the space for a leaf in the table and hides beneath it, catching clothes Stubel and Kurt toss onto the table, throwing them back onto the pile, and, of course flinging many around. The closet with sliding doors allows Corbaccio, Kornblow and sometimes Rusty to hide even while they follow Stubel in and out, Kornblow quipping, "This isn't the first time I've hidden in a closet," either a personal innuendo or an allusion to his closet-hiding scene in *Monkey Business*. And Rusty emerges at least once from the closet wearing a tiara, his hat tip not only to the tiara he stole with a magnet in *Go West*, but to his cross-dressing and gender-bending in films.

While Stubel drinks shots to calm his discombobulated nerves, Rusty manages to provoke a smack on Kurt after taking Stubel's pen, eliciting an apology from Kurt to Stubel. In other words, Kurt accepts punishment for something he didn't do, which, along with the early fencing scene, makes a case for Nazi sado-masochism.

In the penultimate scene, a chase, Harpo again plays a central role. Who else would have the nerve to fly a plane gleefully without knowing how? From Stubel's room, Corbaccio and Rusty packed in one trunk and Kornblow and Beatrice in another are jostled and bounced in a truck toward an airplane waiting to make a getaway in the desert. The cohorts escape, however, as Annette and Pierre have from the police after trying to convince them that Stubel is the villain. They pick up Kornblow, Corbaccio, and Rusty in a car to try to prevent the getaway. The Nazis' truck makes it to the plane, and the Marxes, Annette, and Pierre are left in a cloud of dust. But with Pierre's help they pirate the truck and, driving alongside the plane as it taxis, they use a ladder as a bridge to enter it. Although both the plane and the truck are moving, they climb into the plane one by one, though Kornblow is left hanging upside down on the ladder for a while. By this time, Beatrice has changed sides and is now their ally.

They take over the plane, Rusty knocking out the pilot Emile and seizing the controls. When the plane is off the ground, they revive the Emile, his French name a reference to the Vichy government with its Nazi collaborators. And this reminds us, as does Rusty's harp solo, that there is good and bad, in this case bad, amongst all. But Rusty knocks Emile out again, then flies the plane with wild and naïve enthusiasm, taxiing in circles, then lifting off from the ground. Rusty honks his horn at the police and Stubel following them below.

He even flies "no hands," which causes him to crash the plane into the Casablanca jail, "home again." But consider this: If you are trickster, and you are allowed to take down one building, you might well choose the jail, symbol of authority and sometimes oppression. The demolition of the jail that once held the innocent Pierre and Annette amounts to another of Rusty's accidental accomplishments in the film.

The final scene offers one last fight with Stubel wherein he is stripped of his disguise, the toupee, and his identifying scar is revealed. Following Stubel's arrest, Rusty is wearing a fake beard and so is Kornblow: There was apparently enough toupee to go twice around. As in other Marx Brothers films, the sweethearts, Annette and Pierre, are united, but as in *Horse Feathers,* a film that lacked the schmaltzy romantic uplift of triumphant sweethearts, *A Night in Casablanca* also suggests a polyandrous denouement, or mating at least. For at the very end Harpo joins Groucho and Chico as they chase Beatrice out of the shot.

13

Love Happy (1949)
TRICKSTER'S CAPSTONE
OR HAIL AND FAREWELL

"One day long ago, it came into his mind to dance with a star."
— Erdoes and Ortiz, *American Indian Myths and Legends*[1]

Arthur Marx wrote *Love Happy* for Harpo's character to be the center of the film. It wasn't even intended to be a Marx Brothers film but it become one. In it, Harpo coalesces, comments on, and in some ways transcends his trickster nature. Harpo gives to airy nothing a local habitation and a name: His name is Harpo in the film, and for the first time he is not a picaresque wanderer but lives in an actual home that we get to see the inside of. Chico, ever the Italian immigrant, is Faustino, and Groucho is Detective Sam Grunion but without greasepaint eyebrows and mustache — he too is more himself. Harpo's magic, trickster's in essence, permeates this last Marx Brothers film. He flips over a mirror to see the back of his head, and in the rooftop chase scene, his magic is strangely mixed with corporate symbols. Because of this scene in their last film, Harpo seems to say in parting that trickster nature can and must be at play with the commercial world, a message particularly relevant today when corporate interests dominate both politics and entertainment. If a film is a dream that we dream collectively, and like a dream, offers escape from ordinary life, then films, like art itself, must also be places where we process experience and heal. *Love Happy* tries to make this happen.

Harpo appears after Groucho's Sam Grunion narrates an exposition of the plot, telling us that it will tell a tale of stolen jewels against the backdrop of talented and devoted performers preparing a show without adequate financial backing. The latter sounds like the premise of *Room Service*. And this

159

film, like *A Night in Casablanca,* is full of such allusions, not only to other Marx Brothers films but also to a few iconic films as well, especially to *The Maltese Falcon* (1941). Here again, trickster Harpo and his cohort Chico — Groucho stands off to the side in this film, uninvolved in much of the action and therefore not really a trickster cohort — are on the side of underappreciated and underfunded art as well as struggling love, for the romance blooming between Maggie Phillips and Mike Johnson, the stars of the show, can thrive only if the show itself is able to.

Nurturing young love may be a standard plot element in most Marx Brothers films, but this time the staple of the plot has a twist: Harpo also loves Maggie. He is not beyond human vulnerability though Maggie mistakenly thinks he is, saying, "You live alone; you don't need other people; you don't depend upon them; you never get hurt." We see, on the other hand, that his heart *is* snared. Nevertheless, he loves Maggie unselfishly, and the quality of his devotion is one way that he transcends his trickster nature.

In *Love Happy,* Groucho isn't involved with Harpo and Chico's efforts to fund the production and serve the dual causes of art and love. Nor does he interact with Harpo until the rooftop scene. He is instead to some degree Groucho himself, on his way to his role in *You Bet Your Life,* detached from and ironically commenting on much of the mayhem. Chico as Faustino is, however, Harpo's cohort, so close, in fact, that he is able to read Harpo's mind, which amounts to an interesting riff on Chico as the usual translator of Harpo's mimes. Here Chico goes straight to the source.

But we don't learn about Chico's access to Harpo's mind until after Harpo's first appearance, one that showcases his ability to steal, a trickster proclivity that runs through all of the Marx Brothers films in varying degrees of importance but is here given its own extended *tour de force* scene. In this film, stealing is again depicted as a skill central to Harpo's persona. We first see Harpo from behind, looking like a tramp in his big coat and gazing as if he is hungry into the windows of a delicatessen that is also, Grunion tells us, a front for diamond thieves. Harpo helps customers leaving the deli by carrying their groceries to their cars, first an elderly gentleman whose cigar Harpo lights with a flaming flower in his lapel, again proffering fire. Then he helps an older woman carrying a little dog. While he assists these apparently wealthy people, he helps himself to their food. Yet this isn't just petty pilfering; soon we understand the necessity and benevolence of his thefts, Robin Hood's in nature, for he is feeding the unfunded production's entire cast and crew. He is, in fact, a kind of one-man craft services: The performers and crew would starve if it weren't for his efforts. Only the little dog in Harpo's first scene seems to be wise to his pilfering and barks ferociously until Harpo throws him a Gookie and he dives under his mistress' wrap for cover.

As usual in the films, the police are symbols of order and authority though not necessarily justice, except when trickster educates and illuminates them, like he does Detective Hennessey in *The Cocoanuts*. The *Love Happy* cops are suspicious of Harpo. When one appears in his first scene, the grocery-pilfering Harpo hides by riding the street level elevator down to the delicatessen storeroom behind the men who are delivering the latest shipment of "sardines," their code word for "stolen jewels." The energy in this scene is divided between the proprietor Throckmorton's searching for the can with the Maltese cross signifying that it is the can with the stolen Romanoff necklace inside—this begins the allusion to *The Maltese Falcon*—and Harpo's comic stealing, essentially a choreographed performance in which he catches rejected cans as Throckmorton tosses them in fast motion, sometimes with his hands and sometimes with the huge inside pockets of his coat, while between catches he loads those pockets with sacks of rice and flour. He even uses a grabbing tool to raid high shelves unseen. The gang is so intent on finding the can with the Maltese cross that they don't notice Harpo's audacious stealing. But we do.

Throckmorton eventually finds the can with the Maltese cross, introducing a pattern of irony that will run through the film. The irony is that Harpo, who couldn't care less about it and is ignorant of its contents, ends up with it even though the crooks are desperate to possess it. Ironically, he swaps it from Throckmorton's pocket without his knowing. Ironically, he is trading it for his own ordinary can because he doesn't like its smell. And ironically, he kisses the can, having seen Throckmorton kiss the can with the cross on it although he doesn't know why, in a sort of monkey-see, monkey-do gesture. Moreover, during the course of the film, Harpo, ironically, tries several times to give the can away: to Chico, to an actor, and to Maggie. Then Maggie tries to give it to her beau Mike. But each time it is, ironically, rejected. Finally, in a fit of pique because the show is going under, Mike tosses it, half opened, into the trash. Only the cat seems interested in its contents, so Maggie's friend Bunny takes the trash and the cat out to the alley where the cat continues to slurp up the sardines, leaving the jewels.

Harpo continues stealing from the delicatessen storeroom, escapes on the elevator to the street right behind a policeman's back, then sneaks past two cops discussing his bushy hair and the one thousand dollar reward for his capture, evidence that Throckmorton, having realized that the can with the jewels is gone, has reported Harpo's presence in the storeroom to the police. Madame Egelichi is ringleader of the smuggling operation, and her

devotion to pursuing the necklace has all the monomania of Sidney Green-
street's pursuit of the statue in *The Maltese Falcon*. She is angry over the loss
of the can with the Maltese cross, so orders the Zoto brothers to torture
Throckmorton. This provides an echo of the sado-masochistic inclinations
of Stubel and Kurt in *A Night in Casablanca* even while foreshadowing the
tortures Harpo endures later in the film, heroically or foolishly, it's hard to
know which, at her command.

We can tell that Faustino has a prior connection to Harpo when he appears
for the first time in the rehearsal scene. The motif of their shared history in
the films is taken further: Instead of translating Harpo's mimes, he knows
Harpo so well he reads his mind directly and instantly. Given Harpo's tendency
to overhear dire plots, and his subsequent need to enact arduous mimes to
warn others in prior films, Faustino's talent could, not that it will, prove easier
on them and us too. Harpo is already involved in the stage production as its
volunteer purveyor of food, and furthermore he is sweet on Maggie. Faustino
is only now trying to join the production crew, hoping to sell his dubious
new-age talents to Mike Johnson, Maggie's beau and the show's director.

The famished cast and crew stampede Harpo to get at the food he has
scavenged for them. They leave him curled against a wall, though he revives
enough to feed a string of sausages into the nose hole of a bull, actually two
men in costume, and to offer a ham to an intensely hammy actor, thereby
simultaneously critiquing and punning as well as nurturing. Then he sets a
magic table for Maggie by unfurling a tablecloth with silverware and dishes
attached. Reading Harpo's mind, Faustino reveals his crush on Maggie but
rejects the sardines, accepting instead a "tutsi-frutsi" ice cream cone from the
pocket of Harpo's coat. And it must be a freezer pocket, for the cone is a suspiciously frozen allusion to the tutsi-frutsi-ing Chico gave Groucho in *A Day
at the Races*.

Although silent, Harpo participates in the rehearsal of a musical number,
a song called "Who Stole That Jam" in which he is the prime suspect. He
quivers during the interrogation, and no wonder: The female vocalist has
spanked her doll-children on the basis of no evidence. So when the singer
insists that he "talk," he runs out of the theater, her command foreshadowing
Madame Egelichi's more extreme desires to coax words from the mute Harpo,
two meta-gags on the intransigent silence of his film persona and slightly
reminiscent of the police interrogation Harpo manages to pass in *A Night in
Casablanca*. Pursued by a cop, he hides in the empty theater, but like a Mudhead, that particularly clumsy American Indian trickster, he knocks down
the back row of seats, causing a noisy collapse of all the seats in the theater,
row by row like dominos.

So Harpo is apprehended and brought to Madame Egelichi and Throckmorton to be identified. To learn if he is in possession of the valuable can marked with the Maltese cross, Egelichi has powers at her disposal: both her "whammy," a sexy form of hypnosis, and the tortures meted out by her thugs, the Zoto brothers. But these pragmatics are ultimately useless against Harpo's chaotic, foolishly fearless, and intransigently mute character.

The search of Harpo's pockets, something viewers too have felt an urge to do, dominates the first part of the scene in Madame Egelichi's apartment. After Throckmorton recognizes him, the Zoto brothers, lead by Alphonse Zoto (played by Raymond Burr), begin this slow, methodical search, removing a seemingly endless and meta-cinematic assortment of items from the pockets of his coat, some from former Marx Brothers films, like the block of ice from *Horse Feathers* and the wooden leg from *Monkey Business*, and some artifacts from iconic films, like a sled alluding to Rosebud from *Citizen Kane* (1941). They search without flair, slowly and doggedly, no pun intended even though they do remove a full-grown dog from one of Harpo's deep pockets and it trots away. They also discover a music box, a welcome mat, a mailbox, an inner tube, and two mannequin legs, strangely inert simulacra of Harpo's own alive and swinging leg offered to strangers or familiars, especially in the Paramount films. This particular appearance of the inanimate leg isn't quite enough: We'll see it again. The Zotos even find a can of sardines in his pocket, but without the Maltese cross.

Harpo is susceptible, like trickster, to the allure of female sexuality, so when the aggravated Madame Egelichi gives Harpo "the whammy," a hypnotic state induced by her seductive stares and gestures, Harpo's mouth goes slack and he leans toward her in defiance of gravity, his arms dangling and flopping against her, a bit like his deep backwards leaning due to the spell cast on him in *At the Circus*. But Egelichi cannot get him to talk. Her ignorance that he is mute results in more dramatic irony. And maybe Harpo's audience, hungry to hear his voice after all these years, feels a tad sympathetic to efforts to make him speak.

Madame Egelichi says, "This creature won't talk; there are ways of making him talk," not knowing that there are not, that the character cannot speak because the man playing him is deeply committed to the silence of his persona. So the humor of futility arises from the hyperbolic tortures she orders. He withstands them all, heroic in his defiance, or foolish, or lacking options since he can't talk, or intransigent like trickster: All reflect his ungovernable nature. Egelichi has him slapped; he slaps back — monkey-see, monkey-do again — but he can't or won't explain. She follows this with various hyperbolic tortures but still fails to make him talk.

First he suffers the Hungarian rope torture: being forced to smoke a rope — a pun, perhaps, on smoking marijuana, since both are hemp — for six hours and looking ill, at the point of a knife wielded by a sadistically amused Alphonse Zoto. Then Harpo spends four hours on a spinning rack, not fun for him like the roulette wheel is in *A Night in Casablanca.* The scene is intercut with Madame Egelichi's memorable pacing in platform heels. Next Harpo spends eight hours in a pressure washing machine: We see his face in the round window, turning with confusion in the water, then Alphonse Zoto waiting while a flattened horn honks through the wringer, followed by a flattened hat, metonymic signs that a wrung-out Harpo will emerge next. Then Harpo endures Madame Egelichi's food and water torture: water dripping on the head of a bound Harpo, whose stomach is making cat sounds for he hasn't eaten for days nor slept for a week.

During his last torture, the Apple Test, Harpo, mad with hunger, grabs the apple and eats it, just as he also munched on an apple, though without desperation, while fencing with Kurt in *A Night in Casablanca.* An apple is placed on his head while one of the Zotos fires a gun at it. Then Harpo grabs the gun and points it at his own head: William Tell indeed. He seems brave, with the same imperviousness to mortal danger that we've seen in other films that may also be explained by foolishness, or in this case being driven by intense hunger. Here the gun behaves as his ally, for it doesn't shoot bullets when he pulls the trigger several times with it pointed at his own head. But it does fire inexplicably, or as a result of his trickster luck, when he shoots into the room. In this last test, his gestures proclaim that he'd rather be dead than speak.

Harpo is thrown into a room, still eating that little apple with the ravenousness of a man in the throes of starvation, while back at the theater, Faustino is trying to butter up Lyons to keep him from repossessing the costumes and sets. He does this by getting Lyons to play a duet with him, "Gypsy Love Song," Faustino on the piano and Lyons on the violin. It is delightful for us, but the ploy fails. Lyons shows that he lacks an artist's heart, in spite of his musical tears, by resuming his efforts to repossess the sets and costumes when they finish playing. This scene is intercut with Harpo, still Egelichi's prisoner and desperate to communicate with Faustino, calling him at the theater on a telephone that happens to be in the room he is locked in. And his timing is serendipitous: His phone call stops the repossession from going forward.

Love Happy isn't the first Marx Brothers film to pair Harpo with a telephone, always an absurd and amusing juxtaposition given his muteness. Telephone gags begin in *The Cocoanuts* and occur in subsequent films. Harpo tries to eat telephones, tries to throw one at Groucho, gambles on telephones, and carries on non-verbal conversations on telephones in *Horse Feathers, Duck Soup* and *A Night in Casablanca*. But in this scene locked in a room, the tortured and disheveled Harpo, who seems none the worse for wear except for his wet hair, actually has a telephone conversation with Faustino.

How? By sticking the mouthpiece onto his forehead so his thoughts can travel through the wires to Faustino, with horn honks, foot stomps, and whistles facilitating Faustino's ability to read Harpo's mind, more or less. And it may be less, for there is a good deal of nonsense in Faustino's understanding of the conversation. He is only a little better than we are at reading Harpo's mind, for he "hears" that Harpo is at a party, which goes well beyond euphemism, that the guests are throwing apples at him (he got the apple but otherwise is not even close), and that a woman is in love with him for his sardines (close again but no cigar). Yet Faustino is patient; he is willing to work to get it right. At one point he even tells Harpo, "Clear your head," so Harpo pulls a handkerchief through one ear and out the other, scrubbing back and forth like a yogi.

Yet Faustino intuits enough of the truth of Harpo's situation, which does indeed involve a gathering, an apple, a can of sardines, and Madame Egelichi's passion, for felicitous events to unfold. For example, Faustino thinks Madame Egelichi will save the show with her wealth, so he tells Harpo to bring her to the Winter Theatre where there are lots of sardines and a show that needs saving. Though this is utterly skewed, Egelichi does end up backing the show in hopes of finding the jewels she covets. For without scenery and costumes, Mike Johnson has refused to let the show go on, even though Maggie and others in the cast want it to open with nothing but their raw talent. Mike insists, "Life isn't a fairy tale," when ironically, Madame Egelichi saves the day, arriving in search of the jewels but attempting to disguise her crime by offering to back the show, a fairy godmother in spite of her villainy, just as, reversing the benevolence quotient, Harpo, in spite of being a thief, is kind and generous. In trickster's world, ethical outcomes can be as flexible as knee joints.

The scene in which Mike throws the Maltese cross sardine can in the trash, argues with Maggie, and leaves with Egelichi is intercut with Harpo's escape from the room where the Zotos have locked him. His doing so recalls his and Chico's escape in *Horse Feathers,* but this time he escapes more magically: with a parachute made from the drapes and their rope pulls. In defiance of gravity, he drifts slowly and safely down. Then, intercut with Madame Egelichi and her thugs' opening can after can of sardines searching for the jewels, Harpo finds Maggie's cat in the theater alley eating sardines from the can full of jewels: more serendipitous trickster luck.

Harpo still doesn't know these are the valuable stolen Romanoff jewels, he doesn't even know there are such things, but he sees their beauty so gives the cat a different can of sardines and takes the necklace. Only after this does Throckmorton find the empty can with the Maltese cross, the cat near it licking its chops. Weighing the evidence, he concludes that the jewels are inside the cat. Faustino adds to the confusion, bringing Egelichi a can of anchovies because, according to his Italian immigrant's cultural bias, they're "better than sardines."

Meanwhile, with the gift of the necklace in his pocket, Harpo spiffs up magically for Maggie. He combs the front of his hair while looking at his face in the mirror, then turns the mirror over to see the hair on the back of his head. To make sure we get the surreal gag, he repeats it. He's in fine spirits for someone who has just endured days of torture. But when he goes to Maggie's room and she weeps against him, he wears that expression of helpless dismay we saw in *The Cocoanuts* and in *Go West*.

In the park, Maggie says she envies him because he lives alone and, she thinks, doesn't need other people. But his expression suggests that is not necessarily so. Maggie feels jilted by Mike Johnson, so Harpo clowns around, trying to cheer her up. First he pretends to remove, juggle, and polish his eyes, then put them back into their sockets. But he puts them back on the wrong sides so his eyes are crossed and he must remove them, polish them, and switch them back. We get a close-up of a happy Harpo rolling his eyes around to prove his success. His eyeball trick is stunningly similar to several that turn up in American Indian trickster tales in which trickster learns to remove and retrieve his eyes, even juggle them, but he usually goes too far, loses his eyes and ends up with other creatures' mismatched eyes.[2,3]

A comic sketch based on eyes is particularly relevant because we are made more aware of eyes in *Love Happy*, especially Harpo's and Chico's, due to the film's frequent and sometimes lingering close-ups, more of these than in prior Marx Brothers films. In this scene Maggie describes a brave fantasy of solo Broadway success, without Mike but with Harpo as her agent, just the two of them. While she describes their life, Harpo mimes the entire scenario, using the garbage can and its lid as props to suggest the desk in the office, and he pretends to smoke cigars and even to make phone calls on multiple phones, mouthing unspoken words. But by the end of it, Maggie breaks down, telling Harpo it is her birthday and that she loves Mike Johnson.

Here we see the beginning of some transcendence of Harpo's trickster nature. He has an actual home instead of being a wanderer. And though he continues to cast his lot with the marginalized, and retains a fun-loving nature, we haven't seen him quite as willing until now to set his own needs aside.

To amuse Maggie, Harpo (Harpo Marx) takes out his eyes and juggles them, a trick that American Indian tricksters push too far. *Love Happy,* United Artists, 1949.

Harpo hurries off to fetch his harp to serenade Maggie. This is the first time we get to see where he lives in the films, for he almost always arrives from elsewhere and sometimes wanders off again once he has finished cleansing institutions, values, and cultures.

In *Love Happy* Harpo has his own little dwelling, as does trickster in the periphery of many of the tales once he decides he has had enough of his own shenanigans and goes home. Harpo's home is carved out of nature in the side of a hill in Central Park, a treehouse kind of dwelling with a heart-shaped lock on the door, Harpo's external heart, and furnished with seemingly stolen or scavenged items: a water cooler, beads, and a chandelier. He unlocks the padlock with help from a flashlight with a candle flame. He has an animal friend living there too, a penguin, his doppelgänger.

Why not a duck? We might well ask, and the answer is because this one isn't Groucho or Chico's double but clearly Harpo's, standing on a table wearing a trenchcoat, a crushed top hat, a plaid shirt and patterned tie, all just like Harpo's. The penguin is truly a vision reminding us of the conflation of human and animal in trickster's world, though Harpo's penguin double is as talkative as Harpo is silent, gibbering nonstop. In fact, the penguin doesn't stop talking until Harpo "plays" him a drink of water from his cooler (released by the playing of musical notes on its trombone apparatus). Then Harpo strips his bed to retrieve the harp that doubles as his bedsprings, suggesting that in addition to musical water, Harpo has musical sleep.

He returns to Maggie and plays a movingly shot harp solo. The camera is angled low; we see him behind the strings. Then it shifts to a level side view of Harpo playing "Happy Birthday," then offering Maggie his hand with fingers lit like candles, a gag multiplied beyond its inception in *A Night in Casablanca*. After she blows out the flames, he gives her the Romanoff necklace. She is as oblivious as he is as to the worth of this gift. She says this was her best birthday ever, then weeps. He begins playing "Sewanee," and is so intent on the harp that he does not notice that Maggie's departure until he finishes playing the piece. His face registers surprise.

The Romanoff jewels become the focus of the next scene whose chaos is intensified by the way Harpo makes sure that fake and real remain confused. The rooftop chase scene leaves us with an indelible impression of Harpo's magic and playfulness, and for the first time in the films incorporates, no pun intended though it is apt, what would now be called product placement in film. First, though, Harpo is absent from the film during an interlude in which a young and stunningly beautiful Marilyn Monroe has a short walk-on part. She is seeking the detective Grunion's help because, she says, "men are following me," at the very moment, ironically, that Groucho's own life is being threatened by the Romanoff family's hired thug.

Harpo's absence from this scene is worth noting, for it seems ironic that after chasing so many blondes through the films, he is not there to pursue the quintessence of all beautiful blondes. Yet somehow this seems fitting. First, who knew that Marilyn Monroe would become such an icon? Hers is a small part in a small scene, and she isn't as blonde as she would become. Second, chasing her would undercut Harpo's unique characterization in this film, for he loves Maggie and does not lust indiscriminately after women. Third, and this is after the fact and more about us than Harpo and Marilyn: It is uncomfortable when myths collide. The iconic stature of Harpo Marx combined with the iconic stature of Marilyn Monroe in one scene could cause an icon overdose. Their unique essences are, time has told, too huge to accommodate one another lightly, and the scene with Groucho calls for lightness.

Harpo, as repository of the necklace, at least until he gives it to Maggie, is at the center of the upcoming chase. And what a chase it turns out to be! Harpo and his cohort Faustino have almost succeeded in resolving the major problems. The musical show is opening thanks to Madam Egelichi's backing, and Maggie and Mike's romance is renewed. The necklace, however, poses a threat to Maggie's life, and Harpo is instrumental in both precipitating the danger and saving her from it. Throckmorton's x-rays of the cat reveal no jewels in its gut, but Egelichi's thugs spy Maggie through a window wearing the necklace, in spite of Mike's advice, an ironic and possibly meta-cinematic comment that she should not wear it because the jewels look fake. But when he distracts her with a proposal, embrace, and kiss, the necklace slips from her hand and under the open lid of the grand piano.

Harpo brings a garland of flowers for Maggie. The horseshoe prints on his bum tell us that he fought a winning horse for them. Was it High Hat? But he overhears the Zotos trying to kidnap her and, like in *Animal Crackers, A Day at the Races,* and *A Night in Casablanca,* he has to communicate the danger to Faustino. In a complicated mime involving gestures for "great Dane" and "jaw" for "danger," "mat" and "key" for "Maggie," "eagle" and "itchy" for "Egelichi," and racehorse "mudder" for "murder," Harpo manages to let Faustino know that Egelichi plans to murder Maggie. Telling Faustino is an exhausting effort. Too bad Faustino didn't just read his mind. But Harpo saves Maggie, cast member Bunny, and Mike from the thugs, and thus he saves the show, by seizing another opportunity chance offers: fake jewels on the costume of a passing showgirl's bum. He steals them and dangles them before the thugs, using his feet against the door to trap, then lure them to the roof.

This begins the rooftop chase scene that showcases Harpo's magic. It is a scene that plays with the contrast between the real and fake necklace as well as light and dark, for it is nighttime, but neon billboards intermittently illuminate the roof. When they blink on, the chase proceeds with clarity. But when they blink off, as they often do, Harpo uses the darkness to foil the thugs, whacking them on the head with a metal rudder, tying them to a pole, etc. Harpo enacts much magic on the roof, climbing a statue of the Baby Ruth boy, yawning with him and blowing out his electric torch (which makes only surreal sense), riding lights around the Wheaties billboard even though their rotation is an illusion, and, most memorably, climbing onto the Mobil Oil horse and galloping diagonally up, down, and across the billboard. He swings on the pendulum of the Bulova watch billboard, knocking his pursuers down, then sails through the air, remaining airborne longer than a normal human being could though not trickster, and lands squarely in the mouth of the penguin blowing smoke on the Kool cigarettes billboard. When it swallows him, the Penguin's eyes roll around like Harpo's did when he reinserted his juggled eyes. This is product placement, yes, but product placement dipped in the ambiance of dreams.

Harpo Marx hides in the Kool penguin, conflating the commercial world with the dream world he carries with him. *Love Happy,* United Artists, 1949. Photofest.

    Harpo emerges from the penguin — what a tale he'll have to tell his penguin doppelgänger back home — staggering from saturation in smoke. Then he uses the smoke cloud that clings to him to hide from the thugs. He backs close to the edge of the roof, then overwhelms the Zotos and Throckmorton by blowing smoke at them. So full of Kool penguin smoke is he that, like the steam engine in *Go West,* smoke billows from both of his ears and mouth when he pumps his arms. He is manic with glee over temporarily overcoming them, until he is sucked into an air vent and cleansed of smoke.

Before Harpo lands inside the smoking Penguin and intercut with the rooftop chase, Faustino, banging out chords in his piano solo in the show, inadvertently makes the necklace Maggie dropped inside the piano leap. Madame Egelichi sees it through her lorgnette, and he sees her see it. So as soon as he finishes his number, he absconds with the necklace to the roof. Now there are two necklaces involved in the chase, and three Marxes, for Grunion, wearing a Sherlock Holmes hat — maybe Harpo's from *Duck Soup* and *A Day and the Races* — has also come up there in pursuit of the necklace, perhaps having made a deal with the Romanoffs' hired thug to save his own life. Madame Egelichi comes to the roof too.

Harpo's fake and Faustino's real jewels get mixed up when they collide. Then, bedazzled by the appearance of Madame Egelichi in front of the General Electric neon sun that renders her clothes transparent, Faustino hands her the necklace. But now we don't know whether it is the real or the fake one. Meanwhile, Harpo swings on a rope and is chased up a pole by the Zotos and Throckmorton. In a moment of darkness, Harpo ends up under them on the pole — who knows how? — and lights their bums with the flame from his flower lapel, then braids them to the pole with lengths of rope as if it were May Day. When he finishes, he chops at the pole until they twang and vibrate.

Always musically inclined, Harpo plays a quick tune on the steam pipes on the roof, then plants the jewels, the real ones, perhaps, on Grunion after Madame Egelichi says she would kill for them. He also offers her a leg, not his own but the mannequin leg from the deep pockets of his coat, as if he wants to deny her insight into the power of the hinge. Madame Egelichi picks Groucho's pocket for the jewels while pretending to embrace him, but as they walk away, Harpo grabs them back with the hinged grabbing tool he stole with in the delicatessen scene. And off he skips with the jewels, possibly the real ones.

While Grunion marries to Madame Egelichi and Faustino ends up working for him (or rather, it seems, passing time playing poker with a dog and getting beaten, an amusing allusion to those Coolidge dogs-playing-poker paintings), Harpo's fate isn't as clearly resolved. But that too is consistent with his trickster persona, no matter how much he has learned or matured. We see Harpo last on the rooftop, dancing away like a happy clown close to the neon lights and those other lights, the stars. He doesn't care whether he has the fake or the real jewels for he has one or the other and he never knew the difference anyway. Like trickster, he may have a penchant for stealing, but he is neither mercenary nor greedy. He is reminiscent of another great clown of American cinema in this exit on this urban rooftop amid the neon signs of commerce, alone and heading, we presume, to his little house in a hill in the park.

In *Love Happy*, Harpo has deconstructed neither a lofty institution nor gods on high, unless we count the smugglers and Egelichi as gods with the brute force of the powerful. But in other ways he has done trickster's work: He has stolen with élan and assisted the underdogs — the cast and crew of the musical show, including its lovers. And he has revealed secrets about himself: where he lives and, like the heart-shaped padlock on his house, some of his own heart. He has also played a stringed instrument and some pipes and, most significantly in this film, he has sifted his surreal magic with creations of the commercial world.

He has, in other words, infiltrated the territory of the gods on high who reign today, has penetrated their symbols, found whimsy in them, and mined them for mischief. He has abided in a giant penguin and ridden a flying horse, a Pegasus no less, friend of poets. And the impression of this strange comingling cannot be easily forgotten, mixed as it is with the stuff of dreams.

Conclusion
A Retrospective Montage

"A society without a trickster ossifies into stagnation, death, and doom, while cultures that accept him can continue to change and grow."

— Voth, *Myth in Human History*[1]

In 1933, on his way to the Soviet Union, having been invited there to perform, and while he was at it to deliver a secret message for the U.S. government, Harpo traveled through Germany. He says he "had planned to sort of mosey through Germany and see the sights." Instead he "got across Germany as fast as [he] could go." Why? As he tells it, "I saw the most frightening, most depressing sight I had ever seen — a row of stores with Stars of David and the word '*Jude*' painted on them, and inside, behind half-empty counters, people in a daze, cringing like they didn't know what hit them and didn't know where the next blow would come from. Hitler had been in power only six months, and his boycott was already in full effect. I hadn't been so wholly conscious of being a Jew since my *bar mitzvah*. It was the first time since I'd had the measles that I was too sick to eat."[2]

These are worlds colliding: the magical, mischievous, amusing, and quasi-divine world of Harpo carrying within him trickster on his way to entertain the Russians as envoy of that world, and the grim and heartless world from which the trickster spirit is banished. How uncanny to imagine the Harpo we know in the films stopping in a place so weighted unto death, and skittering so close to a fate that under different circumstances, given his German-Jewish ancestry, might have ensnared him.

When Harpo passes through Germany at the beginning of the horrors of the Reich, the levity and circuitously comic and triumphant spirit that cal-

ibrates cultures collides with a powerful force in the real and tragic world of
history. It is as if the world of dreams (surreal, wild, and full of possibility)
were in a head-on collision with the waking world in its worst nightmare
mode. Harpo floats through Germany, a stunned and powerless witness, something like a messenger of a God who sees but doesn't meddle in human affairs,
except, that is, to offer to humankind uproarious talent and the gifts of the
imagination to fight fascism in all its manifestations. And let's not dwell only
on Nazis because countries are incessantly producing fascist-leaning permu-
tations, including our own. The trickster spirit is a corrective, healing by
challenging power and authority, refreshing and realigning values and institutions by means of life-affirming mischief, and making us well by making
us laugh.

The following retrospective montage offers a composite view of how
Harpo, in his incarnation as the archetypal trickster, accomplishes that benefi-
cial effect. In reviewing what he signifies and how he does it, in summarizing
why we laugh at him, why we love him, and why he seems divine, we see
Harpo's trickster persona emerge as a counterforce to humanity's tendency
to turn against itself. And let's begin this ending with Harpo's angelic nature,
his connection to the divine aspect of trickster.

Harpo's Divine Nature

"Between worlds ... in a world of his own: a symbol of divine qualities which transcend mere trickery"
— Radin, *The Trickster*[3]

Each of the Marx Brothers films offers time and space for trickster to
cavort in. Merry and silly as the films often are, each contains sacred content.
Sparks ignite from the friction of Harpo's touch upon characters and events
in each film.

For example, Harpo raises awareness of talent that deserves recognition,
kudos, and support, whether that talent involves architecture, art, music, or
theater. This happens in *The Cocoanuts, Animal Crackers, Room Service, A
Night at the Opera,* and *Love Happy.* He makes us cognizant of the human
heart's capacity to love in almost every film via its sweetheart subplot and
occasionally in the depiction of filial devotion, like in *Monkey Business* and
Go West. And he heightens our awareness of the perils of nationalism and war
fever via his zany contributions to *Duck Soup.* Harpo helps us learn to recognize the destructiveness of greed in *The Cocoanuts, A Day at the Races, At
the Circus, Go West, The Big Store,* and *A Night in Casablanca.* And he helps

us learn to appreciate art's origins in the lives of the masses in *A Night at the Opera, A Day at the Races,* and *At the Circus.* Finally, he exposes us to the dignity of workers and the beauty of human diversity in *The Big Store, A Day at the Races* and *At the Circus.*

It goes without saying that each film's harp solo connects Harpo to the divine by making him resemble an angel. He even drops a feather from invisible wings in *A Night in Casablanca.* It's perhaps a warped syllogism to say that angels play harps, Harpo plays a harp, therefore Harpo is an angel, but if he isn't exactly an angel, at least we can agree that his harp solos elevate the tone of the films along with Harpo's status in them. For he is often a bum with a smashed top hat who performs some sort of lowly job or merely steals. But when he plays the harp, he awes others; they are swept up in both his reverence for the instrument and in the music he liberates from its strings. In addition, he draws out music from others, like the Indian chief who accompanies him on flute in *Go West* and the chorus that sings as he plays in *At the Circus.* Divided lovers or the marginalized forget their troubles while he plays the harp. And playing, Harpo sheds negative epithets hurled at him, like "bum" or "riff raff" even while he elevates sensibilities and liberates others, including the audience, from their cares.

To acknowledge the divine in Harpo's persona, viewers learn to exercise negative capability, acknowledging his contradictions while accepting his inconsistencies, for in truth he misbehaves in many ways, from destroying mail to stealing the silverware to sneezing a room into disarray. Yet in spite of his misbehavior, a sacred quality clings to him, Hyde's "paradoxical quality of sacred amorality,"[4] due in part to his vow of silence. And being a buffoon does not disqualify him from partaking of the sacred either. So what if he is foolish? The holy fool is an old and related archetype. Radin reminds us that "laughter and belief in the divinity of the laughed-at are not mutually exclusive."[5]

Finally, like trickster of myth, Harpo's character evolves as he goes along in the thirteen Marx Brothers films. By the time we get to the last film, *Love Happy,* Harpo loves selflessly, and his mischief is done solely in the service of others.

Harpo's Hunger

> "And he began to eat with them, and eat more than they."
> — Koén-Serano, *Folktales of Joha: Jewish Trickster*[6]

In many Marx Brothers films, Harpo exhibits a hyperbolic hunger for food. Like trickster of myth and like most of us, he is often seeking his next

Harpo and his cohorts stow away as kippered herrings, a fishy ruse, and while he's at it, Harpo impersonates a female herring. Left to right: Harpo Marx as Harpo, Zeppo Marx as Zeppo, Chico Marx as Chico, and Groucho Marx as Groucho on a poster for a film billed as *The Stowaways*, consisting of scenes from *Monkey Business*.

meal. When he finds it, he often eats outlandish quantities, including, sometimes, non-food items. His voracious appetite is perhaps the first trickster trait Harpo manifests.

At the hotel in *The Cocoanuts,* the Marx Brothers' first film, Harpo eats a bellhop's buttons, then at the desk he consumes a blotter with paste and a buckwheat flower, and subsequently takes a bite out of the telephone and drinks the ink. In *Monkey Business* Harpo and his cohorts are identified with food because they are hiding in barrels labeled "kippered herring." In

Horse Feathers Harpo shares a bouquet of flowers and a bag of oats with his horse, and he drinks a lot of booze in the speakeasy, pouring a fifth into his own bottle with a bottomless shot glass that functions as a funnel. He also eats many bananas, one with a surreal zipper so he can save it for later, and he eats bananas and a hot dog while playing in the Huxley-Darwin football game, once even trying to substitute MacHardie's finger for his lost hot dog.

His capacity for eating intensifies in some of the films, most notably in *A Night at the Opera* when Groucho orders everything on the menu and adds numerous hard-boiled eggs multiplied by Harpo's honks in the stateroom scene, and when Harpo and his cohorts eat the opulent Italian dinner in steerage that is so generously offered. There are also those phallic salamis that Harpo and Chico exchange as gifts, Harpo taking a bite from the circumcised tip. In a later breakfast scene, he plays with most of the food on the table, eating pancakes along with a tie and a cup. In *A Day at the Races* Harpo continues to consume things that aren't food, munching on the thermometer. In *Love Happy,* he eats an apple ravenously, as he does in *A Night in Casablanca,* both while in peril.

Harpo becomes a veritable eating-machine in *Room Service,* whose very title focuses our attention on food. When Harpo and his starving cohorts finagle a meal, they all rush to the table, but only Harpo rhythmically stokes his mouth, taking food from others, his arm not ceasing its plate-to-mouth motion until all of the food is gone. And as soon as more appears, he is at it again, this time eating a sandwich, wax paper and all, and concluding with a banana from his pocket, an ironic indication that while the others were hungry, he had a private stash.

In *The Cocoanuts, Horse Feathers,* and *Go West,* Harpo's thirst is hyperbolic: in the former he is driven to the punch bowl by odious speechifying; in the latter he drinks from the horses' water trough, lights a match on his parched tongue, and intercepts mint juleps from women framing his cohorts. In *A Night in Casablanca,* Harpo is a guinea pig making sure Groucho's meal isn't poisoned, but he's really a goat, eating a candle, a cup and saucer, and salting the telephone.

The significant evolution of Harpo's relationship to hunger in *Love Happy* is worth noting: in this last film, Harpo's thefts consist almost entirely of food, not for himself but for the hungry cast and crew of the struggling musical production. He is, one could say, feeling voracious and stealing food on behalf of others.

Harpo's Lust and Harpo's Love of Love

> "An ageless and Priapus-like protagonist strutting across the scene, attempting, successfully and unsuccessfully, to gratify his uninhibited sexuality."
>
> — Radin, *The Trickster*[7]

Harpo chases blondes through many scenes in various films, sometimes pausing in the midst of other mischief to take off after women, though the women usually flee and he rarely catches up with them. He seems unable to control his impulse to chase women, perhaps because he doesn't have to worry about catching them. The urge is even powerful enough to awaken him from chloroform-induced sleep in *Animal Crackers* and to keep him groping women while he sleeps in the stateroom in *A Night at the Opera.*

Harpo enters *The Cocoanuts,* for example, on the heels of a woman. When he realizes that ringing the bell at the hotel desk will summon female bellhops, he rings and rings and rings until women fill the lobby, then he chases them as they scatter. In *Animal Crackers,* he pursues Mrs. Rittenhouse's female guests, revives from chloroform-induced sleep when a blonde passes by, and later strategically chloroforms himself so he can lie down next to her. In *Monkey Business*, although Harpo and his cohorts may be hiding in barrels labeled "kippered herrings," it is as a man and not as a fish that Harpo chases a blonde on a bicycle. Though he focuses on food and drink in *Horse Feathers*, Harpo pauses to flirt with the college widow Connie Baily, and in the end tackles her in a pile-up with her other grooms. While his blonde-chasing is pretty consistent in the films, Harpo actually ends up in bed with a woman, or at least in the bed next to hers, only in *Duck Soup*. And he misses the most iconic of blondes in *Love Happy.*

In spite of the emphasis on Harpo's lust, it is important to recognize that he approves of young love, watching sweethearts tenderly and assisting them when he can. Of all the films, only *Horse Feathers* and *Duck Soup* lack the sweethearts subplot: in *Horse Feathers,* Connie Baily draws all the men to her, and in *Duck Soup,* war usurps the ardor that might have stoked lovers, leaving enough only for trysts, like Harpo's on his Paul Revere ride. In most of the films, though, he sides with sweethearts and works to remove the barriers between them that are often caused by people in power who must overcome bias, or by crooks who need to get out of the way.

In *The Cocoanuts,* Bob has to gain recognition as an architect to be considered a worthy suitor of Polly. In *Animal Crackers,* John Parker has to prove his worth as an artist to marry Arabella Rittenhouse. (In both films, a snob of a mother stands between them.) In *Monkey Business,* Zeppo courts Mary, who is in danger from her father's gangster rivals. In *A Night at the Opera,* Ricardo and Rosa's love can flourish only when Ricardo's singing career thrives. In *Room Service,* Leo and Hilda's future plans depend upon the success of his play. In *A Day at the Races,* Gil and Judy must save the sanitarium to salvage their love; as a singer, Gil doesn't make *bubkas,* so he needs his racehorse High Hat to win big and bail them out. In *At the Circus,* Jeff and Julie can't wed unless the circus runs in the black. In *Go West,* Eve and Terry must heal their families' feud by selling her grandfather's property to the railroad. In *The Big Store,* Tommy and Joan's future, plus the music academy, are threatened by crooks. In *A Night in Casablanca,* Pierre and Annette are likewise endangered. And in *Love Happy,* the vicissitudes of Maggie and Mike's relationship are tied to those of the musical show. Harpo helps all of these young lovers' problems go away.

It is striking how often the union of young lovers is entangled with artistic expression and, second most often, criminal antagonists. Harpo joins the fight in support of art and against crooks. Ultimately, by implication, in serving love as in exhibiting lust, Harpo serves the procreant urge, which is trickster's natural tendency because it assures the continuation of life.

Harpo's Androgyny and Shape-Shifting

"It is often said that well-known tricksters are not male but androgynous."

— Lewis Hyde, *Trickster Makes This World*[8]

When one goes through the films with an eye to Harpo's cross-dressing, gender-bending, and shape-shifting, evidence of these abounds. Though he chases women in the films, Harpo also hugs and kisses men in bursts of affection, joy, and mischief. He also plays tricks predicated on gender confusion, he dresses in drag, and he impersonates women. His androgyny, a kind of shape-shifting, evokes trickster's physical inchoateness, as in early Winnebago trickster tales when he carries his external penis in a box and even sends it for a swim, or when he transforms himself into a woman, crafting female organs from meat, marrying the chief's son, bearing children, then suddenly dropping the pretense to return to his wife and original family.

Often Harpo's behavior develops the gender-bending theme. In *The Cocoanuts,* for example, the bellhop becomes part of a little drama almost too subtle to notice when Harpo offers the bellhop his leg, the same bellhop whose buttons he earlier ate, and they exit together. Harpo is next seen getting off the elevator and playing "When My Dreams Come True" on a clarinet; the bellhop now running the elevator, wears a satisfied expression but is unwilling to let Harpo back on the elevator with Penelope, instead taking her to her floor before returning for Harpo. He opens the elevator door Harpo is leaning on, making him fall in.

In *Duck Soup,* Harpo sits in Ambassador Trentino's chair and pulls him onto his lap. In *A Night at the Opera,* Harpo kisses both men and women on the departing ship with great vigor. In *Room Service,* Harpo lifts Leo's coat to make a pun, but he may also be checking out his bum. And in *At the Circus,* Harpo, told to act out the scene near Gibraltar's cage, kisses Chico and lays him down for more kisses, as if *acting* could refer only to love scenes. Finally, in *A Night in Casablanca,* Harpo, having won big at roulette, kisses a random man on the lips; we see the man in the corner of the frame, affronted and trying to wipe off Harpo's kiss.

In some films, Harpo plays tricks based on gender. In *Monkey Business,* he stands in front of the women's restroom, blocking the "WO" part of "WOMEN" so that an unpresuming male thinks he is entering the men's room and gets tossed out; only then does Harpo step aside to reveal the rest of the sign. At a party, Harpo emerges from a wreath meant for Mary. He also sneaks around disguised as a bustle, cleaving to women's bottoms while offering an interesting spin on cross-dressing because he's not *in* drag but is drag itself.

Often, though, the androgynous theme involves cross-dressing. In *Animal Crackers,* for example, Harpo concludes an anarchic game of bridge wearing, much to her surprise and ours, Mrs. Whitehead's shoes. Later, when his brothers are singing "Old Kentucky Home," he steps forward in what may be a woman's dress. In *A Night at the Opera,* Harpo tries on layers of costumes, and when Lassparri orders them off, Harpo strips down to the innermost layer, a female costume. Later in the film, Harpo and Chico infiltrate *Il Trovatore* dressed as female gypsies. In the stagecoach scene in *Go West,* Harpo creates mass confusion with hats, he himself ending up wearing Lulubelle's chiffon-draped hat and bustle. As a footnote to all this, Harpo emerges from Stubel's closet in *A Night in Casablanca* wearing a tiara like the one he stole with a magnet in *Go West,* though this one is presumably Stubel's.

Finally, the gender-bending theme is developed by Harpo's impersonations of women, and this goes beyond clothes to include gestures. In *A Night at the Opera* at breakfast in Groucho's hotel suite, Harpo imitates a woman making up her face like he did as a kippered herring, applying ketchup lipstick with his pinkie finger and sugar powder with a pancake. In the same scene, he plays the role of an old Gookie-faced crone doing needlework in a rocking chair. And in *A Night in Casablanca*, Harpo imitates Beatrice smoking a long cigarette from a cigarette holder, gazing back at her suspiciously through a lorgnette that matches hers.

In these ways Harpo interrogates the concept of gender, exhibiting trickster's malleable gender while also satirizing rigid sex-role divisions just as he satirizes other rigid notions about identity, even while having fun playing at being a woman.

Harpo's Animal Mates

> "He liked the stable, he did! There were horses here with nice long manes for him to braid."
>
> — Sherman, *Trickster Tales*[9]

In cultures all over the world, trickster is portrayed as an anthropomorphic version of various animals: coyote, hare, raven, fox, spider, or monkey, to name a few. Moreover, especially in American Indian mythology, human beings are not ranked above animals but share the world with them as siblings. And this is the very spirit that is manifested in Harpo's relationships with animals in the films. He does not claim dominion over animals, nor is he a shaman trying to draw powers from their spirits, but rather he is an animal, or a friend, a collaborator, and sometimes even a sweetheart.

While Harpo exhibits traits of various animal tricksters, he seems most closely associated with Rabbit or Great Hare, because he can evoke magic. He is likened to animals repeatedly in the films, like when he drinks from the horse's trough in *Go West,* when he tells Groucho he lives in a doghouse in *Duck Soup,* when he is a mad dog in *A Night in Casablanca,* and when he has a penguin double in *Love Happy.* Harpo's bond with animals is also a motif in the films, running the gamut from companion to beloved. The horse sweetheart, linking him to the lutin, a French trickster "particularly fond of horses,"[10] is a motif introduced in *Animal Crackers* by means of a photograph, developed to his actual canoodling with a horse in *Horse Feathers,* and culminating in his being in bed with a horse in *Duck Soup.* But it doesn't end there. In *A Day at the Races,* Harpo twice kisses High Hat, the kiss of a friend showing gratitude.

Harpo's connections to animals also extend beyond the four-legged nations. In *Monkey Business*, a frog abides under his hat. In *Room Service*, he poaches a turkey from a contest he is judging, intending it for food, but the turkey escapes though seems unable to leave Harpo, hovering near the window and ending up back inside. In *At the Circus,* Harpo is on amiable terms with the gorilla Gibraltar, but his special friends are the seal who coaches him at checkers and spanks him when he loses the match, a lamb who helps him sleep, and the ostrich he rides into battle.

Harpo's physical ease with animals in all the films — even when he is a dogcatcher in *Horse Feathers,* which would seem to place him in a position of enmity but somehow doesn't and may even explain the dog emptied from his pocket in *A Night in Casablanca*— suggests the depth of the bond. He reflects a love and camaraderie that transcends species and is sweet, spontaneous, and ingenuous.

Harpo's Magic

> Trickster takes "delight in floating fiction in the face of stern reality"
>   — Lewis Hyde, *Trickster Makes This World*[11]

Harpo's magic, the quality that relates him to Rabbit or Great Hare, is also a major way he surpasses the trickster natures of his cohorts Groucho and Chico. For only Harpo is able to transcend human limitations and the laws of physics, entering the realm of magic and the surreal. This capacity occurs in almost every film and develops as we move from film to film.

Harpo reveals his other-worldly talents early on. In *The Cocoanuts,* he bends the metal bars of the jail cell to free himself after foolishly locking himself in. In addition, he swims out of Penelope's room at the hotel spouting water, and rows away from the auction on land. In *Animal Crackers,* his magic becomes even more surreal: He makes smoke appear solid, produces chocolate smoke on request, animates inanimate statues and the clock's cuckoo and, best of all, steals a birthmark from Roscoe Chandler and affixes it to his own arm. In the same film, he opens a door on one side of a room to a sunny day and a door on the other side of the room to a stormy night.

Magic and the surreal continue to be associated with only Harpo, not his brothers, in the films. In *Horse Feathers* he wins money playing a telephone like a slot machine. In *Duck Soup,* Harpo responds to questions via a lexicon of tattoos, but in one of them, a real dog barks from his doghouse tattoo, an example of "imaginary gardens with real toads in them"[12] if there ever was one, simultaneously establishing Harpo as a poet, something we already suspect because of his adroit use of metonymy.

The same scene introduces a trick like the one associated with the Afro-

Carribean trickster Eshu whose hat, white on one side and black on the other, confuses witnesses and causes fights among them: Zeppo enters wearing half of a hat after passing the be-scissored Harpo on his way in. It appears to be whole from one side and no hat at all from the other. Finally, in *Duck Soup* Harpo takes the wondrously clever mirror scene with Groucho into the realm of magic once or twice, for we wonder not only how he anticipates Groucho's every move but also how their hats, one black and one white, become the same color.

In *A Day at the Races,* Harpo's tricks reflect hyperbole and magic when he digs so deeply in the sheriff's pockets that he pulls up his socks, when he bangs so hard on the piano that he liberates its sound board and plays it like a harp, when he catapults himself into the pond by spinning the piano stool, and ultimately when he is identified as Gabriel. Significantly, he recalls trickster Eshu again in the blackface scene when he blackens only half of his face with axle grease in the barn when the cohorts are trying to escape from corrupt law enforcers. Because from one side he appears to be white and from the other black, his gesture is eloquent in its implications about identity, witness reliability, the instability of racial categories, and maybe even the status of Jews in America.

In *At the Circus* we have more of the magical, both when the leopard's head hanging from the crotch of Harpo's costume rises up to growl at the lions, and when Harpo is called "Swingali" because of his music's hypnotic effect on lions. When the African American circus workers try a counter-spell on him, we see Harpo lean backwards in defiance of gravity.

Magic and surreal tendencies continue throughout the films. In *A Night at the Opera*, Harpo runs *up* a curtain to escape the authorities converging from both wings to nab him on the stage. In *Go West*, he fires a shot from a whisk broom, gets into an argument with a roll-top desk, and his body stretches when he replaces the coupling between train cars. He also gets thrown into the furnace and emerges without being burnt like his Biblical forbears, though Harpo has nothing to prove or die for.

In *The Big Store*, not only does Harpo's typewriter carriage extend beyond the machine to hover in the air, but Harpo later plays a baroque trio with mirror images of himself in a surreal musical sequence with his nonconformist trickster reflections. In *A Night in Casablanca,* he lets go of the building he is sarcastically accused of holding up and it falls down; he also transfers a candle flame to his own fingertips, survives impossible tortures, has his thoughts sucked out of his head by a telephone, and cleans the inside of his head from ear to ear with a handkerchief. Finally, in *Love Happy,* Harpo unfurls a table cloth with place settings attached, sees the back of his hair by flipping over his mirror, and removes, polishes, and juggles his eyes to amuse Maggie, a trick that echoes both trickster Hare's and Coyote's removal and juggling of their eyes. And Harpo accomplishes tricks in the rooftop chase that can be described only as surreal: riding lights around a billboard, swinging on the Bulova Watch pendulum, flying through the air, reversing his locations in mere seconds of darkness, being catapulted into the Kool cigarette penguin's mouth and emerging hidden in a cloud of smoke. Best of all, he rides diagonally across a billboard on the Mobil Oil Pegasus.

Harpo is, again, the only Marx with a zipper on his banana. In other words, he is the only Marx with talent for magic and the surreal, which is to say that he does not inhabit the sphere of ordinary men.

Harpo and Fire

> "Iureke" steals fire and hides it "one half in one tree, one half in another. 'If people are clever,' he said, 'they will figure out this trick.'"
>
> — Sherman, *Trickster Tales*[13]

Trickster tales from many parts of the world include a celebration of trickster as cultural hero who gives fire to human beings, sometimes at the risk of angering gods. Iureke, quoted above, is a Venezuelan trickster; Loki gives fire to humans in Norse mythology, Prometheus in Greek mythology, Maui in Polynesian tales, and Great Hare in American Indian tales. Harpo too is associated with fire in the films, and offers it, as he does his leg, frequently. He is associated with other elements as well, but none so prominently as fire.

At times Harpo offers fire implausibly from the pockets of his coat, like the candle burning from both ends in *Horse Feathers*, the film in which he also burns books, shoveling mass quantities into the flames. In *Duck Soup* he uses a blowtorch to light a cigar, and he burns the lemonade vendor's hat in his popcorn machine flame. He wears a miner's lit candle on his hat during the long penultimate sequence in *Room Service,* and he lights cigars with enormous matches in *At the Circus*. He lights a match on his tongue in *Go West* where he also stokes the trains engine with kerosene, wood, popcorn, himself, and the train's own wooden structure. He wears a flower-lapel cigarette lighter, lighting both a cigar and the Zoto brothers' bottoms in *Love Happy* where he also uses a flashlight flame to unlock the padlock to his little home.

Harpo is associated with the other elements in the films too: earth, when he goes prospecting in *Go West;* water when he floods the examination room in *A Day at the Races*; and wind in his flatulence and when he sneezes a hurricane in *At the Circus*. But most frequently, fire is Harpo's on-screen element.

Harpo's Luck

> The agile mind is pleased to find what it is not looking for.
> — Lewis Hyde, *Trickster Makes This World*[14]

Again and again in the films, Harpo makes use of what appears before him on his path. Like trickster, he thinks fast and with a hinged mind, so he is able to capitalize on the serendipitous. We see this capacity when he recognizes the disguise potential of the three aviators' beards in *A Night at the Opera* and steals them, and when he exploits the escape potential of the proto-skateboard in *Monkey Business*.

Harpo gets into the speakeasy more quickly than Groucho and Chico by saying the password "swordfish" with props and gestures. Harpo Marx as Pinky and Frank Rice as the speakeasy doorman. *Horse Feathers*, Paramount Pictures, 1931.

He furthermore outwits circumstances with the panoply of props in the pockets and lining of his coat, like when a homeless man asks him for change for a cup of coffee in *Horse Feathers* and he hands him a steaming cup of coffee instead, or when he needs to get into a speakeasy and mimes the password *swordfish* with a sword and a fish, pulling both from the repository of his coat. That coat, which he wears from film to film, is, like John Cage's music, "a net to catch contingency."[15] Harpo comes prepared to capitalize on what circumstances offer.

Sometimes Harpo uses the props in his pockets for the simple fun that accident affords. For example, in *At the Circus*, after he cuts open Goliath's pillow while searching for stolen money and the fan creates a blizzard of feathers, Harpo transforms himself into a Salvation Army Santa, improvising a beard from the feathers and giving himself and Chico a break for levity in the midst of danger. Sometimes Harpo has to force chance to yield its bounty by combining it with stealing, like when he and Chico get themselves to the football game in *Horse Feathers*. Harpo takes a chiffon scarf from a woman, wraps it around his head with the ends streaming, then steals the garbage collector's horse-drawn refuse can. Did he absolutely need the scarf? No, but because of it, he arrives at the game looking more dramatically ancient and Roman.

And we cannot ignore Harpo's gambling luck. In *Horse Feathers* he wins big, not only playing the slot machine in the speakeasy but also playing the telephone and the coin-changer on a man's belt; these involve magic. In *A Day at the Races,* he rides High High to first place in the race against odds that render all of the underdogs who bet on him big winners. And in *A Night in Casablanca,* Harpo wins again and again at the roulette wheel. His extraordinary luck makes us think the heavens smile on him.

Harpo's Flexible Joint

> "Humor oils the joint where contradictions meet."
> —Lewis Hyde, *Trickster Makes This World*[16]

Harpo is a generous persona with his leg. He offers it to strangers and familiars again and again, both in the films and beyond. Usually characters hold it until they become aware that they are holding it. And how others respond to it gives us insight into them: antagonists throw down the leg, exasperated and disgusted; protagonists are amused. Whomsoever is holding it, Harpo swings his leg at the hinge of the knee. He does this so often that we suspect there's a lesson in it. Moreover, sometimes in the films Harpo riffs on the trope of the leg, developing a meta-discourse, like when he offers a mannequin leg, hingeless and rigid, in *Monkey Business* and *Love Happy.*

Harpo introduces the trope in the Marx Brothers' first film, *The Cocoanuts,* where he risks running it into the ground, offering his leg to others nine times, a record in the films: to the bellhop, a woman in the lobby, Margaret Dumont's Mrs. Potter, Chico, and Chico and Penelope simultaneously. In *Animal Crackers,* he gives Groucho his leg, and notably Mrs. Whitehead to distract her when she is angling for the painting. In *Duck Soup,* Harpo gives his leg to Chico in the spirit of affection, and to the lemonade vendor in the spirit of nudnikery. In *Monkey Business* he introduces the mannequin leg to foil the ship's authorities in the Punch and Judy show, playing on the confusion between puppet and human, inanimate and animate. Later in the film, when he offers his own leg to the gangster Joe, Joe smiles, telling us instantly that he is a good guy. But when Harpo offers his leg to the ship's

Harpo Marx offers Madame Egelichi (Ilona Massey) a mannequin leg instead of his own, denying her the lesson of the flexible joint in a meta-cinematic riff on his own trope. *Love Happy,* United Artists, 1949. Photofest.

officer who rejects it in the passport scene, this tells us to beware of officials bearing rubber stamps.

Then Harpo takes a break from offering his leg in the films, returning to the trope in *A Night in Casablanca* when he tricks a woman in the hotel lobby into holding his leg and eventually scares her away, and in *Love Happy*, when he offers a mannequin leg to Madame Egelichi, apparently the leg the Zoto brothers found deep in his pockets on their rummaging expedition. Thus he simultaneously puns on his own trope while pronouncing Egelichi unworthy of initiation into knowledge of the hinge.

Because the human leg has a joint allowing it to bend and swing, Harpo's trope offers two related insights. First, joints are vulnerable, so when trickster wants to disturb or attack, he goes for the joint, which Hyde calls the "hidden weakness."[17] But joints are also flexible, so Harpo's trope also suggests a posture to strike in a precarious situation, relaxed and malleable. Figuratively, a "joint-working consciousness"[18] can make use of opportunities and contradictions; this is the hinged mind so essential for survival and pleasure in an imperfect world. The joint, loose and flexible, can help a body leap, not necessarily away from danger but sometimes toward insight, connection, and metaphor, and this suggests the link between "art-making and the hinged mind."[19] The human leg with its flexible knee joint, then, becomes a metaphor for the hinged mind along with trickster's work of both disturbing and recalibrating, all the while striking an efficacious posture.

Harpo's proffered leg is disorderly, socially inappropriate, generous, playful, and alive. What happens when the leg is wooden and incapable of these attributes? We see precisely what, in the march of the Nazi goosestep toward inflexibility, hatred, and death.

Harpo's Craft

> "He exhibits craft in cheating and destroying the enemy."
> Erdoes and Ortiz, *American Indian Myths and Legends*[20]

Harpo's leg, the deft way he slips it into the hands of the unsuspecting, is one aspect of his craft, but he has much more up his sleeves and pants legs to amuse and provoke change. His craft also involves the many props in the deep pockets and lining of his shoplifter's trenchcoat (see *Harpo's Silence*). In addition, Harpo's miming and facial expressions are intrinsic aspects of his craft. And his music is too, most memorably on harp but also on flute, piccolo, clarinet, and harmonica. Music, however, deserves and will have its own discussion (see *Harpo's Harp*, following).

Examples of Harpo's craft are too numerous to detail: Every moment he is on-screen, everything he does involves the application of craft, whether miming, wielding props, moving, mugging, standing still, or even sleeping. So a few examples must suffice to suggest his repertoire.

In *The Cocoanuts*, Harpo snags evidence to clear Bob's name and indict the crooks with a strategic swoop of his top hat, vestiary marker of wealth ironically worn. And undressing is also part of Harpo's craft, for he is prone to nudity, stripping down to his underwear in *Animal Crackers* and *Horse Feathers*. He also changes form completely: In *Monkey Business* Harpo hides from the ship's police in a Punch and Judy show, proving himself an apt puppet. Shape-shifting via physical movement, including the movement of his facial features (note how he uses the Gookie face as his puppet mask), is sometimes an aspect of his craft. Yet Harpo's body is agile: He does gymnastics throughout the *Il Trovatore* scene in *A Night at the Opera*. In *A Day at the Races*, Harpo uses a photograph of Morgan's face to spur High Hat on to greater speed, helping him win the race. So transferring signification from one context to another is part of his comic craft.

Studying and imitating another's gestures to the point of being able to anticipate them are also part of Harpo's craft. He combines props and movement when he impersonates Maurice Chevalier, strapping a phonograph to his back and lip-syncing "You Brought a New Kind of Love to Me." He imitates the gait of the Italian patriarch in the bed department scene in *The Big Store*. He impersonates Groucho as his mirror image with uncanny accuracy. And he impersonates Beatrice in *A Night in Casablanca,* smoking a long cigarette and spying through a lorgnette until he deconstructs his own efforts, blowing bubbles, then snapping at them like a dog.

Socially inappropriate and audacious behaviors are also part of Harpo's craft. In *Animal Crackers* he cheats his way through a bridge game with an endless supply of aces of spades, and he manages to call Margaret Dumont's Mrs. Rittenhouse a "dummy" even though he doesn't speak. In *Duck Soup* he washes his feet, much to the dismay of the thirsty factory workers, in a rival vendor's lemonade. He leaps upon and kisses strangers of various genders in *A Night at the Opera*, and he sits on Trentino's lap in *Duck Soup,* wherein he also hides from a woman's husband underwater in the man's own bathtub.

Harpo's horn is a staple of his craft. He uses it to speak, and does so even on the telephone in *Horse Feathers*. He suggests flatulence with it, when he bumps bellies with the vendor in *Duck Soup* and various others. He multiplies the order for hard-boiled eggs with it, even while he sleeps, in *A Night at the Opera.* He uses his horn as a baton and a mute and later a weapon in *At the Circus.* And when he carries it with the bulb end sticking out of the top of his trousers, it suggests a phallus.

Harpo's interaction with animals is part of his craft: horses in *Animal Crackers,* picnicking with his horse in *Horse Feathers,* being a jockey in *A Day at the Races,* getting coached at checkers by a seal, and vanquishing the saboteurs of the circus from the back of an ostrich in *At the Circus.*

Harpo uses pictures as part of his craft: He steals a poster of a circus ballerina in *Horse Feathers,* hanging it on walls wherever he may be. He shows a picture of his nemesis Morgan to High Hat, thus spurring him on to win the race in *A Day at the Races.* He steals a Rembrandt portrait because he has a crush on its female subject in *A Night in Casablanca,* and this ends up saving the day because it reveals the stash of stolen art. He gathers all of the paintings in *Animal Crackers.* And Harpo appears on a few wanted posters as well.

Craft-wise, Harpo does some other interesting things. He comes close to dancing with the stars like trickster Coyote in the rooftop scene in *Love Happy,* where he also hides inside the Kool penguin, then in the smoke that saturates him after he emerges from it. And he cracks Jewish jokes using his lexicon of props and gestures, once by circumcising a phallic salami, and once by blowing the shofar on a American Indian's ceremonial headdress horns while they are on his head. The list goes on.

Harpo's Harp

> "Honestly three things seem mixed together in this music: humor
> and eros and sweet sleep."
> — Lewis Hyde, *Trickster Makes This World* [21]

On a Madison Avenue Bus between 42nd and 68th Streets, I overheard an elderly music professor telling a young African American harp student to watch the Marx Brothers films to see Harpo playing the harp backwards. This struck me as interesting because not only is the harp a descendant of trickster Hermes' lyre, but also *backwards* is precisely Hermes' trick to disguise his theft of Apollo's cattle. Harpo, like Hermes, taught himself to play and thus developed his own technique, tuning the harp differently and playing his own way all his life. Did he play it backwards? I don't know. But he bears watching and listening to, for the range of his repertoire, from popular standards to blues to jazz to classical, for his unique glissandos, and for his rapture and transport while playing. Like Hermes, and the Biblical David too, Harpo casts a spell with his music.

Also like Hermes, who was "eager to know another art, and made himself the shepherd's pipes, whose music carries great distances,"[22] Harpo makes music with wind instruments, playing a clarinet in *The Cocoanuts*, a flute in *A Day at the Races*, a harmonica in *Go West,* and pianos in several films. In *A Day at the Races,* in fact, Harpo plays Rachmaninoff's "C-Sharp Minor Prelude" so vigorously that the piano falls or is driven apart, which ironically brings him back to his essential love, for he lifts the soundboard out of the piano's ruins and *voila*, a harp. Harpo claims that in the scenes where he plays the harp, he isn't acting: the man playing the harp is him.[23]

Harpo's harp interludes, one in each of the films except *Duck Soup* and *Room Service,* have a calming effect on him, on other characters, and on his audience. He plays popular melodies, classical pieces, jazz and blues. His solos, often preceded by comic shenanigans, are often sublime, like his duet on a harp improvised from a blanket loom in *Go West*. Harpo and the flute-playing chief's rendition of "From the Land of the Sky-Blue Water" by Charles Wakefield Cadman, based on a Dakota song, offers homage to American Indians in a scene otherwise satirical of the depiction of Indians by non–Indians in Hollywood films, and concludes with the chief's gentle hand on Harpo's shoulder. Also memorable is Harpo's harp variation on "Blue Moon" by Richard Rodgers, accompanied by an African American chorus in *At the Circus*. And in *A Night in Casablanca*, in a room between floors in the hotel, an angel feather drifts down as Harpo begins to play Franz Liszt's "Hungarian Rhapsody No. 2."

In some of the films a harp simply appears for Harpo to play, like in *The Cocoanuts, Animal Crackers, Monkey Business, Horse Feathers, A Night at the Opera, At the Circus, The Big Store,* and *A Night in Casablanca*. In some films, however, he must improvise a harp. When that happens and with little regard for continuity, those improvised harps morph into the real thing, like in *A Day at the Races* and in *Go West*. Finally, in *Love Happy,* Harpo keeps his harp under his mattress where it doubles as bedsprings in his own little house.

Harpo also plays wind instruments, answering the question, "Who Dat Man?" in *At the Circus* with notes sounding like "It's Gabriel"; even without his harp, Harpo continues to be identified as an angel. He plays the harmonica in *Go West* because it is portable, the musical interlude taking place on horseback en route to the train. Harpo even plays in a musical trio with himself in *The Big Store,* beginning with his solo on harp reflected in two mirrors but morphing, for his reflections, tricksters too, are not under his control. One plays a cello and the other a violin while the surprised Harpo accepts their autonomy and they make music together.

Harpo's relationship with music can be complicated, like his irreverent but ultimately restorative deconstruction of *Il Trovatore* in *A Night at the Opera,* or his phonograph-assisted impersonation of Maurice Chevalier in *Monkey Business.* Sometimes his playing stylizes and reiterates a film's romantic theme song, like in *Animal Crackers.* But music is always a major way that Harpo communicates, and each time he offers us beauty and tranquility via the universal language of music.

Harpo's Thefts

> "When he ... steals, it isn't so much to get away with something or get rich as to disturb the established categories of truth and property, and, by doing so, open the road to possible new worlds."
> — Lewis Hyde, *Trickster Makes This World*[24]

Stealing is one of Harpo's most salient trickster traits. And like Hermes and Coyote, he is adept at it. He uses his hands, his teeth, and his tools to accomplish his thefts, and his huge coat is often the repository of his loot. Furthermore, because of the varied and outlandish inventory of his pockets, we know that as a character he has been pinching all kinds of things in his extra-diegetic life, those presumed fictional adventures between and around the ones depicted in the films. Sometimes Harpo steals for the fun of it, often returning what he has stolen. Sometimes he steals to get what others won't give up and therefore can't be obtained in any other way. And sometimes he steals to help himself or others.

His thefts force us to accept his status as one who abides outside the pale of the law. He is essentially an outlaw who usually escapes arrest because of his wit, whimsical good nature, and generosity, although he sees the insides of jail cells in *The Cocoanuts* and *A Night in Casablanca,* and is running or hiding from police in other films. He acknowledges neither rules nor authority. In fact, he questions these even while exhibiting ethical impulses. In this way he lives with contradictions and teaches us to do so too, liberating us from foolish consistencies and ultimately demonstrating the necessity of suspending simplistic definitions of *good* and *evil.*

He is like the Arabic-Jewish trickster Joha, who at his trial for stealing, said to the king, "There will be many others who will say of you, Majesty, that you are unjust, because Joha is a poor unfortunate who was convicted for a stealing a bauble"[25]: When Harpo steals, he forces us to reconsider the relative impact of the theft as well as who owns what and by what authority. Thus our minds become hinged and thoughtful and maybe even radicalized.

Harpo's thefts in the first film, *The Cocoanuts*, land us right inside this ethical complexity, for he steals a lot (a man's suit jacket, Bob's handkerchief, and Detective Hennessey's shirt, among other things) for the sport of it. He also clarifies the difference between his essentially benign stealing and the damaging thefts of Harvey and Penelope, including their attempted theft of Bob's good name along with his fiancée. In *Animal Crackers*, Harpo steals the paintings, but we could also say that he is gathering them, for in the end his having them all together — the original *After the Hunt* and the two imitations — is the pragmatic by which John Parker's talent is revealed. He also steals Groucho's watch, Grace Carpenter's shoes and, in his own extra-diegetic moments lacking clear connection to the plot, most of the silverware in the mansion. We know this because it rains from his sleeve when Detective Hennessey (yes, the name Hennessey again, though not the same actor) shakes his hand and asks him if he wants to be a crook. Harpo nods a gleeful and adamant "yes."

Sometimes Harpo uses ingenious methods, like a bottomless shot glass as a funnel to steal booze at the speakeasy in *Horse Feathers*, a film wherein he also steals a chiffon scarf and a horse-drawn garbage can on wheels for his classical arrival at the big game. He steals money from the sheriff's pockets in *A Day at the Races* and from Groucho's pockets in *Go West*, having handed over money with literal strings attached. His theft of the Rembrandt in *A Night in Casablanca*, motivated by attraction to the woman in the portrait, accomplishes the good work of clearing Pierre of suspicion and revealing the Nazis' stolen treasures. And in *Love Happy*, Harpo's thefts of food from the delicatessen that is really a front for stolen jewels — he is stealing from thieves — are accomplished with entertaining dexterity and with the admirable motive of feeding the cast and crew of a struggling musical show.

Finally, some of Harpo's thefts are surreal, like his theft of the birthmark in *Animal Crackers* and his theft of the aviators' beards in *A Night at the Opera* and the professor's beard in *Horse Feathers*, these receiving a meta-cinematic send-up at the end of *A Night in Casablanca* when Harpo and Groucho sport beards made from Stubel's toupee. But is this last one theft or a souvenir?

Harpo's Flatulence

"In any case I am a great man even if I do expel a little gas!"
— Paul Radin, *The Trickster*[26]

Some of the tales in the Winnebago Trickster Cycle involve amusing episodes of hyperbolic flatulence, Coyote's gas propelling him so high that he must cling to the upper branches of a tree to keep from being blown away altogether. Because producing and expelling gas occasionally is part of the human condition, we are able to relate. And because farting combines elements of surprise, embarrassment, and an undeniable odor, it is, from a certain point of view, amusing. Because social protocol insists that we neither pass gas nor speak of doing so in polite company, the intensity of repression renders the subject, when it escapes, no pun intended, all the more fraught with humor.

Harpo's flatulence is expressed metonymically in the films. Although his horn is usually his mouthpiece, occasionally it is his *tuchus* piece, a trope introduced in the very first film, *The Cocoanuts,* when Harpo honks his horn and Groucho and Chico run out of the room. In *A Night in Casablanca,* something similar happens, though this time the bulb of the horn and its stick, stuck inside of Harpo's trousers, may be a metonymic sign of a phallic order, especially because it is a woman who flees the hotel lobby. In *Duck Soup,* Harpo bumps bellies with the lemonade vendor, his horn honking with each bump, thereby associating the digestive tract with the sound. He honks similar belly bumps in other films too.

But the most developed trope for flatulence occurs in the stateroom scene in *A Night at the Opera.* Harpo may be asleep, but sleeping never stopped a person from farting, nor does sleeping prevent Harpo from expressing his trickster's essence. His ill-timed somnolence is trickster's; his groping women even while asleep in the crowded and chaotic setting is trickster's too. So when each time Groucho adds an item to the steward's order and Chico says, "and a hard-boiled egg," the sleeping Harpo honks his horn, and Groucho translates the honk as "make that two hard-boiled eggs," we suspect an allusion to flatulence. Maybe an egg is just an egg, but it is difficult to add up the elements (a small enclosed space, the sound the horn makes, and the sulfurous odor of hard-boiled eggs) and not come up with farting.

Near the end of Groucho's interchange with the steward, Harpo issues a series of honks, then a single one, which Groucho translates as "twelve more hard-boiled eggs" then "a duck egg." Here we have something like a grand finale and a final metonymic joke.

Harpo's Cleansing of the Gods on High

> "Joha went and put his behind in the new window in the wall. 'What is this?' said the sultan."
> — Koen-Serano, *Folktales of Joha, Jewish Trickster*[27]

In myth and legend, trickster unsettles established order and authority and rattles hierarchies. This is often done by or on behalf of the powerless or the poor, and is enacted against the powerful, proud, or wealthy. Though they seem revolutionary, trickster's rebellions neither abolish nor necessarily overthrow order and power. Rather, the debasing cleanses and renews; the chaos refreshes and realigns. Rigidity is unhealthy and does not nurture creative energies, so the status quo needs shaking up from time to time to prevent cultural stagnation. Because those in power are not necessarily wise, trickster's challenges can be good medicine.

This theme is at the heart of every Marx Brothers film, and Harpo's trickster antics play a huge part in generating the chaos that eventually results in a more just equilibrium. In *The Cocoanuts, Animal Crackers, A Night at the Opera,* and *At the Circus,* societies too keen on money and status and therefore impervious to genuine worth need to be shaken up and cleansed. The false values of the wealthy are often represented inimically by Margaret Dumont, but she can be reformed. The inhumane tendencies of bureaucratic orders like those of ships, duchies, or colleges are another matter. They must be cleansed by means of chaos in *Monkey Business, Horse Feathers,* and *Duck Soup.* And the violence and greed of criminals, or wolves hiding in sheep's clothing in other ways, or hiding behind sheep, are also under assault in the films.

In *Horse Feathers,* corruption in academia, including collegiate sports, is satirized. In *Monkey Business,* the microcosm of the ship, with its hierarchies and rigid protocols, is under assault. In *Duck Soup,* Harpo and his cohorts move beyond the surrogate war of football in *Horse Feathers* to satirize actual war and the nationalism that stokes it. In *A Night at the Opera,* high art along with its snob contingent of patrons are cleansed and renewed, not to mention made more aware of worthy talent. In *A Day at the Races, At the Circus, Go West,* and *The Big Store,* Harpo and his cohorts fight for the marginalized, often those lacking money, and in *Room Service* they do battle against ambition and greed that threaten to frustrate the triple needs for food, shelter, and artistic sustenance. In *The Cocoanuts, The Big Store, A Night in Casablanca,* and *Love Happy,* Harpo and his cohorts also take on powerful crooks — gods, perhaps, of the underworld.

Because the police are the summoned enforcers of order and the status quo, Harpo's many confrontations with them symbolize his trickster role. These occur in almost every film, from his theft of Hennessey's shirt in *The Cocoanuts,* his silverware bust in *Animal Crackers,* his Punch and Judy and customs scenes' confrontations in *Monkey Business,* his police-dog chase scene in *Horse Feathers,* his mid–*Il Trovatore* bust in *A Night at the Opera,* his half-blackface escape in *A Day at the Races,* his fake hydrant in *The Big Store,* and his arrests in *A Night in Casablanca* and *Love Happy.* He often outwits cops and spoofs the symbols of their power. And when he lands in jail, as he does in *The Cocoanuts* and *A Night in Casablanca,* he gets out with tricks.

We feel vicarious satisfaction when Harpo and company assault the gods on high. We cheer their efforts and successes. In their way, the films celebrate and invigorate the rebellious spirit within each of us, a spirit that keeps insisting that we acknowledge our humanity, fight greed, and redistribute wealth and opportunity.

Harpo's Trickster Cohorts

"Maybe because they are so very much alike, they are friends, except when they try to trick each other."
— Erdoes and Ortiz, *American Indian Myths and Legends*[28]

Like the American Indian trickster Coyote, whose pal Iktome is also a trickster, Harpo has trickster friends. Harpo's trickster cohorts Groucho and Chico recognize him instantly in the films, they greet him warmly, they understand his mischief, and they collaborate with him. Even if they start out on different sides and even twit or scam each other, like in *Duck Soup* and *Go West,* they end up collaborating in the effort to undermine the powerful and assist the marginalized who are sometimes also young lovers.

The film's antagonists recognize Harpo immediately as an outsider, more so than Groucho and Chico. But Groucho and Chico aren't far behind; they are outsiders too, Chico because of his immigrant status and Groucho because of his wisecracking audacity. Harpo hangs out with them and collaborates with them, but he isn't completely dependent upon them for companionship, for he has warm relationships with animals. He is a loner, though not alone in nature.

In *The Cocoanuts,* the three go in circles in the hotel lobby shaking hands, immediately recognizing their kindred spirits, although presumably Harpo and Chico, already companions, have never met Groucho and Zeppo before. Groucho even hands Harpo mail to tear up, entering easily into his manic irreverence. In *Animal Crackers,* all three — Zeppo is just a guy whose status rises to romantic lead in *Monkey Business*— unite in the cause of John and Arabella's love, even though they are seemingly strangers to one another: Groucho an African explorer, Chico a musician, and Harpo appearing suddenly on the scene as the Professor. In *Monkey Business,* however, they are connected somehow, traveling together as stowaways in barrels labeled KIPPERED HERRING.

In many of the films, like *A Day at the Races,* Chico and Harpo have a close prior connection. In *Duck Soup* they are working together as inept spies for Trentino, in *Horse Feathers* they deliver booze for the speakeasy, and in *At the Circus*, they are employed by the circus. In *A Night at the Opera* they know each other from music school, and In *Go West* and *The Big Store*, they are brothers sharing evident affection: in the former they enter holding hands, in the latter Chico scratches Harpo's back and they play a duet together just like old times. In *Love Happy*, they are such close friends that Chico can read Harpo's mind, more or less. Often Groucho is not related to them, but sometimes Harpo works for him, as his chauffeur in *Duck Soup* and *The Big Store* where he is also office chicken farmer, cook, image enhancer, and secretary. Even without a prior connection, however, Groucho recognizes the *simpatico* and is quick to join them.

And that is the point. While Harpo, like trickster of myth, tends to be a loner, an outsider, not a pack animal though perhaps an animal, he and his trickster cohorts hang out together for a while because each is social, adaptable, and opportunistic. And they remain together for the duration of the films based on recognition of their kindred natures and goals. They are willing to lob the full force of their comic spirit, all of its tricks, at the mighty. When their work is done, they sometimes part ways, except, perhaps, when they all marry the college widow like in *Horse Feathers* or chase the same woman out of the shot, as in *A Night in Casablanca*. In the last film, *Love Happy*, Chico ends up working for Groucho, but Harpo skips away, utterly on his own, except, perhaps, for his penguin doppelgänger.

Harpo as Picaro

> "Coyote was going along..."
> — Lewis Hyde, *Trickster Makes This World*[29]

Until *Love Happy*, where Harpo appears to have roots, living in a little hillside house in the park, he is usually a picaresque figure who simply turns up in the film. Like the Lone Ranger, he comes to town, restores justice, and punishes evil. But Harpo does so comically, and unlike the Lone Ranger, he doesn't come to town with that purpose in mind. He is simply a wanderer who ends up getting involved. Some films hint at a backstory for him, some none. But once Harpo enters the world of the film, usually about ten minutes in, once the milieu and its discontents have been established, he figures out whom to cast his luck with pretty quickly: the underdogs and divided lovers. And he gains our sympathy because with them our sympathies already reside.

For example, Harpo arrives at the *Cocoanuts* hotel with Chico, a backstory implied because of the stolen articles from other hotels that fall from his coat. In *Animal Crackers*, Harpo, simply appears. In *Monkey Business*, the cohorts are already bonded; they are traveling together as stowaways in barrels from who-knows-where. In *Horse Feathers*, Harpo isn't exactly a wanderer; he has a regular job as a dogcatcher and another delivering ice, but he ends up on campus because he is mistakenly recruited at the speakeasy to play football for Huxley College. In *Duck Soup* Harpo is also already a resident, this time of Freedonia, with three jobs: spying for Sylvania, selling peanuts and popcorn below Groucho's window (perhaps a front for spying), and driving the president. Nevertheless, he retains that fly-by-night quality.

In *A Night at the Opera*, Harpo seems to be returning from somewhere. He and Chico show great joy upon meeting again. In *Room Service*, Harpo is so transient that he is in the process of being evicted from a homeless shelter when he moves into the hotel with Groucho and Chico, with whom he has a prior friendship. In *A Day at the Races*, Harpo works at the track as a stable boy and jockey, a flimsy sort of stability. In *At the Circus*, Harpo works for the circus as the strongman Goliath's assistant; he has a job and a residence, yet the circus is, by nature, nomadic.

In *Go West,* Harpo's brother is sending him west, so again he is on the road. In *The Big Store,* Harpo works for Groucho and lives with him in his office as short order cook, typist, chauffeur, and manipulator of props to make Groucho look important, but it is clear that neither has a permanent home. *A Night in Casablanca* places Harpo as trickster in the world's crossroads of conspiracy where he is labeled a *vagrant* by the police, and he looks like a vagrant, leaning on a wall, even though it turns out that he's actually holding it up.

So again, only in *Love Happy* does Harpo's life seem rooted, or, at any rate, it's the first time he has a little house and we get to see inside of it, with its random, perhaps stolen musical furnishings, and his roommate, a penguin, a feathered double dressed exactly like him, but vociferous in contrast to Harpo's silence. Yet in spite of this relative domestic stability, in the closing shot of this last Marx Brothers film, Harpo skips off with the Romanoff jewels on a rooftop like Chaplin's Tramp on the road, that wanderer's essence still clinging to him.

Harpo and Liminal Spaces

> "Eshu and Legba are both wanderers, living in spaces between things; their special areas are crossroads, thresholds, and boundaries."
> — Voth, *Myth in Human History*[30]

Harpo often shows a predilection for doorways, places where land and water meet, and thresholds. In other words, it seems natural for him to loiter in liminal spaces, spaces that are intermediate and transitional, waiting and watching to see what might occur. Perhaps this is because his nature is like this too, negotiating the world of men and the world of the divine, male and female, good and bad, rich and poor, black and white, colonizer and indigenous. He crosses the boundaries that divide people, he shape-shifts, impersonates, and bends gender. So it shouldn't surprise us that he expresses his liminal essence on a physical, even geographical level, visiting a hotel where land and water meet, hanging out in lobbies, on elevators, in doorways, on stairways, traveling on ocean liners, and idling where traffic of all kinds intersects. He seems to know things will happen in such places, being no respecter of boundaries and relishing the conditional status of the threshold.

Here are a few summary examples. *The Cocoanuts* and *A Night in Casablanca* are set in hotels, one where land and water meet, the other at an international crossroads. In both, Harpo is just hanging around, taking in the traffic, and chasing it if it is female and blonde. *Monkey Business* and *A Night at the Opera* offer major sequences set on ocean liners, and what could be more transitional than a ship sailing between continents and cultures? Harpo is often seen, or sees others, at windows or portholes, like in *Duck Soup, A Night at the Opera, At the Circus, Room Service,* and *Horse Feathers.* In *Love Happy* he negotiates rooftops and their billboards with the agility of one used to moving above earth, in the sky. In *Go West,* Harpo actually becomes so intimate with the train that he fuels it with timber from its own walls and floors, and he uses his own body to join cars. And trains themselves are border crossers, as are airplanes, cars, motorcycles, bicycles, and skateboards, all vehicles that Harpo rides in the films.

In a surreal little scene in *Go West,* Harpo is temporarily off the train, "off the threshold and into the house,"[31] when the farmer's house gets caught on the cowcatcher. Harpo is standing still, but the front door swallows him, then the back door spits him out. Like trickster, he cannot stay in the house for long.

Harpo's Silence

> "The injunction to silence is the speech act by which a particular narrator is made sacred."
> — Lewis Hyde, *Trickster Makes This World*[32]

Despite claims that Harpo spoke in the 1925 film *Too Many Kisses,* it was a silent film so it certainly does not challenge the gestalt of Harpo's silence.

His muteness, the most striking aspect of his persona, has an interesting and complex bearing on his trickster essence, reminding us of "the force field of the spiritual world," and both reflecting and eliciting "reverence and awe."[33]

Behind the persona, we know that three things converged to silence the performer Arthur Marx: his Uncle Al's advice about the potential benefit to the act of his miming, a vaudeville review that praised his "pantomime" but panned "the effect ... when he speaks," and his own realization that he "simply couldn't outtalk Groucho or Chico." After the bad review, he "never uttered another word, onstage or in front of a camera, as a Marx Brother."[34] But how does Harpo's silence relate to his trickster essence? And is it really silence?

First, Harpo's silence is rebellious: He refuses to plead with the powerful against injustice. Adornoesque in its hint of soulful despair, Harpo's silence is also triumphant because he doesn't mute his behavior; on the contrary, he communicates loudly and flamboyantly with props, mime, music, magic, and mischief. With props and mime, he makes sophisticated puns, ironic comments, and even satirizes language itself. With magic he expands our notions of what is real. And with music he casts an esthetic, emotional, and spiritual spell. As for his mischief, we don't fail to hear it. It's silly, irreverent, absurd, revolutionary, and often sweet. Furthermore, like trickster, who is a guide to seeing, Harpo helps us focus in the meditative stillness of his wordlessness.

Who else speaks the language of silence? Souls, infants, animals, the powerless, visual artists, God. Silence is forced upon immigrants, who must learn the new language of their adopted country (Harpo's refusal to privilege English offers them ready access to his humor). In addition, *voice* is often the very thing denied the oppressed, so Harpo, with his muteness, expresses solidarity with those deprived of voice. All of these groups, then — souls, infants, animals, immigrants, and the oppressed — tend to respond to him, instinctively understanding that he is casting his lot with them. Marginalized members of the population welcome him onto their turf, most significantly in *A Day at the Races, At the Circus,* and *Go West.* The soul is inebriated by his antics and children, not yet distanced from the flexible pre-linguistic omniscient state of infancy, are ecstatic in his presence. Just look again at scenes with children in *Monkey Business, A Night at the Opera, A Day at the Races, At the Circus,* and *The Big Store,* to witness the camaraderie between Harpo and children. Animals bond with him, not only horses but also dogs, a lamb, a frog, a seal, and an ostrich.

And Harpo has a special relationship with artists whose tools are not words, fighting for recognition for an architect in *The Cocoanuts* and a painter in *Animal Crackers,* admiring a Rembrandt portrait in *A Night in Casablanca,* and showing homage to the power of photographs when he kisses one of his horse and when he uses one to make High Hat run faster: in that case, suggesting somewhat philosophically that a picture of a man *is* the man. He is also allied with musicians in numerous films, helping tenors prevail in both *A Night at the Opera* and *The Big Store,* and drawing the camera to jazz, swing, and blues performances in *A Day at the Races* and *At the Circus.*

At the time the Marx Brothers started making movies, the medium had recently transitioned to sound. In *The Cocoanuts,* Harpo alone seems unconcerned with the problems of early sound. Moreover, being a mute character doesn't stop him from commenting on technology, especially technology that delivers the human voice to others. Harpo has an extended relationship with telephones throughout the films, taking a bite out of one in *The Cocoanuts,* playing one like a slot machine in *Horse Feathers,* having a horn-assisted conversation on one in *Duck Soup,* salting one to eat in *A Night in Casablanca,* and applying one to his forehead so Chico can read his thoughts in *Love Happy.*

Groucho's verbal dexterity is a foil for Harpo's silence, and Chico's immigrant English and homonym errors follow up with a lesson about *voice,* as in claiming the language as one's own and stamping it with one's nuanced history and character. Certainly, this has implications for poets and writers. But Harpo's miming is deeply eloquent too and essentially poetic. And he kept it up. In a 1961 interview on *The Today Show,* Harpo still doesn't speak. In fact, until a stage performance at which he announced his retirement, then started giving his Bar Mitzvah speech[35] (as if thirteen was the age he turned off his voice so turns it on again precisely then), most of the public never heard Harpo speak.

Harpo presents us with a few enigmas regarding his silence too. Does he lend his voice to the barbershop quartets in *Monkey Business* and *Duck Soup?* Does he sing while scrubbing up with Groucho and Chico in *A Day at the Races?* Furthermore, with his lexicon of props, which includes tattoos, he riffs a lot, arguing with Professor Wagstaff, for example, that one *can* burn the candle at both ends simply by pulling a candle burning from both ends out of his coat pocket, and showing Groucho where he lives in *Duck Soup* by displaying the tattoo of a doghouse on his chest. When Groucho tries to top that, meowing at the tattoo, a real dog lunges from it, barking at him. In the end, Harpo speaks in his own way, and he does so resoundingly.

Finally, Harpo took a vow of silence and stuck to it, and this connects him to trickster's divinity because it places him in the company of a variety of religious sects that practice silence. It takes discipline to persevere in such a vow, for the self-imposed restriction of silence involves denial of a very human impulse. Contemplative orders of Catholic monks and Carmelite nuns practice silence in order to focus on meditation and prayer, to keep the airways to the divine uninterrupted, a practice also followed in Buddhism, Hinduism, and Islam. Ironically, Jews, a loquacious people, tend to embrace the opposite means, preferring reading and intense discussion to connect with the divine. Perhaps that explains Harpo's loquacious kind of silence in these wild, anarchic, comic films. He transcends his self-imposed vow of silence, reminding us how free of limitations a liberated persona can be.

Harpo as Fool

> "Impossible to tell where his cunning ends and his stupidity begins."
>
> — Paul Radin, *The Trickster*[36]

In addition to dishing it out, trickster takes it. He himself often gets tricked or foiled, on occasion by himself. That is part of his nature. And he sometimes learns a few things in the process. But Harpo comes to us late in the trickster tradition. A long line of tricksters have preceded him, so he does not need, perhaps, to recapitulate the entire process of trickster's development from inchoate to individuated to educated. He is already called "The Professor" in the second film, *Animal Crackers,* though he regresses to being a student shooting peas at Professor Wagstaff, such as he is, in a Huxley College classroom in *Horse Feathers.* So is Harpo stupid or cunning? A savior or a buffoon? The answer is *yes.*

On the one hand, he often sabotages his own efforts and gets a come-uppance. For example, in *Duck Soup,* the angry vendor sticks Harpo's lemonade-filled horn down his pants and honks it, making Harpo metonymically piss his pants. In the same film Harpo undermines his and Chico's spying efforts by making a racket, first setting all the clocks to go off at midnight, then being unable to turn off a radio blasting Sousa music. Later he lights a match while he's locked in an ammunition closet.

Similarly, after creating ingenious disguises for himself and the other stowaways in *A Night at the Opera,* Harpo drinks so much water so sloppily at the radio broadcast microphone that he washes the glue from his chin, and his stolen beard adheres to the face of the cop he embraces. In *Room Service,* Harpo chases his poached turkey with a baseball bat, knocking out the agent of the play's backer whose check will not only pay their room and board but also fund the production. In *At the Circus,* when he and Chico are snooping for stolen money in the giant Goliath's room, Harpo does several silly things that wake him up, despite common knowledge that it's unwise to wake a sleeping giant. In *Go West* he uncouples the wrong car, then has to keep it attached to the train by *becoming* the train coupling. Harpo also accidentally pours kerosene instead of water into the engine, giving the train a burst of speed when it needs to stop to pick up the lovebirds Terry and Eve. And he dumps the train's fuel off the train in a thoughtless moment and ends up having to feed the train itself to keep it running. Harpo messes up plenty.

Sleeping excessively or at inappropriate times is part of this buffoon aspect of Harpo's trickster nature. *Animal Crackers* references tricksters' propensity for sleep three times: Harpo puts himself to sleep while accompanying John and Arabella's love song on his harp; he spends a night outdoors on a bench instead of indoors on a bed in a hotel room, using the stolen painting as a blanket and birds for his alarm clock; and he chloroforms the guests, then himself after positioning himself next to the blonde he has been unable to catch. He sleeps inopportunely in *At the Circus* while searching Goliath's room when he drinks the sleeping potion Chico mixed to put Goliath back to sleep. And he sleeps most memorably in the stateroom scene in *A Night at the Opera,* his trickster nature expressed thoroughly even while he sleeps. The behavior is reversed in *Monkey Business* where it isn't Harpo who sleeps at an inappropriate time but the ship's officer who comes into the barbershop for a trim and pays for his lapse of consciousness by forfeiting his entire mustache to Chico's cockamamie instructions and Harpo's excessive snips.

Does Harpo learn anything during the films and thus progress from his buffoon status? Is he, like trickster, educated, for example, by his hunger? From his hunger, Harpo seems to learn only to eat as much as he can whenever he can. Nevertheless, by the final film, even though he is still stealing, in this case food, he is doing so not to stoke his own appetite but to feed his friends, the musical performers in an unfunded show. So, yes, perhaps he does become educated: he seems less self-involved than the Harpo of *Room Service* who doesn't share the banana stashed in his pocket while his cohorts are starving. Overall, though, he probably doesn't learn much. Harpo shares some this aspect of his essence with residents of Chelm, a town celebrated in Ashkenazi Jewish folklore that is populated entirely by "foolish people" though "maybe the people in Chelm are really wise, after all."[37] If Harpo learned too much, he would cease to be a fool, and that is no small thing, for fools border on the comic and the sacred.

Harpo's Wildness, Mania, and Fun

> "He is what the best-behaved and most circumspect person may
> secretly wish to be."
> — Erdoes and Ortiz, *American Indian Myths and Legends*[38]

When she was still a teenager, my sister-in-law Kathi attended a Marx
Brothers retrospective at a local theater. She was slapping her leg so hard
while laughing during the film that her leg was black and blue the next
day. And that was the effect of watching only one film! Indeed, each Marx
Brothers film contains scenes involving such manic hijinks that viewers risk
suffocating with laughter. Sometimes even the cameramen filming scenes
ended up doubled over on the floor because the brothers would indulge in
unscripted and spontaneous mayhem. But that doesn't mean the wildness is
without significance. For when comic disorder mixes with quotidian order,
first there is chaos, then the frenzy subsides and relationships (of individuals,
societies, and institutions) are recalibrated. Energy, insight, and even artistic
creation result from these spontaneous disruptions. Let's look again at just a
few.

In *The Cocoanuts,* a funny manic scene occurs in Penelope's hotel room.
It has a door joining it to Mrs. Potter's room, and both also have exits to the
hall. So these rooms qualify as liminal spaces, places of change and flux where
the unexpected can occur. Indeed, the ante is upped as the principal characters
go in and out of both rooms through all three doors, sometimes just missing
each other. Harpo violates privacy throughout this scene, entering both rooms
according to his whims. The scene is rich with choreographed chaos, as funny
as Groucho and Chico's "Why a duck?" dialogue but this time not dependent
on spoken language, Harpo's destruction of the mail, the foiled-by-Chico
auction of lots, Detective Hennessey's "I Want My Shirt" aria, and Harpo's
increasingly more besotted forays to the punch bowl, offer other examples of
chaos in the film. But in this particular scene, Harpo snags the evidence that
will expose the antagonists and realign values.

Chaos is also embedded in *Animal Crackers,* in the core of its plot involving the thefts and confusions of paintings which are all in Harpo's hands by
the end. One of its zaniest scenes, though, is the outing of Roscoe Chandler
as Abie the Fishman, a scene that achieves surreal impact when Harpo steals
his birthmark. Another is the bridge game that Harpo and Chico play, or
perhaps un-play, with Grace Carpenter and Mrs. Rittenhouse. It is absolutely
loaded with gags, some self-deprecating about gambling and cheating, some
against the upper class, most of the nonsense very much coming from Harpo.

The stolen silverware cascading from Harpo's sleeve at the film's end doesn't hurt the cause of mayhem either.

Monkey Business offers wild scenes in the Punch, Harpo, and Judy show and the barbershop-mustache-trim fiasco, but its apogee is the scene in which Harpo and his cohorts try to exit the ship with Maurice Chevalier's passport. That is funny in itself, considering what an icon Chevalier is, but Harpo blows the scene into a whirlwind of chaos when the Chevalier ploy fails and he resorts to destroying all premises of order, tossing around official documents and using the inkpad and stamp to render the head of a bald officer official.

In *Horse Feathers*, the football game sequence, appearing on ESPN's list of great football scenes, gives collegiate football a treatment it may never recover from. And *Duck Soup* has a number of manic scenes. The one that saved Woody Allen's character from suicide in *Annie Hall* (1977) with its dose of fun-loving mayhem is the war-fever musical scene, but other restoratives are Harpo's Paul Revere ride, his mini-war with the lemonade vendor, his tricks on Groucho with the motorcycle sidecar, the bunker escapades during the Freedonia-Sylvania war, and most of all and for posterity, Harpo's mirror scene with Groucho with its touches of surrealism and realism that let us know there really is no mirror there, that these really are two guys who look uncannily alike — we knew Harpo and Chico look alike, but Harpo and Groucho? — at the film's peak.

Of all the Marx Brothers films, *A Night at the Opera* may be the most iconic in terms of wildness and mania. The stateroom scene, with its continuous addition of people to the small space, the mopping up, the making of the bed, the fixing of pipes, the manicuring, the food-ordering, and the passing around and balancing of the sleeping Harpo (who is all the while honking and groping women), makes it worthy of its classic status. Registering close on the hilarity-meter are the bearded stowaways' radio speeches and the deconstruction of *Il Trovatore*, replete with costumes, gymnastics, scrim changes, police chases, and surreal coups contributing to prolonged oxygen deprivation due to laughter.

A Day at the Races offers at least two big scenes of mayhem: the assignation with Flo in Groucho's room at the sanitarium that ends up being foiled by Harpo and Chico's wallpapering, and the examination of Mrs. Upjohn. The latter scene bursts with chaos from repeated scrubbings-up, Harpo's reverse bows, the insulted and sputtering Dr. Steinberg, and physical outrages perpetrated upon the hypochondriac rich lady (Dumont) who gets more attention, in addition to a shave and a shoeshine, than she bargained for.

Even *Room Service*, somewhat off the Marx Brothers' trajectory, has a good turkey chase. And feeding the sick guy, Harpo swapped for Leo Davis, whose illness morphs from measles to a tapeworm, is rich, as is the prolonged fake suicide scene precipitating a second fake suicide, the candle on Harpo's hat meanwhile burning with quiet intensity, not unlike our amusement.

At the Circus, sometimes criticized for lacking the necessary friction of a staid milieu as context for the antics of Harpo and his cohorts, can make an unsuspecting viewer weep with laughter in the scene where Harpo's sneeze has the impact of a hurricane in the Little Professor's scaled-down abode, in the scene wherein Harpo and Chico search for stolen money while Goliath sleeps, and the zany high wire–trapeze act that several non-circus performers are drafted into.

Go West, my personal favorite, has two indelibly hilarious scenes: the stagecoach ride involving a manic forced swapping of hats, a trope presented in other films but intensified in this small space and combined with gender confusion and the twitting and thwarting of the antagonist Beecher. Nothing tops the marvelous train sequence, though: the efforts to speed up and slow down the train, its re-routing through an oblivious farmer's homestead with a bull in residence, Harpo as train coupling, and Harpo's philosophically rich dismantling of the train to feed it to itself to keep it running toward its destination.

The Big Store gives us an unforgettable bed department scene that is affectionate and whimsical in its celebration of children and cultural diversity even while Harpo and Chico revel in wildness while Groucho sleeps it out. The later chase scene, exploiting as it does the opulence of the department store setting for gags, isn't bad either, even if doubles are performing the Marx Brothers' stunts.

The last two films have their delightful manic moments too. In *A Night in Casablanca,* the most prolonged and therefore inebriating is Stubel's packing scene; he is sabotaged by the undetected Harpo, Chico, Groucho, and the shafted chanteuse Beatrice. Stubel is driven mad by the tendency of his packed clothes to unpack themselves, drawers to go upside-down, empty closets to fill up again, and filled trunks to empty. And *Love Happy* has Madame Egelichi's varied tortures of Harpo to make him speak when her whammy fails to have the desired effect. The rooftop scene in the film, while not laugh-out-loud funny, is nevertheless wild, exotic, and surreal in its imaginative use of commercial symbols like the Mobil horse and the Kool penguin as Harpo's playgrounds. In fact, Harpo sweeps those commercial symbols into the realm of imaginative play, reminding us of the lack of demarcation between the ordinary and extraordinary, the quotidian and the mysterious, the secular and the divine.

Ultimately the supercharged wildness in the films celebrates human energy, spontaneity, imagination, audacity, irreverence, and even luck. Just by sitting in our seats watching, we feel energized. That is, our psyches get a workout, as do our politics and our philosophical premises. And the medicine goes down easy because trickster stories "let us observe through the eyes of humor."[39] "The audience ... undergoes ... a loosening and breathing of the psychic boundaries."[40]

Final Thoughts

> "He has not left the scene."
> — Lewis Hyde, *Trickster Makes This World*[41]

Navigating daily life takes a good deal of mental agility, balance, and humor. Trickster, in tales throughout the world, shows us how to go along, have our adventures, maybe get into some difficulties, but ultimately survive. The plot arc of trickster tales is quasi-picaresque: Trickster arrives from somewhere else, then gets involved in complications or has to confront some powerful person or force, often while trying to satisfy a need, and often that need is for food or sex. Chaos escalates and eventually order is restored. Though relationships don't remain quite the same, they're better. For in shaking up the world he inhabits, trickster cleanses and renews it. He bestows fire. He promotes life. Life seesaws between disruption and balance for trickster. It does for us too.

Harpo's traits are essentially trickster's: his hunger, his lust, his musicality, his support for the underdog, his penchant for stealing, his joint work, his silence, his shape-shifting and gender-bending, his animal *simpatico*, his capacity for magic and the surreal, his attraction to liminal spaces, his exploitation of chance and luck, and his irreverence for the powerful, whether people or institutions. When we examine them, we also see that these qualities do not remain discrete from one another, just as Harpo himself resists classification. He embodies them all more or less simultaneously and glides between them: sometimes he manifests one, sometimes many; he flows from one to another.

His attraction to liminal spaces like doorways, elevators and hotel lobbies, opens him up to chance events, accidents, and opportunities. This is like working the joint, finding the flexible space in which to maneuver, and it applies to the joints of the mind as well. His shape-shifting capacity is related to this too, as is his talent for magic. And his magic is related to his conflation of animate and inanimate, male and female, animal and human. His refusal to abide by rules, social and legal, underlies his penchant for stealing, which is sometimes pragmatic and sometimes political. His outsider social behaviors incline him to offer his leg to strangers and even make the gesture seem, from a certain point of view, generous and meaningful. And his refusal to abide by ordinary rules helps him navigate easily between high and low, from harp melody to flatulent honk.

In addition to the fluidity of Harpo's trickster persona, he is also flexible in the way he occupies the medium of film. Meta-commentary on technology and the medium of film itself enters the films early and continues throughout, from his tasting the telephone and attempting to throw it at Groucho in *The Cocoanuts* to his playing a telephone like a slot machine in *Horse Feathers* to his salting one in *A Night in Casablanca*; from his battle to silence the radio in *Duck Soup* to his muteness before the microphone in *A Night at the Opera*. And he comments on the Marx Brothers films too, from the proffering of his leg in the earlier films to the tug of war with the wooden leg in *Monkey Business* and the wooden leg's reappearance in *Love Happy*; and in his breaking the fourth wall via allusions to his and Chico's brotherly affection in *Go West* and *The Big Store*, the sibling rivalry depicted in fighting gags in *Duck Soup* and *Monkey Business,* and their card playing in *Horse Feathers* and *Monkey Business.*

Harpo is performing in a visual medium that, in the first film, had recently incorporated sound. He is not without the sounds of music and horn, whistle and lip pops, but he does not speak, so many of his gags play off of his muteness and celebrate his amusing ability to cash in on muteness in a medium that made an arduous transition to sound. That is the resonant metaphor, the joke in fact, of money pouring from the telephone when Harpo plays it like a slot machine in *Horse Feathers.*

Harpo has a variety of names in the films, but he begins and ends with his own: He is Harpo in *The Cocoanuts,* The Professor in *Animal Crackers,* Harpo again in *Monkey Business,* Pinky in *Horse Feathers,* and *Duck Soup,* Tomasso in *A Night at the Opera,* Stuffy in *A Day at the Races,* Faker in *Room Service,* Punchy in *At the Circus,* Rusty in *Go West* and *A Night in Casablanca,* Wacky in *The Big Store,* and Harpo once and for all in *Love Happy.*

Other motifs besides the classic trickster ones accrue in the films and contribute to Harpo's trickster status. For example, Harpo is prone to nudity, sometimes wearing nothing but underwear beneath his coat. In *Room Service,* Chico says, "he doesn't believe in shirts"; apparently he doesn't always believe in pants. In the first several films he evokes Revolutionary War iconography (as does Groucho): marching with a piccolo and using his horn as a gun, and thus reminding us that the impact of this humor, trickster's in nature, is essentially revolutionary. He sets off explosions in closets in *Duck Soup* and *The Big Store*; he causes a sprinkler system to rain torrents at the sanitarium in *A Day at the Races*; he sneezes a hurricane in *At the Circus*.

Other motifs involve the confusion Harpo causes with hats, identity markers whose muddling interrogates identity. This happens in *Duck Soup, A Day at the Races,* and *Go West*. The autonomous life of facial hair is a motif in *Monkey Business, A Night at the Opera,* and *A Night in Casablanca*. These seem endlessly engaging to Harpo, and he uses them to provoke and accomplish various unmaskings. Finally, Harpo makes an uncanny sort of mischief with mirrors in three films: *Duck Soup, The Big Store,* and *Love Happy*.

When we add up his metaphors and metonymies, like the trope of his proffered leg and the horn whose meaning runs the gamut from expressing sexual desire to communicating to farting, and when we consider the implications of his imaginary doghouse with a real dog in it, we suspect that Harpo limns his trickster essence with that of a poet. For he speaks as poets do. And we know that this trickster is a poet once and for all when he rides the Mobil billboard's horse with wings, a Pegasus, "the horse of the Muses, [that] has always been at the service of poets."[42]

In the end, it is fitting to return to Harpo's most frequent trope for its historical, social, and philosophical implications: his proffered leg. With this trickster for his own time as well as ours, perhaps for any time, "there is laughter amid tears."[43] His gesture demonstrates the power of the hinge over and over again: what it looks like and how it works, telling us not only to seek the vulnerable place within a culture's or institution's power, but also to aspire to flexibility, to learn to hang loose if we want to strike an efficacious posture in a troubled world. Moreover, joints must be lubricated and exercised to move well and painlessly, which is trickster's work in cultures. And there is no other trope that Harpo injects into the films more frequently and with more quiet insistence than the trope of his proffered leg swinging at the knee, a lesson taken to heart in England in a precarious time.

Notes

Introduction

1. Lewis Hyde, *Trickster Makes This World* (New York: North Point Press, a division of Farrar, Straus, and Giroux, 1998). Hyde's book provided scaffolding and vocabulary for this project, and for that I am deeply indebted.

2. This and other tidbits from Harpo's life are from Harpo Marx and Roland Barber, *Harpo Speaks* (New York: Limelight Editions, 1961).

3. Or, as Hyde puts it, "When human culture turns against human beings themselves the trickster appears as a kind of savior" (279).

4. Coyote and Hare are incarnations of trickster in Native American cycles of tales.

5. Carl Joseph Jung says that trickster is "a forerunner of the savior, and, like him, God, man, and animal at once. He is both subhuman and superhuman, a bestial and divine being..." Paul Radin, *The Trickster: A Study of American Indian Mythology* (New York: Schocken Books, 1956), 203.

6. One example of stage skit material inserted into Marx Brothers films is described as "the flash bit" in *Harpo Speaks*. He and Chico "are onstage looking for something we've dropped. Chico asks me for a flashlight. I act dumb. 'The flash!' he says. Where's-a flash?' I am very eager and anxious to please, but I keep pulling the wrong thing out of my coat—a flask, a flag, a fish, a flush (poker hand), a flute, everything but a flash. Finally Chico says, 'You're-a impossible. Come on. Help me look for it.' Whereupon I haul out a flashlight, turn it on, and help him look for it" (383). This skit is used verbatim in *Animal Crackers*.

7. For an interesting discussion of the contrast between the ancient Greek trickster Hermes and the Winnebago trickster see Karl Kerenyi's "The Trickster in Relation to Greek Mythology" in Paul Radin, *The Trickster: A Study of American Indian Mythology* (New York: Schocken Books, 1956).

8. Stories about both Ashkenasic and Sephardic tricksters can be found in Sheldon Oberman and Peninnah Schram's *Solomon and the Ant and Other Jewish Folktakes* (Honesdale, Pennsylvania: Boyds Mills Press, 2006). See also Peninnah Schram, *The Hungry Clothes and Other Jewish Folktales* (New York: Sterling, 2008) and Nathan Ausubel, ed., *A Treasury of Jewish Folklore* (New York: Crown, 1948).

9. The trickster Eshu, wearing a hat that is black on one side and white on the other (sometimes white and red), would confound witnesses, causing them to fight over what they had actually seen: a man in a white hat or a man in a black hat? Coincidentally, the double-sided hat motif is evoked several times in the films: in Zeppo's half-hat after an encounter with the scissors-wielding Harpo in *Duck Soup*; in Groucho and Harpo's hats, one white and one black, in the mirror scene in *Duck Soup;* and most significantly in Harpo's blacking of half of his face with axle grease (the protagonists' stratagem to escape the law by blending in with the black community). In this way Harpo interrogates the notion of racial identity—who is he? and according to whose point of view?—in an otherwise uncomfortable scene.

10. Paul Radin's *The Trickster: A Study of American Indian Mythology* provided many parallels to Harpo's antics in its cycles of trickster tales.

11. Marx and Barber, *Harpo Speaks*, 11.

12. Mudheads are "sacred clowns" in Pueblo tradition who "break tension with ridiculous antics and silly pantomimes." David M. Jones and Brian L. Molyneuax, *Mythology of the American Nations* (London: Hermes House, 2006).

13. Joe Adamson. *Groucho, Harpo, Chico and Sometimes Zeppo: A Celebration of the Marx Brothers* (New York: Simon & Schuster, 1973), 84.

14. Harpo refuses to participate in the sort of dialogue characterized here: "In both Plato and Job the relationship between human and the divine is no longer played out in dramatic form, but is orchestrated in imposing intellectual dialogues, which rationalize the very basis of our civilization." Stanley Diamond, "Introductory Essay: Job and the Trickster," Paul Radin's *The Trickster*.

15. Theodore Adorno famously said that to write poetry after Auschwitz is barbaric.

16. Harpo says, "I announced to Minnie that I would never speak another word on stage" after a reviewer noted, "the effect is spoiled when he speaks." Harpo continues, "I went silent. I never uttered another word, onstage or in front of a camera, as a Marx Brother." Marx and Barber, *Harpo Speaks,* 121–122.

17. "We might say, then, that in many traditions the injunction to silence is the speech act by which a particular narrative is made sacred." Hyde, *Trickster Makes This World*, 156.

18. Jack Kerouac, "To Harpo Marx," Jason Shinder, ed., *Lights, Camera, Poetry! American Movie Poems, the First Hundred Years* (New York: Harcourt Brace, 1996), 41.

19. In Tale 16 of the Winnebago Trickster Cycle, trickster carries his penis in a box, and in one instance, sends it across the water to have intercourse with the chief's daughter.

20. "The Homeric Hymn to Hermes," Lewis Hyde, trans. *Trickster Makes This World*, 317–331. Hyde also discusses Krishna as trickster within.

21. In Tale 23 of the Winnebago Trickster Cycle, trickster becomes so flatulent after eating a laxative bulb that he has to cling to the top of a poplar tree to keep from blowing away while his feet flop in the air.

22. Hyde's discussion of joints, joint-work, the hinge, and hinged minds is signally relevant to Harpo's trope of the knee and the way that trope symbolizes his trickster work in general in the films. See Hyde, *Trickster Makes This World*, 205, 252–272, and 307–311.

23. Richard Erdoes and Alfonso Ortiz, *American Indian Myths and Legends* (New York: Pantheon, 1984). They define trickster stories as those involving "tricks and pranks, especially when played by the lowly, small, and poor on the proud, big, and rich," and trickster as "a rebel against authority and the breaker of all taboos" (335). And Hyde says that "tricksters in general begin by muddying the high gods" (90).

24. See Hyde, chapter 7, "Speechless Shame and Shameless Speech."

25. Marx and Barber, *Harpo Speaks*, 52–53.

Chapter 1

1. Grant L. Voth, *Myth in Human History* (Chantilly, Virginia: The Great Courses, 2010), 103.

2. Hyde, *Trickster Makes This World*, 307.

3. Adamson, *Groucho, Harpo, Chico and Sometimes Zeppo*, 82.

4. Hyde's translation of the "The Homeric Hymn to Hermes" describes Hermes' creation of the lyre from a turtle shell and his masterful playing of it.

5. On a Madison Avenue bus in New York, I overheard a conversation between an older music professor and a young African American student of the harp. He was advising her to watch the Marx Brothers films to see Harpo play the harp backwards. Does he?

Chapter 2

1. Schram, *The Hungry Clothes and Other Jewish Folktales*, 75.

Chapter 3

1. Radin, *The Trickster*, 189.

2. The poet John Keats defined *negative capability* as "capable of being in uncertainties, mysteries, doubts, without any irritable reaching after fact and reason —...." *The Letters of John Keats*, ed. Hyder Edward Rollins (Cambridge: Harvard University Press, 1958, Volume I), 193.

3. John Keats, "Ode on a Grecian Urn," *The Wadsworth Anthology of Poetry,* ed. Jay Parini (Boston: Thompson Higher Education, 2006), 421–422. "Heard melodies are sweet, but those unheard/ Are sweeter; therefore, ye soft pipes, play on" ll. 11–12.

4. In his "Prefatory Notes" to *The Trickster,* Paul Radin specifically relates trickster to Punch and Judy: "Many of the Trickster's traits were perpetuated in the figure of the mediaeval jester, and have survived right up to the present day in the Punch-and-Judy plays and in the clown" (xxiii). So although it may seem like an odd juxtaposition, it makes perfect sense that Harpo appears with them.

5. In Nikolai Gogol's "The Nose," *The Overcoat and Other Tales of Good and Evil,* trans. David Magarshack (New York: W.W. Norton, 1957), the protagonist's nose sneaks away from his body while he is asleep and runs around town, a very strange doppelgänger having a life of its own.

6. In Tale 20 of the Winnebago Trickster Cycle, trickster transforms himself into a female, making a vulva out of an elk's liver and breasts from elk's kidneys. He wears a dress, marries the chief's son, and bears children. Later he wonders why he's doing all this and returns to his wife.

7. I suspect a vestigial trace of Ashkenazic Jewish folklore here: the tale of the Baal Shem Tov's trust of an impulse that leads him to wander for days to a river, there to discover an unusually large frog who is really a scholar suffering punishment for the sin of concealing an ancient scroll. See Howard Schwartz, "The Tale of the Frog," *Gabriel's Palace: Jewish Mystical Tales* (New York: Oxford University Press, 1993).

8. Early in the Winnebago Trickster Cycle of tales, trickster violates the sanctity of war rituals in a number of ways: as chief, he shouldn't be going on the warpath, he shouldn't have intercourse before battle, he shouldn't leave the feast before his guests, yet he does all these things.

9. Jack Kerouac, "To Harpo Marx," *Lights, Camera, Poetry! American Movie Poems, the First Hundred Years,* ed. Jason Shinder (New York: Harcourt Brace, 1996).

Chapter 4

1. Voth, *Myth in Human History,* 94.

Chapter 5

1. Radin, *The Trickster,* 147.

2. Adamson, *Groucho, Harpo, Chico and Sometimes Zeppo,* 224.

3. Marianne Moore, "Poetry," *The Complete Poems* (New York: Macmillan/Penguin, 1994), 36. In his doghouse tattoo, Harpo satisfies Moore's poetics criteria. Moore says we won't have poetry "till the poets among us can be/ 'literalists of/ the imagination'/—above/ insolence and triviality and can present/ for inspection, imaginary gardens with real toads in them." Here Harpo presents for inspection an imaginary doghouse with a real dog in it.

Chapter 6

1. Hyde, *Trickster Makes This World,* 90.

2. In his exuberant embrace of strangers, alliance with "the procreant urge," celebration of "the flesh and the appetites," willingness to "live with the animals," and picaresque tendency to "tramp a perpetual journey"—in these and other ways, Harpo suggests *simpatico* with Whitman's "Song of Myself." Walt Whitman, "Song of Myself," *Leaves of Grass* (New York: Signet Classics, 2000), 24, 44, 50, and 72.

3. See Lawrence Kramer, "Glottis Envy," *Musical Meaning: Toward a Critical History* (Berkeley: University of California Press, 2002).

Chapter 7

1. Hyde, *Trickster Makes This World,* 356.

2. Whitey's Lindy Hoppers, young swing dancers from Harlem, danced at the Savoy and the Cotton Club as well as in film. They also performed in Europe and Australia. Judy Pritchett and Frank Manning, "Whitey's Lindy Hoppers," *Archives of Early Lindy Hop,* http://www .savoystyle.com/whiteys_lindy_hoppers.html.

3. Susan Gubar, *Race Changes: White Skin, Black Face in American Culture* (New York: Oxford University Press, 1997), xiv.

Chapter 8

1. Erdoes and Ortiz, *American Indian Myths and Legends*, 335.
2. Who can forget Daisy Buchanan's emotion and tears as she examines Jay Gatsby's mound of elegant shirts as if they represent a belief system, these correlatives of his extravagant aspirations, in F. Scott Fitzgerald's *The Great Gatsby*?

Chapter 9

1. Erdoes and Ortiz, *American Indian Myths and Legends*, 336.
2. See Auden's poem at http://www.poets.org/viewmedia.php/prmMID/15545.
3. Seventy-six years after the Emancipation Proclamation, which did not immediately free the slaves but did shift the impetus of the Civil War, it is conceivable that some members of this chorus are the children or grandchildren of slaves. The lines of the harp strings that members of the chorus are standing behind suggest, among other things, lack of freedom. At the end of his number, Harpo swings around to join them there, thus casting his fate with them. But the harp strings also signify making music from travail, blues issuing from harp and human voice and offering the spirit of liberation. It is no accident that we see the sign declaring "Refreshment" as the "make it a blues" sequence begins. Harpo plays the harp like an angel joined by a chorus of angels. In a letter to Abraham Lincoln about the Emancipation Proclamation, a Northern black soldier's mother's said, "When you are dead and in Heaven, in a thousand years that action of yours will make the Angels sing your praises" http://www.archives.gov/exhibits/american_originals_iv/sections/nonjavatext_emancipation.html.

Chapter 10

1. Hyde, *Trickster Makes This World*, 14.
2. Thoreau once said, "We do not ride upon the railroad; it rides upon us," seeing, early on that technology could be a double-edged sword. Henry David Thoreau, *Walden* (Boston: Houghton Mifflin, Riverside edition, 1960), 63.

Chapter 11

1. Voth, *Myth in Human History*, 97.
2. Allen Eyles, *The Marx Brothers: Their World of Comedy* (New York: A. S. Barnes, 1969), 130.
3. W.H. Auden, in his elegy "In Memory of William Butler Yeats," reminds us that art travels through time, and can "be punished under a foreign code of conscience./ The words of a dead man/ Are modified in the guts of the living." Read the entire poem at http://www.poets.org/viewmedia.php/prmMID/15544.
4. See Bruno Schulz, *The Street of Crocodiles and Other Stories* (New York: Penguin, 2008), for rich imaginative development of this theme.
5. William Blake, "The Chimney Sweeper," *Songs of Innocence*, and "The Chimney Sweeper," *Songs of Experience*, in *The Poetry and Prose of William Blake* (New York: Doubleday, 1965), 10 and 22.

Chapter 12

1. Erdoes and Ortiz, *American Indian Myths and Legends*, 335.

Chapter 13

1. "Coyote Dances with a Star," Erdoes and Ortiz, *American Indian Myths and Legends*, 385.
2. "Inktonmi learns the eye-juggling trick of four boys, who warn him not to practice it too frequently.... He tries the eye-juggling trick once too often, and loses his eyes; the boys restore them to him, but take away his power" ("Summary of the Assiniboine Trickster Myth," Radin, 100).

3. Veeho, a trickster in Northern Cheyenne tales, learns the trick from a medicine man of commanding his eyeballs to "fly out of [his] head and hang on that tree over there," and then retrieve them, commanding them to "come back where you belong." He is given a similar prohibition: "don't do this trick more than four times a day." But Veeho does it once too often and loses his eyes. On the way home, he begs an eye from a mouse and another from a buffalo. When he gets home, his wife, with delicious understatement, says, "I believe your eyes are a little mismatched" ("Doing a Trick with Eyeballs," in Erdoes and Ortiz, 379–381).

Conclusion

1. Voth, *Myth in Human History*, 94.
2. Marx and Barber, *Harpo Speaks,* 301.
3. Radin, *The Trickster*, 189.
4. Hyde, *Trickster Makes This World*, 10.
5. Radin, *The Trickster*, 186.
6. Mathilda Koén-Serano, ed. *Folktales of Joha: Jewish Trickster* (Philadelphia: The Jewish Publication Society, 2003), 253.
7. Radin, *The Trickster*, 167–8.
8. Hyde, *Trickster Makes This World*, 335.
9. Josepha Sherman, "The Lutin's Pranks," *Trickster Tales: Forty Folk Stories from Around the World* (Little Rock: August House, 1996), 38.
10. Sherman, "Lutin or Not? Two Tales from French Canada," *Trickster Tales*, 129.
11. Hyde, *Trickster Makes This World*, 71.
12. Moore, "Poetry," 36.
13. Sherman, *Trickster Tales*, 105.
14. Hyde, *Trickster Makes This World*, 131.
15. Ibid., 140.
16. Ibid., 274.
17. Ibid., 256.
18. Ibid., 297.
19. Ibid., 311.
20. Erdoes and Ortiz, *American Indian Myths and Legends*, 355.
21. Apollo on Hermes' lyre, as quoted in Hyde, *Trickster Makes This World*, 328.
22. Hyde, *Trickster Makes This World*, 329.
23. Marx and Barber, *Harpo Speaks,* 12.
24. Hyde, *Trickster Makes This World*, 13.
25. Koén-Serano, ed., *Folktales of Joha*, 142.
26. Radin, *The Trickster*, From "Winnebago Trickster Cycle."
27. Koén-Serano, ed., *Folktales of Joha*, 148.
28. Erdoes and Ortiz, *American Indian Myths and Legends*, 339.
29. Hyde, *Trickster Makes This World*, 220.
30. Voth, *Myth in Human History*, 103.
31. Hyde, *Trickster Makes This World*, 221.
32. Ibid., 156.
33. Ibid., 157.
34. Marx and Barber, *Harpo Speaks,* 121–122.
35. Bill Marx, *Son of Harpo Speaks* (Milwaukee: Applause Theatre & Cinema Books, 2010), 168.
36. Radin, *The Trickster*, 180.
37. Schram, *The Hungry Clothes and Other Jewish Folktales,* 61.
38. Erdoes and Ortiz, *American Indian Myths and Legends*, 335.
39. Tim Tingle, editor of *Trickster: Native American Tales—A Graphic Collection*, April 20, 2011, interview online.
40. Hyde, *Trickster Makes This World*, 267.
41. Ibid., 8.
42. Thomas Bulfinch, *Bulfinch's Mythology* (New York: Barnes & Noble, 2006), 123.
43. Erdoes and Ortiz, *American Indian Myths and Legends*, 336.

Bibliography

Adamson, Joe. *Groucho, Harpo, Chico and Sometimes Zeppo: A Celebration of the Marx Brothers.* New York: Simon & Schuster, 1973. Print.

Animal Crackers. Dir. Leo McCarey. Perf. Harpo, Chico, Groucho, and Zeppo Marx. Paramount, 1930.

At the Circus. Dir. Edward Buzzell. Perf. Harpo, Chico, and Groucho Marx with Kenny Baker and Florence Rice. MGM, 1939. Warner Bros. Entertainment, 2004.

Auden, W.H. "In Memory of William Butler Yeats." Web. http://www.poets.org/viewmedia.php/prmMID/15544.

_____. "September 1, 1939." Web. http://www.poets.org/viewmedia.php/prmMID/15545.

Ausubel, Nathan. *A Treasury of Jewish Folklore.* New York: Crown, 1948. Print.

Belcher, Stephen. *African Myths of Origin.* London: Penguin, 2005. Print.

The Big Store. Dir. Charles Riesner. Perf. Harpo, Chico, and Groucho Marx with Tony Martin. MGM, 1941.

Blake, William. "The Chimney Sweeper" from *Songs of Innocence* and "The Chimney Sweeper" from *Songs of Experience.* Ed. David V. Erdman. *The Poetry and Prose of William Blake.* New York: Doubleday, 1965. Print.

Blount Jr., Roy. *Hail, Hail, Euphoria: Presenting the Marx Brothers in Duck Soup: The Greatest War Movie Ever Made.* New York: HarperCollins, 2010. Print.

Bulfinch, Thomas. *Bulfinch's Mythology.* New York: Barnes & Noble, 2006. Print.

The Cocoanuts. Dir. Joseph Santley and Robert Florey. Perf. Harpo, Chico, Groucho, and Zeppo Marx. Paramount, 1929.

A Day at the Races. Dir. Sam Wood. Perf. Harpo, Chico, and Groucho Marx with Allan Jones and Maureen O'Sullivan. MGM, 1937.

Dembriki, Matt, ed. *Trickster: Native American Tales: A Graphic Collection.* Golden, Colorado: Fulcrum, 2010. Print.

Duck Soup. Dir. Leo McCarey. Perf. Harpo, Chico, Groucho, and Zeppo Marx. Paramount, 1933.

Erdoes, Richard, and Alfonso Ortiz. *American Indian Myths and Legends.* New York: Pantheon, 1984. Print.

Eyles, Allen. *The Marx Brothers: Their World of Comedy.* New York: A. S. Barnes, 1969. Print.

Fitzgerald, F. Scott. *The Great Gatsby.* New York: Charles Scribner's Sons, 1925. Print.

Go West. Dir. Edward Buzzell. Perf. Harpo, Chico, and Groucho Marx. MGM, 1940.

Gogol, Nikolai. "The Nose." In *The Overcoat and Other Tales of Good and Evil.* Trans. David Magarshack. New York: W.W. Norton, 1957. Print.

Gubar, Susan. *Race Changes: White Skin, Black Face in American Culture.* New York: Oxford University Press, 1997. Print.

216

Hathaway, Nancy. *The Friendly Guide to Mythology*. New York: Viking, 2001. Print.
"The Homeric Hymn to Hermes." Trans. Lewis Hyde. *Trickster Makes This World* by Lewis Hyde. New York: North Point Press, a division of Farrar, Straus, and Giroux, 1998. Print.
Horse Feathers. Dir. Norman McLeod. Perf. Harpo, Chico, Groucho, and Zeppo Marx. Paramount, 1932.
Hyde, Lewis. *Trickster Makes This World*. New York: North Point Press, a division of Farrar, Straus and Giroux, 1998. Print.
"Ivie Anderson." http://en.wikipedia.org/wiki/Ivie_Anderson. Web.
Jones, David M., and Brian L. Molyneaux. *Mythology of the American Nations*. London: Hermes House, 2006. Print.
Jung, Carl Joseph. "On the Psychology of the Trickster Figure." *The Trickster: A Study of American Indian Mythology* by Paul Radin. New York: Schocken Books, 1956. Print.
Keats, John. *The Letters of John Keats*. Edited by Hyder Edward Rollins. Cambridge: Harvard University Press, 1958, Volume I. Print.
_____. "Ode on a Grecian Urn." *The Wadsworth Anthology of Poetry*. Ed. Jay Parini. Boston: Thompson Higher Education, 2006, 421–2. Print.
Kerenyi, Karl. "The Trickster in Relation to Greek Mythology." *The Trickster: A Study of American Indian Mythology*. By Paul Radin. New York: Schocken Books, 1956. 171–191. Print.
Kerouac, Jack. "To Harpo Marx." *Lights, Camera, Poetry! American Movie Poems, the First Hundred Years*. Ed. Jason Shinder. New York: Harcourt Brace, 1996. Print.
Koén-Sarano, Matilda, ed. *Folktales of Joha: Jewish Trickster*. Philadelphia: The Jewish Publication Society, 2003. Print.
Koestenbaum, Wayne. *The Anatomy of Harpo Marx*. Berkeley: University of California Press, 2012. Print.
Kramer, Lawrence. "Glottis Envy." *Musical Meaning: Toward a Critical History*. Berkeley: University of California Press, 2002. Print.
Love Happy. Dir. David Miller. Perf. Harpo, Chico, and Groucho Marx with Vera-Ellen, Raymond Burr, and Eric Blore. United Artists, 1949.
Marx, Bill. *Son of Harpo Speaks*. Milwaukee: Applause Theatre & Cinema Books, 2010. Print.
Marx, Groucho. *The Groucho Phile: An Illustrated Life*. New York: Bobbs-Merrill, 1976. Print.
Marx, Harpo, and Roland Barber. *Harpo Speaks*. New York: Limelight Editions, 1961. Print.
Mills, Joseph, ed. *A Century of the Marx Brothers*. Newcastle: Cambridge Scholars, 2007.
Monkey Business. Dir. Norman Z. McLeod. Perf. Harpo, Chico, Groucho, and Zeppo Marx. Paramount, 1931.
Moore, Marianne. "Poetry." *The Complete Poems* by Marianne Moore. New York: Macmillan/Penguin, 1994. 36. Print.
A Night at the Opera. Dir. Sam Wood. Perf. Harpo, Chico, and Groucho Marx with Kitty Carlisle and Allan Jones. MGM, 1935.
A Night in Casablanca. Dir. Archie Mayo. Perf. Harpo, Chico, and Groucho Marx with Sig Ruman. Loma Vista Productions, 1946.
Oberman, Sheldon, and Peninnah Schram. *Solomon and the Ant and Other Jewish Folktales*. Honesdale, Pennsylvania: Boyds Mills Press, 2006. Print.
Leo Pavlát. *Jewish Folk Tales*. New York: Greenwich House, 1986. Print.
Pritchett, Judy, and Frank Manning. "Whitey's Lindy Hoppers." *Archives of Early Lindy Hop*. 20 December 2011. Web. http://www.savoystyle.com/whiteys_lindy_hoppers.html.
Radin, Paul. *The Trickster: A Study of American Indian Mythology*. New York: Schocken Books, 1956. Print.

Room Service. Dir. William A. Seiter. Perf. Harpo, Chico, and Groucho Marx with Lucille Ball, Ann Miller, and Frank Albertson. RKO Radio Pictures, 1938.

Schulz, Bruno. *The Street of Crocodiles and Other Stories.* Trans. Celina Wieniewska. New York: Penguin, 2008. Print.

Schram, Peninnah. *The Hungry Clothes and Other Jewish Folktales.* New York: Sterling, 2008. Print.

Schwartz, Howard. *Gabriel's Palace: Jewish Mystical Tales.* New York: Oxford University Press, 1993. Print.

Sherman, Josepha. *Trickster Tales: Forty Folks Stories from Around the World.* Little Rock: August House, 1996. Print.

Thoreau, Henry David. *Walden.* Boston: Houghton Mifflin, Riverside edition, 1960. Print.

Tingle, Tim, author of *Trickster: Native American Tales — A Graphic Collection.* April 20, 2011 interview. Web.

Voth, Grant L. *Myth in Human History.* Chantilly, Virginia: The Great Courses, 2010. Print.

Whitman, Walt. "Song of Myself." *Leaves of Grass.* New York: Signet Classics, 2000. 22–78. Print.

Index

Numbers in **_bold italics_** indicate pages with photographs.

219